The Father Who Redeems and the Son Who Obeys

The Father Who Redeems *and the* Son Who Obeys

Consideration of Paul's Teaching in Romans

Svetlana Khobnya

Foreword by
John Nolland

☙PICKWICK *Publications* · Eugene, Oregon

THE FATHER WHO REDEEMS AND THE SON WHO OBEYS
Consideration of Paul's Teaching in Romans

Copyright © 2013 Svetlana Khobnya. All rights reserved. Except for brief quotations in critical publications or reviews, no part of this book may be reproduced in any manner without prior written permission from the publisher. Write: Permissions, Wipf and Stock Publishers, 199 W. 8th Ave., Suite 3, Eugene, OR 97401.

A part of chapter 2 was published under the title "God the Father in the Old Testament" *European Journal of Theology* 20 (2011) 139–48.

Revised Standard Version of the Bible, copyright 1952 [2nd edition, 1971] by the Division of Christian Education of the National Council of the Churches of Christ in the United States of America. Used by permission. All rights reserved.

Pickwick Publications
An Imprint of Wipf and Stock Publishers
199 W. 8th Ave., Suite 3
Eugene, OR 97401

www.wipfandstock.com

ISBN 13: 978-71-62032-170-6

Cataloguing-in-Publication data:

Khobnya, Svetlana.

The father who redeems and the son who obeys : consideration of Paul's teaching in romans / Svetlana Khobnya, with a foreword by John Nolland.

xviii + 182 pp. ; 23 cm. Includes bibliographical references.

ISBN 13: 978-71-62032-170-6

1. Bible. Romans—Criticism, interpretation, etc. 2. God—Biblical teaching. 3. Son of God—Biblical teaching. 3. Jesus Christ—Biblical teaching. I. Title.

BS2665.2 K53 2013

Manufactured in the U.S.A.

Contents

Foreword by John Nolland | vii
Preface | xi
List of Abbreviations | xiii

I   Introduction | 1
II God the Father in Jewish Tradition | 19
III God the Father Revealed in Christ | 45
IV Christ's Faithfulness as Fulfillment of the Father's Faithfulness | 82
V   Christ's Obedience and Abraham's Faith | 116
VI Christ's Obedience versus Adam's Disobedience | 149
VII Conclusions | 164

Bibliography | 169
Author Index | 183
Ancient Document Index | 185

Foreword

THE FRESH CONTRIBUTION OF this study to an understanding of Paul's letter to the Romans is rooted in the seriousness with which it takes Old Testament and Second Temple Jewish traditions of the Fatherhood of God. It has been all too easy for Christians, in understanding the Fatherhood of God christologically, to shortchange the Jewish heritage and invest everything in the newness of the Abba-Father relationship opened up by Jesus. Khobnya has redressed the balance in the case of Romans. True, the Jewish heritage has been reinterpreted in the light of Christ, but the point is that there was something solid to reinterpret and expand.

Intertextuality is an important dimension of the approach adopted. The "illegitimate totality transfer" identified in earlier study of biblical words led scholarship into a period of austerity where meaning was stripped down to a bare minimum. The credibility of this minimalism was undergirded by a rather narrow conceptual focus in the understanding of meaning; the discovery of the reader and rediscovery of rhetoric, among other things, have moved us on from that. An exploration of the way in which texts echo earlier texts and create meaning, in part by exploiting levels of precision and imprecision in the textual links, has been one way in which the scholarly pendulum has been swinging back to a more fulsome approach. When one is talking of resonance with multiple texts rather than reference to a single text, issues of meaning become more complicated, but also much richer.

And if a text like Romans resonates with a large body of OT texts and Jewish traditions, various elements in the text of Romans can also have relationships of resonance with one another (intratextuality). Khobnya takes full advantage of this possibility in Romans. The richness is undeniable, but the challenge is to demonstrate that wild imagination has not taken the place of chilly minimizing. Khobnya keeps back from extremes and makes her own attempt at offering a reasoned case for a considerable degree of flexible and plural readings.

Romans is not as such a narrative text, but the point has been made often enough that it implies a narrative, a salvation-historical narrative that draws heavily on OT patterns and motifs and finds its completion in Christ. It is an implied-narrative approach that adds another kind of richness to this study of the role of the Father-Son relationship of God and Jesus in Romans. Intertextuality and implied-narrative work hand in glove.

The importance of the Jewish background for Romans is understood by Khobnya in worldview or symbolic world terms. Since the symbolic world represents the very air breathed by those who share it, it is rarely explained, but it is often the all but invisible vital clue to understanding. Vital aspects of the meaning potential of a text cannot be accessed without appreciation of the appropriate symbolic world. An appreciation of the symbolic world clears up obscurities and non-sequitors in texts, but it also expands the range and depth of meaning.

Unfortunately many of the surviving Jewish traditions can only be definitely traced to a period beyond the writing of Romans. Perhaps many of them existed earlier, but Khobnya takes another approach: what is done with texts later demonstrates a potentiality of the text; and a potentiality recognized later could also have been recognized earlier. This strand of thinking becomes of particular importance for her appeal to the Jewish Aqedah traditions.

With Jewish traditions of God as Father as vital background, Khobnya explores how in Romans God the Father is revealed in Christ. Paul is shown to be involved in some redefining. God as Father in Romans corresponds primarily to Christ as Son. God fulfills his promises in this Son: messianic promises, including making the nations the king's heritage. God is also father of his people, now redefined in terms of Jews and Gentiles, able to address God as Abba through the Spirit. They are sons now through conformity to the obedient son, Jesus. Where now to look for the faithfulness of the Father? Redefinition again. Without loss of the Jewish history, God's faithfulness = his righteousness must now embrace a place in the covenant for Gentiles, and it must take account of the widespread Jewish failure to embrace Jesus. Old Testament resources are available to assist in the necessary rethinking. For Paul Christ is the means of demonstrating God's covenant faithfulness to Israel, for the sake of Israel, but also for the benefit of the Gentiles.

Working from Rom 1:5; 1:16–17 (with a major focus on the quotation from Hab 2:4); and 3:21–26, Khobnya argues that Christ's faithfulness is intended to be seen as fulfilment of the Father's faithfulness. The role of πίστις is called upon to carry the main burden in the case being made. It is helpful for Khobnya's case that πίστις is used of God's faithfulness in 3:3, but surprising that it is not used elsewhere in the NT or in the OT in this way (except as echoed in one place name); and elsewhere in Romans δικαιοσύνη is preferred for God's faithfulness.

In the author's hands intertextuality (and intratextuality) tends here toward maximizing readings, with what have previously been seen as competing readings tending to be asserted simultaneously. So, for example, "the obedience of faith" of 1:5 seems to be both the obedience that is faith, but also faithful obedience in the pattern of Jesus, and as well acting in light of the eschatological situation with its new covenant realities. For Hab 2:4 there seems to be a similar adding up of the various options. Perhaps there is an important corrective here to overanalyzed conceptual meanings. In relation to the discussion of Hab 2:4 there is a question of whether expansiveness of meaning should be allowed to include syntactical indeterminacy. Khobnya aligns herself firmly with those who read "faithfulness of Christ" in Rom 3:22 and not "faith in Christ." This is the key to her understanding of Rom 3:21–26: Christ undertakes the redemption God intends; God is demonstrating his faithfulness in as much as Christ is faithfully fulfilling God's redeeming intention.

In the study of Rom 4:1–25 Khobnya sets Abraham's example into the Pauline context, and in particular Paul's concern for Gentile inclusion. She looks at Abraham in Gen 15 and 17 and in Jewish tradition. For Paul God acts in power and grace; and faith is faith in God's faithfulness thus expressed. Abraham's faith anticipates the shape of Christian faith. Of special interest, however, is that alongside this main thrust Khobnya identifies a thread that wants to make Abraham's faith, acted upon in obedience, anticipatory for that of Jesus. Some will see this as an unsatisfactory maximizing reading, but it gains at least some thematic traction from what follows (only thematic traction, because in what follows the correspondence is between Isaac and Jesus, not Abraham and Jesus). In an extended treatment of Christ's redemptive death and the Aqedah motif, Khobnya argues that Paul offers a radical rereading of the Aqedah as God's story of redemption that comes about in Christ's obedience to the Father.

Christ's obedience versus Adam's disobedience is explored with a focus on Rom 5:12–21, but reaching wider and beginning with Adam's disobedience in Scripture and tradition. Christ's obedience is equated with his faithfulness. And Christ's obedience here is seen as the obedience of the son. Are we therefore to see Adam's disobedience in terms of Adam as son of God? Traditions of Adam as son of God might have been explored here, but have not; they might have strengthened the case being made.

The use of the Fatherhood of God as a lens through which to explore Romans is as far as I am aware unparalleled. Khobnya has made it fruitful, producing new insights into this much studied letter. Both in terms of method and substance this is a book that deserves our attention.

Revd Professor John Nolland
Trinity College, Bristol

Preface

THIS MONOGRAPH IS A slightly revised version of a PhD thesis carried out at the Nazarene Theological College (NTC) and submitted to the University of Manchester in 2011. I am thankful to Pickwick Publications for accepting my manuscript for publication.

Many people have made the completion of this book possible and I want to express my greatest gratitude to all of them. I am thankful to the NTC faculty and staff for their support throughout the years of my research. I want to thank especially my supervisor, Dr. K. E. Brower, not only for his attentive and thorough supervision but also for the initial encouragement to pursue my dream of a higher education. His comments on my work as it progressed were very insightful, helpful, and encouraging. His personal scholarly work and life have always been an example for me.

I am thankful to my many friends at NTC and Ehrhardt Seminar at the University of Manchester whose perceptive comments and questions always stimulated further research and new discoveries. I am especially grateful for those who proofread this manuscript. Their care and attention to detail saved the book from too much semantic interference from my mother tongue. Those traces that remain are my responsibility alone.

I am thankful to all my friends for their spiritual and financial support. I could not have even dreamed of moving to England and undertaking research that lasted years without the support of anonymous donors. Their belief in me and their generosity toward my family and me have put us forever in their debt. The years of studies and research at NTC became precious for my academic and pastoral experience. If I have become a more careful reader of scripture and a better scholar, I have them to thank.

Finally, I want to thank my husband, Andrey, for his faithful support and great encouragement on a daily basis. This monograph would not have been accomplished without the loving support of my husband and my son, Artem. I dedicate this book to them.

Soli Deo gloria
Svetlana Khobnya
January, 2013

Abbreviations

Primary Sources

Ant.	*Jewish Antiquities* by Josephus
Apoc. Ab.	*Apocalypse of Abraham*
Apoc. Ezek.	*Apocryphon of Ezekiel*
Apoc. Bar.	*Apocalypse of Baruch*
2 Bar.	*2 Baruch*
4 Bar.	*4 Baruch*
Bib.Ant.	*Liber Antiquitatum Biblicarum* by Pseudo-Philo
CD-A	*Damascus Document*
DSS	Dead Sea Scrolls
1 En.	*1 Enoch*
Exod. Rab.	*Exodus Rabbah*
Gen. Rab.	*Genesis Rabbah*
HB	Hebrew Bible
Jos. As.	*Joseph and Aseneth*
Jub.	*Jubilees*
Levi Rab.	*Leviticus Rabbah*
L. A. E.	*Life of Adam and Eve*
LXX	Septuagint
1 Macc	1 Maccabees
2 Macc	2 Maccabees

Abbreviations

3 Macc.	3 Maccabees
4 Macc.	4 Maccabees
MT	Masoretic text
MS	Manuscript
MSS	Manuscripts
NT	New Testament
OT	Old Testament
Pss. Sol.	*Psalms of Solomon*
1Q-11Q	Qumran Scrolls from Caves 1–11
4Q372	*Apocryphon of Joseph*
4QFlor	*Florilegium (4Q174)*
1QH	*The Thanksgiving Hymns*
1QpHab	*Pesher on Habakkuk*
4QMMT	*Halakhic Letter*
1QS	*The Community Rule*
Sib. Or.	*Sibylline Oracles*
Sif. Deut.	*Sifre Deuteronomy*
Sir	*The Wisdom of Jesus Son of Sirach*
T. Benj.	*Testament of Benjamin*
T. Dan	*Testament of Dan*
T. Gad	*Testament of Gad*
T. Job	*Testament of Job*
T. Jud.	*Testament of Judah*
T. Levi	*Testament of Levi*
T. Mos.	*Testament of Moses*
Tob	Tobit
T. 12 Patr.	*Testament of the Twelve Patriarchs*
Wis	Wisdom of Solomon

Contemporary Sources

AB	Anchor Bible
BECNT	Baker Exegetical Commentary on the New Testament
BRev	Bible Review
BibInt	Biblical Interpretation
BST	Bible Speaks Today
CBQ	Catholic Biblical Quarterly
CBR	Currents in Biblical Research
DNTT	*Dictionary of New Testament Theology.* Edited by Colin Brown. 4 vols. Exeter: Paternoster, 1975–1978
DJD	Discoveries in the Judaean Desert
DSD	Dead Sea Discoveries
DPL	*Dictionary of Paul and His Letters.* Edited by G. F. Hawthorne and R. P. Martin. Downers Grove, IL: InterVarsity, 1993
FB	Forschung zur Bibel
HCOT	Historical Commentary on the Old Testament
HTR	Harvard Theological Review
ICC	International Critical Commentary
JBL	Journal of Biblical Literature
JETS	Journal of the Evangelical Theological Society
JJS	Journal of Jewish Studies
JRS	Journal of Ritual Studies
JSJ	Journal for the Study of Judaism
JSJSup	Journal for the Study of Judaism: Supplement Series
JSNT	Journal for the Study of the New Testament
JSNTSup	Journal for the Study of the New Testament: Supplement Series
JSOT	Journal for the Study of the Old Testament

JSOTSup	Journal for the Study of the Old Testament: Supplement Series
JSP	*Journal for the Study of the Pseudepigrapha*
JTS	*Journal of Theological Studies*
JR	*Journal of Religion*
LBNTS	Library of New Testament Studies
NCB	New Century Bible.
NIB	*The New Interpreter's Bible*
NIBC	New International Bible Commentary
NICNT	New International Critical Commentary
NICOT	New International Commentary on the Old Testament
NIDOTTE	*New International Dictionary of Old Testament Theology and Exegesis.* Edited by Willem A. Van Gemeren. 5 vols. Grand Rapids: Zondervan, 1997
NIGTC	New International Greek Testament Commentary
NIVAC	New International Version Application Commentary
NovT	*Novum Testamentum*
NTS	New Testament Studies
OBC	Oxford Bible Commentary
RS	*Religious Studies*
RevQ	*Revue de Qumran*
SBET	Scottish Bulletin of Evangelical Theology
SBL	Society of Biblical Literature
SBLDS	Society of Biblical Literature Dissertation Series
SBLMS	Society of Biblical Literature Monograph Series
SBLSymS	Society of Biblical Literature Symposium Series
SCM	Student Christian Movement
SJT	*Scottish Journal of Theology*
SNT	Studien zum Neuen Testament

SNTSMS	Society for New Testament Studies Monograph Series
SPCK	Society for Promoting Christian Knowledge
STDJ	Studies on the Texts of the Desert of Judah
TDNT	*Theological Dictionary of the New Testament*. Edited by G. Kittel and G. Friedrich. Translated by G. W. Bromiley. 10 vols. Grand Rapids: Eerdmans, 1964–1976
TDOT	*Theological Dictionary of the Old Testament*. Edited by G. J. Botterweck and H. Ringgren. Translated by J. T. Willis et al. 8 vols. Grand Rapids: Eerdmans, 1974–1978
TS	*Theological Studies*
TynBul	*Tyndale Bulletin*
VT	*Vetus Testamentum*
WBC	Word Biblical Commentary
WTJ	*Westminster Theological Journal*
WUNT	Wissenschaftliche Untersuchungen zum Neuen Testament
ZNW	*Zeitschrift für die neutestamentliche Wissenschaft und die Kunde der älteren Kirche*

Chapter 1

Introduction

"Although theologians have written about God the Father for centuries, the endeavor has been largely Christological, rather than a focus on the Father-God motif. Therefore there has been little apparent progress in understanding the concept, and by default it has assumed increasingly negative connotations."[1] This study takes up Tasker's challenge to keep this Christological perspective in balance with the Father-God motif that has its roots in OT and is prominent in the Second Temple period (hereafter 2TP). It argues that for Paul God is the Father who redeems. The OT imagery that shaped Israel's conception of God's interaction with them, and was a basis for God's future restoration of the nation despite their unfaithfulness, is central to Paul's explanation of the new salvific act of God the Father in Christ, the faithful and obedient Son.

---

1. Tasker, *Ancient*, 4. There is a problem with fatherhood language in relation to God because it interferes semantically with a human image of fatherhood that may have negative connotations. Although I acknowledge the problem, I do not focus on issues raised by feminist theologians, sociologists, psychologists, or anthropologists in relation to fatherhood language. I take the view that God the Father is a biblical term that renders divine reality rather than a secondary model that is created on the basis of negative human experience. I attempt to draw a biblical picture of God the Father gaining the theological content from the character of God and from the narrative identification of God who is involved with his people and wants to redeem them. See more on that below in "Statement of the Problem".

Background Assumptions

The initial data that includes the reasons for writing a letter or the actual social, cultural, and religious context of Paul's thought is helpful when studying Paul's teaching in Romans.[2]

It is commonly recognized that the letter was written by Paul in the middle to late 50s of the first century, from Corinth or somewhere nearby. Paul had never visited Rome despite his intentions to go to Jerusalem and thereafter to Rome and thence to Spain (1:8–15; 15:14–33).[3] Nevertheless, he claims to be their apostle as he is the apostle for all the Gentiles, and is eager to fulfill his responsibility in declaring the gospel of God's Son (1:1, 9, 15; cf. 1 Cor 10–13).

Paul wants understanding and appreciation of the message he proclaimed for the nations. He needs the support and backing of the Roman Christians in the venture of the mission of God to Jerusalem, to Spain and to Rome itself.[4] J. Crafton shows that this reflects Paul's "theological purpose in the epistle (namely the uniting of the nations in Jesus), which demonstrate[s] explicitly Paul's own function within the rhetorical world of the text, and which invite[s] participation by the Romans in that world."[5] Paul calls Roman Christians to participate in his vision—moreover in God's bigger vision—to bring all the nations into the obedience of faith that Paul gradually discloses in his letter.

The recipients of Paul's letter are identified by scholars as a community consisting of both Jews and Gentiles.[6] The Roman church was originally strongly Jewish in character and combined belief in Christ with an adherence to the Jewish law in whole or in part. This form of Christianity may have been espoused by some Gentiles who had already been in contact with the Jewish synagogues or some Jews who had been in frequent contact with Jews in Jerusalem and Palestine.

But other mostly Gentile Christians were dispensing with the need for obedience to the Jewish law as such. This group grew especially when the Jewish stream within the Roman church had been seriously weakened by Claudius' disciplinary measures against members of the

---

2. Wedderburn, *The Reasons*; Jewett, *Romans*, 1–91.
3. References to scripture without indication of the book will be to Romans.
4. Well presented by Jewett, *Romans*. See also Wedderburn, *The Reasons*, 22.
5. Crafton, "Paul's Rhetorical Vision," 326.
6. Wedderburn, *The Reasons*, 50; D. Moo, *Romans*, 9–13; Crafton, "Paul's Rhetorical Vision," 317–39; Jewett, *Romans*, 18–20, 58–59, 70–72.

Jewish community.⁷ By the time Paul wrote, Claudius was dead and the Jews could freely move back into Rome. As a result, the Jewish tradition in the church would be increased again, bringing "further troubles in the form of friction between proponents of the Law-free gospel and their Jewish and Judaizing neighbours."⁸ The conflict situation in Rome is clearly seen in the discussion of the relations between the strong and the weak (14:1—15:7). Paul's warnings to the Jews against taking pride in the possession of the law and circumcision (2:17-24; 3:27), and to the Gentiles against placing themselves above the Jews (11:17-21), as well as his admonitions to both parties not to think of themselves more highly than they ought (12:3), are evidence that these were problems among the Roman Christians.

At the same time Paul does not suggest that the Roman Christians deserve rebuke for any deficiency, for they are filled with all knowledge and are able to instruct each other (15:14; 16:17-20). Paul writes to those who are already saved and holy (1:1-15) but who are probably "being threatened by another salvific scheme, hence their assurance of salvation is being threatened"⁹ in the sense of whether the followers of Christ still have to follow the Jewish practices (cf. 3:27-31).

Paul writes to both Jews and Gentiles to affirm and to clarify the roots of their belief and practice. His message is the gospel of God that was promised beforehand and is now revealed in Christ. What has happened in Christ that is so important for Paul and for his audience? God has sent his Son to deal with sin (8:3). Christ is raised by the glory of the Father (6:4). God's righteousness has been revealed through the faithfulness of Jesus Christ (3:22).¹⁰ Through Christ's obedience many will become righteous (5:19). Paul shows that Christ's obedience is crucial in fulfilling the promise of the Father, which is redemption¹¹ for the Jews and

---

7. Tobin, *Paul's Rhetoric*, 17; Jewett, *Romans*, 18-20.

8. Wedderburn, *The Reasons*, 65; Jewett, *Romans*, 72; Crafton, "Paul's Rhetorical Vision," 322.

9. Campbell, *The Quest*, 205.

10. More on the faith of Christ in chapter 4.

11. Redemption has its background in the OT imagery of the exodus story. God's redemption is the deliverance of the people of Israel so that they can be his possession, people, even more importantly, his family (Exod 4:22). More generally, it is divine deliverance from the bondage of slavery, suffering and affliction; it is God's saving activity toward Israel. See chapter 2 below. Although the word ἀπολύτρωσις (redemption) itself appears a couple of times in Romans (3:24; 8:23), divine redemption as God's deliverance in Christ is prominent in Paul. Redemption in Paul, as we shall see

the Gentiles (3:21–26; 5:1–21). Christ is the fulfillment of the law (10:4). Paul wants to ensure that the Roman Christians continue following the gospel of God revealed in Christ and continue or join the mission of God, the one that Paul himself is on. Although Paul writes to the Romans, his message extends to all actual readers for they are part of God's eternal plan involving all the peoples of the earth, even all creation (8:1–27).

Statement of the Problem

Paul's encounter with the risen Christ did not change his faith orientation but did precipitate a significant change in nuance in his understanding of God. Hays, Dunn, Grieb, Witherington III, and Wright[12] all argue that Jesus did not bring a new concept of God, "but he demonstrated in action the full extent of God's redemptive will for the world which was from the beginning."[13] In this light, "a hope depicted in the prophets as the return of the exiles to their home and as the return of the children of Israel to God as Father" has been realized in Christ.[14] But precisely because this hope has been realized in Christ, the apostle Paul unfolds it in reference to the renewal and restoration of Israel as children of God and to the inclusion of the Gentiles as a part of God's bigger purposes from the very beginning.

The first part of the claim is essential to the question of God's faithfulness or truthfulness to the promises given to Israel. The second part raises the question of God's character and relation to the whole world. The two questions are related. The starting point for both questions is God, his relation to and redemption of the Jews and the Gentiles in Christ and it shapes the direction of Paul's argument.

---

in this research, is referred to in terms of deliverance from sins (6:18), justification and salvation through Christ's blood (5:9), reconciliation with God through Christ (5:11) as God's righteousness revealed through Christ (1:17; 3:21), and adoption into the family of God (8:14–17). See also Morris, "Redemption," 784–86; Schneider and Brown, "λύτρον," 189–223.

12. Hays, *Echoes*, xiii; Dunn, *Romans 1–8*, lxxi-lxxii; Grieb, *The Story of Romans*, xxii-xxiii; Witherington III, *Paul's Narrative*, 81–85; Wright, "The Letter to the Romans," 397–405.

13. Childs, *Biblical Theology*, 358.

14. M. Thompson, *The Promise*, 18.

Paul assumes many axioms about God without expounding them but they nevertheless flow from the overall context of his beliefs.[15] One of these axioms is that God the Father who redeems Israel out of Egyptian and Babylonian captivity, and who promises to redeem and restore Israel in the future, is the One who acts in his Son Jesus Christ calling people from all the nations into obedience of faith.

Traditionally, scholars have recognized the father image as a central "doctrine of God's nature and work" through Christ in the NT in general, and in Paul in particular.[16] In fact, it has become the dominant figure to describe God in his relationship to Jesus and to his followers. God the Father has been described from "the point of Christological confession" that begins with the NT and moves on from there without deep engagement with the whole of scripture.[17] Moreover, it has been viewed as original, creative and wholly new.[18] However, the idea of God the Father that is rooted in the OT and prominent in the 2TP, has received insufficient attention[19] and consequently is "in danger of being eclipsed without . . . the hope of the final realization of the promises of God made to Israel and guaranteed in Israel's Messiah, Jesus of Nazareth."[20] Thus, the concept of God's fatherhood is "not just another idea peripheral to the central core of biblical teaching and needs to be recognized as such."[21]

M. Thompson offers a careful study of the meaning of the fatherhood of God in the biblical narratives. She emphasizes the concept of God's fatherhood not as new or original in the NT but as a concept that evokes Israel's ancient and corporate hope of God's saving power and covenant faithfulness.[22] The idea of God's fatherhood in the OT illuminated by the role of the father in Israelite society has three distinctive

---

15. Dunn, *The Theology*, 28–29.

16. Machen, *The Origin*, 162–64; Hamerton-Kelly, *God the Father*, 82ff. He reaffirms his position in the later article "God the Father," 101; Jeremias, *Prayers*. Also, Barr, "Abba," 28–47. However, no systematic work has been offered on God's fatherhood in Paul, especially in Romans.

17. M. Thompson, *The Promise*, 157.

18. Lidgett, *The Fatherhood of God*," 2. Bousset, *Jesu Predigt*, 242; Jeremias, *Prayers*; Kittel, "ἀββα," 6.

19. Nunnally emphasizes this fact in his dissertation, "The Fatherhood." See also Tasker, *Ancient*; M. Thompson, *The Promise*, 3–15, 156; D'Angelo, "Abba," 611–30.

20. M. Thompson, *The Promise*, 157.

21. Tasker, *Ancient*, 1.

22. M. Thompson, *The Promise*, 164.

characteristics according to Thompson. God the Father is the origin of the family who also provides an inheritance (whether land or eternal life) for his children. God the Father protects and provides for his children. He is also the figure of authority to whom obedience and honor are properly rendered.[23] From these perspectives Thompson considers the idea in NT teaching. For Paul God the Father is the founder of the family who gives an inheritance to his children (8:14–17).[24] The very love and mercy of God that elected Israel now elects all those in Christ, including the Gentiles who are also honored children of Abraham.[25] God called them to be saints and to belong to Christ granting them a new status.

Thompson argues that all three characteristics in Paul appeal not to what God is but what he does, namely to God's mercy and righteousness, his saving actions in Christ in whom God's promises made to Abraham open up the orientation toward the future.[26] Following this discussion two important ideas become worth further exploration. First, to speak of God as Father is to emphasize the redemptive work of God that Paul displays in a rich vocabulary, including reconciliation, adoption, and salvation. Second, the relationship of God the Father with his children for Paul is the result of the redemptive activity of God through his Son. Therefore, it is impossible to speak about God the Father who redeems without addressing the actions of the Son, particularly his faithful obedience to the Father. While the idea of God the Father who redeems in the OT and in Romans will be addressed more thoroughly in chapters 2 and 3, and the obedience of the Son will be discussed in chapter 4 and 6, one more explanation in relation to the language of God's fatherhood needs to be pondered.

The term "father" for God is problematic since it evokes "male" imagery. Contemporary feminist theologians see male imagery for God as idolatrous and anti-women.[27] Therefore, some of them attempt to consider God as Father in combination with other images that are not exclusively male, such as "mother," or "parent."[28] Others believe that this issue cannot be so easily resolved and continue to emphasize the problem

23. Ibid., 38, 54.
24. Ibid., 116.
25. Ibid., 121.
26. Ibid., 132.
27. E. A. Johnson, *She Who Is*, 33–41; Hampson, *Theology and Feminism*; M. Thompson, *The Promise*, 3–13.
28. Van Wijk-Bos, *Reimagining God*, ix.

of male imagery for God that legitimizes patriarchy and provides a paradigm of male hierarchy.[29]

Although this study is not engaged in feminist discussion, as stated earlier, it holds the opinion that naming God according to our conception of human fathers relegates God to the level of a human construct. The significance of calling God the Father goes much deeper than a helpful analogy; it begins with God.[30] The proposition of this study is that in the OT and Judaism God as Father is used as a family concept and corporately, that God is like a Father of Israel, like a loving parent (embracing fatherly and motherly characteristics as, for example, in Isa 49:14–16) of his people or of the righteous ones within Israel. Moreover, God as Father is the One who acts on behalf of his people and redeems them. In this respect the words of Thompson are significant, when she says that understanding "God the Father has less to do with certain attributes or characteristics that might be assigned to God, and much more to do with the way in which God's mercy and faithfulness persistently seek out a people as heirs of the divine promises."[31]

The NT and Paul in particular call God the Father of Christ and of those who are in Christ, because it is a reality for those in Christ, when his Father becomes our Father. This concept emphasizes corporate, covenant and family relationships. God the Father redeems through his Son so that we all (Jews and Gentiles, male and female) may have access into his family. God the Father language describes a reality that exceeds "the capacity of ordinary," "commonsense discourse," this reality is of God's "suffering love."[32] God's fatherhood and his redemption in and through Christ concern all people and rather express a universal, cosmic and gender-neutral inclusion. The idea of the Son if viewed as the embodiment of Israel and humanity also helps to overcome the maleness of the word.

The second part of this research focuses on how God's faithfulness is extended to the Gentiles and how God deals with Israel's unfaithfulness. Two recent scholars look carefully at the faithfulness issue but their work leaves these questions unanswered.

---

29. Erickson, *God the Father Almighty*, 23; Brown and Bohn, eds., *Christianity, Patriarchy*; M. Daly, *Beyond God the Father*.

30. Widdicombe, *The Fatherhood of God*, viii–xv; 255–61.

31. M. Thompson, "Mercy upon All," 207.

32. Davis and Hays, eds., *The Art*, 13.

Johnson suggests that the idea of God's faithfulness toward his people is expressed especially in Paul's account of chapter 9–11, where Paul insists on God's faithfulness to Israel despite its faithlessness and God's purposes toward the Gentiles. She stresses a tension in the relationship of God's faithfulness to Israel with his impartiality and notes that this is present throughout Israel's history. This tension does not allow God's faithfulness to overcome God's impartiality and *vice versa*. She writes that God's faithfulness is impartial, inclusive, and independent of human right or worth. This is the tension that allows Paul to declare the inclusion of the believing Gentiles without excluding unbelieving Jews.[33] The inclusion of the Gentiles has been accomplished in the same terms as God's call of Israel, namely at God's initiative. Johnson implies that an explanation for God's faithfulness to Israel may be found in the beginning of Israel's history when God calls them a nation and redeems them out of Egypt. God's election is independent of human worth and thus, it is as true of the Gentiles as of Israel.[34] This means that "God's impartial treatment of Jews and Gentiles is therefore a demonstration of God's faithfulness to Israel rather than an abrogation of it."[35] Johnson is right in identifying the divine character and relationship to Israel and to the world as a starting point for Paul's discussion. However, she does not directly answer how God's call and faithfulness to Israel extend to the Gentiles and how Paul deals with Israel's failure to attain the righteousness of God. Nor does she discuss the role of Christ in God's purposes.[36] The question is then where does Christ's faithfulness find its place in the whole discussion? This underlines the importance of considering Paul's whole narrative, his bigger picture and not only chapters 9–11. Second, what role does Christ play in relation to God's faithfulness and eventually in relation to both Jews and Gentiles? And finally, who are the children of God according to Paul?

Caroline Hodge takes a different approach. She studies the idea of the inclusion of the Gentiles into the people of God and of God's redeeming purposes for Israel from an ethnic point of view. While underlining ethnicity and kinship as crucial to Paul's understanding of the relationship between the God of Israel and humans, she believes that Jews and

---

33. E. E. Johnson, "Romans 9–11," 225.
34. Ibid., 224.
35. Ibid., 227.
36. Ibid., 230.

Gentiles as different ethnic groups do not collapse into one but have a relationship that can be rearranged and renegotiated. This becomes a key for unfolding Paul's idea of the renewal and restoration of Israel as children of God and for the inclusion of the Gentiles.

Hodge suggests that "polar opposites" (Jews and Gentiles in Romans) are connected by sharing common ancestry descending from Abraham and having a shared God but that they are not merged.[37] By using the phrase "first the Jews, then the Gentiles" Paul does not join these groups together but maintains the hierarchy, placing Jews at the top. This cultivated tension between them propels Paul's "version of salvation history, ultimately bringing about the salvation of both peoples."[38] While Jews and the Gentiles, as branches of the same tree, are descendants of the same ancestor, as separate branches they are independent in genealogy. This leads her to conclude that, "Jews and gentiles are distinct peoples and remain so; the Jews claim their link to Abraham by birth (and God's promises) and the gentiles by adoption (and God's promises)."[39] As the "natural" branches the Jews are higher in hierarchy.[40] Ultimately, God will restore the Gentiles to a subordinate rank, when the full number of them responds. Then all Israel will be saved. Thus, for Hodge, God's choice of Israel, as his first people, is the means to bring in the Gentiles.[41] So, the overall tension between Jews and Gentiles in Paul describes the process of the restoration of Israel. The Gentiles' reconciliation to God through Christ serves this larger goal.[42]

Caroline Hodge rightly re-addresses the issue between Jews and Gentiles in relationship to God as relating to their origin: how the peoples become God's in the first place. This idea again raises the question of God's fatherhood. Secondly, Hodge is correct that Paul recognizes Israel's "special relationship" with God. Paul reminds his reader that

---

37. Hodge, *If Sons*, 138.
38. Ibid.
39. Ibid., 146–47.
40. The language of ethnic, status and gender distinction, according to Hodge, is also seen in passages like Gal 2:15 (Paul's distinction from the Gentiles), Gal 2:7–9 ("the spread of the gospel as segregated ethnically"), Gal 4:21–31 (master/slave relationship, the role of women as mothers and the distinction between chosen and non-chosen lineage). She underlines that Paul's focus on ethnicity is vivid in his "stay as you are" advice. See ibid., 128–29.
41. Hodge agrees with Nanos on this. Nanos, *The Mystery of Romans*.
42. Hodge, *If Sons*, 147. See also Nanos, *The Mystery of Romans*, 223.

theirs is still the adoption, the divine glory, the covenants, the receiving of the law, etc. (9:4–5). Jewish identity as a part of Israel's destiny is a positive value for Paul. Christ himself is a Jew by physical descent (9:5; cf. 1:3; 11:1). The universally gracious God would not be trustworthy if he were not faithful to Israel.

For Paul, however, this special relationship does not describe a superiority of the Jews in relation to God through Christ. Paul affirms sinfulness of both Jews and Gentiles before God (1:18—3:20) and that the Jews are no better than the Gentiles (3:1–9). They all need to receive a spirit of adoption and be children of God (8:14–17). As Esler convincingly shows, "prior to their recategorization as believers in Christ, the Jews and Greeks are equal in respect to a negative status, their subjection to sin, although from entirely different routes—the Greek apart from the law and the Jews under the law."[43] Although ethnicity remains, Jews and Gentiles are equal in the status that they have attained in Christ through whose obedience they have now received reconciliation (5:11) and have become children of God's family (8:14–17).

Perhaps Hodge's model of hierarchical relationship and superiority of the Jews over the Gentiles derives from her narrow understanding of the role of Christ in Paul. She describes Christ Jesus only as a way for the Gentiles to join in Israel as additional people.[44] She does not emphasize the significance of Christ for the Jews. They will be saved when the full number of the Gentiles comes in (11:25) but they are already God's people.

Hodge's view is problematic at this key point: in Paul the centrality of Jesus' work and his obedience to God the Father serves as the means for unfolding God's purposes not only for Israel but to Israel and through Israel for the whole world from the very beginning. Paul's whole logic of arguing that Jews and Gentiles are children of Abraham and of God himself corresponds with the idea of their adoption and the inheritance of both parties. Paul's message of God's redemptive activity is inseparable from God's acceptance of both Jews and Gentiles into his family as children and accordingly heirs (8:14–17). These are the key points that will be investigated more fully later on.

Although from different perspectives both Hodge and Johnson attempt to study God's nature and work in relation to humanity, they lessen the significance of Christ in Paul's scheme. This consequently does not

---

43. Esler, *Conflict*, 360–61.
44. Hodge, *If Sons*, 147.

clarify how God's call and faithfulness to Israel extends to the Gentiles and how Paul deals with Israel's failure to attain the righteousness of God.

This study focuses on how God redeems Israel and the nations without losing the "eschatological trajectory," meaning that Christ through his obedience fulfills his Father's promises to his people, "first Israel and then also the Israel of the renewed covenant."[45]

Paul's extensive comparison between Adam and Christ (5:12–21) points to placing all people under Adam and under sin because of Adam's disobedience (cf. 1:18—3:20). The whole point of the obedience of the Son is that he enters the age that was begun by Adam and "through his obedience shatters its power and inaugurates a new age of human history."[46] Through Christ's obedience many will become righteous (5:19). Paul builds up his argument in Romans in such a way that Christ's obedience in 5:12–21 in God's redemptive purposes becomes an explicit explanation of Christ's faithfulness, πίστις Χριστοῦ, as he has unveiled it beforehand (especially in 3:22) and that deserves special attention.

Since the Reformation Romans has often been read with an emphasis on the faith of the believers through which the ungodly are justified by God's grace. Luther was struggling with the medieval religious system that seemed to place people in the position of having to earn God's favor by doing various rites. In Romans he found the explanation of "justification by faith" in Christ alone. This understanding has exercised a powerful influence on the subsequent reading of Romans. Critical to this has been the translations of Paul's phrase, πίστις Χριστοῦ (faith of Christ) in 3:22, 26 and other letters as an objective genitive where Christ is seen as the object of faith. So faith is the faith of the believers through which they are justified by God's grace. It leads, in a sense, to reading Paul "as putting one human activity (fulfilling stipulations of the law) over against another human activity (believing)."[47] Besides, Luther's explanation has little room for understanding God's redemption as interpreted against the Jewish background where the theme of faithfulness and obedience is a prevailing factor for the people of God. The question of God's redeeming activity through the faithful obedience of Christ was left largely unexplored.

At the beginning of the century Adolf Deissmann notices that Paul's faith indicates a mystical fellowship with Christ and in this fellowship

---

45. M. Thompson, *The Promise*, 156.
46. Cousar, *The Letters of Paul*, 128.
47. Ibid., 130.

is union with God.⁴⁸ Consequently, it is difficult to find an acceptable translation for πίστις Χριστοῦ (German *Christusglauben* implies both faith in and of Christ himself). Even though Deissmann does not explain whether the phrase implies Christ's faith or faith in Christ, he observes that through πίστις Χριστοῦ there is a "fellowship" with God and it is a mystical unity.

Another German scholar, Adolf Schlatter, pointed more in the direction of the subjective understanding of faith saying, "But faith arises from what Christ is and does. It is based on Christ's conduct toward mankind."⁴⁹ However, Schlatter does not develop this understanding in a coherent way.

A shift of understanding πίστις Χριστοῦ as a subjective genitive in modern scholarship is associated with the ground-breaking research of Richard Hays. It is the faith that Christ himself has. In his *The Faith of Christ* Hays begins with Gal 3:22 but then also refers to the letter to the Romans. He argues that Paul uses both the subjective genitive in reference to the faith of God, πίστιν τοῦ θεοῦ (3:3) and from the faith of Abraham, ἐκ πίστεως Ἀβραάμ (4:12, 16). There is no indication in the surrounding context of 3:21–26 that Jesus Christ is to be considered the object of faith. Christ's faith is surrounded by two notions of "an atoning sacrifice" and "his blood" that focus on Christ rather than a believer. Accordingly, all three terms are descriptive of Jesus in his obedient death on the cross. There is an addition to Jesus' faith, the phrase that refers to the believers separately: to all who believe, εἰς πάντας τοὺς πιστεύοντας (3:22b). So, it makes sense to read the beginning of the verse as the righteousness of God revealed through the faithfulness of Christ.⁵⁰

The Greek word πίστις for "faith" has a broad range of meaning, including not only trust or faith, but also obedience, faithfulness, reliability, and fidelity. Paul connects faith and obedience in ways that make them virtually synonymous (1:5; 16:26). If the subjective reading is in view then the possibility of being righteous comes through the faithfulness of Jesus Christ, through his faithful obedience to the will of God so that because of that the many will be made righteous (5:19; cf. Phil 2:8). This certainly does not deny the necessity of Christians to have faith in Christ as 3:22b (cf. Gal 2:16; Phil 1:29) shows, but it indicates that God's

---

48. Deissmann, *Religion of Jesus*, 205–6.
49. Schlatter, *The Theology of the Apostles*, 24.
50. Hays, *The Faith*, 170–74.

redemptive purpose is fulfilled through Christ's faithful obedience. Since the publication of the first edition of Hays's PhD dissertation the debate over the meaning of πίστις Χριστοῦ has intensified.[51]

This study argues that the subjective reading fits Paul's overall narrative in terms of the obedience and submission of the Son to the loving will of the Father (5:12–21; cf. Phil 2:5–11).

Mark Reasoner is afraid that "the subjective reading can run the risk of making human participation in Christ's faithfulness a work that eclipses the mystery of the redemption accomplished by Christ's death."[52] However, this does nothing to diminish the mystery of redemption. Paul himself admits the mystery of God's revelation (16:25–26). It just shows that there are no simple answers to the concept of redemption. Perhaps, we need to look at Christ's act with new eyes within God's redeeming activity and consider it against its Jewish background. The Christological understanding of πίστις Χριστοῦ can bring a change in which "salvation, the Law and the righteousness of God take on new meanings."[53]

As the debate concerning πίστις Χριστοῦ continues,[54] this study may be a further contribution to the subjective understanding of it as a part of Paul's bigger theme of the divine initiative and redemptive purposes accomplished through Christ's obedience.

Methodology

There are four approaches that are essential for this particular research.

---

51. B. Longenecker, "ΠΙΣΤΙΣ" 478–80; L. T. Johnson, "Romans 3:21–26," 77–90; Hooker, "PISTIS CRISTOU," 321–42; Keck, "'Jesus' in Romans," 443–60; Gorman, *Inhabiting the Cruciform God*, 57–85. For the objective understanding of faith, see Hultgren, "The *Pistis Christou*," 248–63; Dunn, "ΕΚ ΠΙΣΤΕΩΣ"; Esler, *Conflict*, 159; Reasoner, *Romans in Full Circle*, 39; Porter and Pitts, "Πίστις," 33–53; Matlock, "Saving Faith," 73–89; Watson, "By Faith (of Christ)," 147–63. Some scholars present a "third view" on πίστις Χριστοῦ, namely, as the gospel message about Christ. However, in essence they do not depart far from the subjective understanding of faith. They just emphasize more precisely that the subjective understanding does not exclude the objectivity of faith in Christ. See Sprinkle, "Πίστις Χριστοῦ," 165–84; Schliesser, *Abraham's Faith*," 263. For further bibliography on the debate of the meaning of πίστις Χριστοῦ, see also online, "Faith(fulness) in/of Christ Bibliography," Paul's Epistle to the Galatians, http://epistletothegalatians.wordpress.com/faithfulness-inof-christ-bibliography.htm.

52. Reasoner, *Romans in Full Circle*, 39.

53. Stubbs, "The Shape of Soteriology," 139.

54. See the collection of essays in Bird and Sprinkle, eds., *The Faith*.

A key approach of this study is intertextuality. Intertextuality is defined as "the imbedding of fragments of an earlier text within a later one."[55] In relation to Paul, this approach is particularly fruitful because Paul is a Jew and his theology is rooted in the Jewish scriptures. He repeatedly refers to Israel's scriptures. They determine the "subtext that plays a constitutive role in shaping his literary production."[56]

Within intertextuality, according to R. Hays, there are both obvious intertextual references such as quotations or allusions and subtler ones such as echoes.[57] Although scholars realize that this criterion is complicated and it is often difficult to be certain that particular scriptural passages lie behind certain NT texts, yet intertextuality needs to be undertaken because earlier texts have left their marks in the NT in very concrete ways.[58] The intertextual correspondence between texts is characterized by linguistic and contextual parallels,[59] or by "overlap in shared intertextual exegetical combinations."[60]

Moreover, intertextuality denotes the "transposition of earlier material to something new;" it is about "observing the transformation of influences."[61] R. Hays observes in this regard that, "if we are to arrive at a properly nuanced estimate of Paul's theological stance toward his own people and their sacred texts, we must engage him on his own terms, by following his readings of the text in which he heard the word of God."[62]

Paul reads the scripture through his own understanding of the gospel. At first glance, it may appear that Paul re-writes the story of Israel to fit into his own scheme (see, for instance the bald statement, "and that rock was Christ" in 1 Cor 10:4 in reference to the rock in the wilderness from Num 20:8–10). However, Paul re-reads Israel's entire story in the light of Christ because in his view the action of God has always been centered in Christ. Consequently, the gospel concerning his Son is now indispensible for a proper understanding of the words of the scripture. In Paul's view, he now sees history clearly for the first time rather than

---

55. Hays, *Echoes*, 14.
56. Ibid., 15–16.
57. Ibid., 23–29.
58. Brooke, *The Dead Sea Scrolls*, 70; Hays, *Echoes*, 23, 70–71.
59. Beavis, "The Resurrection," 51.
60. Brooke, *The Dead Sea Scrolls*, 93.
61. Ibid., 73.
62. Hays, *Echoes*, x.

revises it. As Cousar concludes, "Paul provides a radical reading of Israel's history and scriptures in terms of the revealed gospel. It is the latter that defines the former, and not *vice versa*."[63] Paul's keen awareness of living in the time when the OT pronouncements are being fulfilled in Christ, allows him "imaginative" freedom in the usage of the OT in his teaching.[64] Paul's Christological approach provides the essential hermeneutical lens.[65] For him the Jewish scriptures serve in God's plan as a witness to the gospel, which is to be the final revelatory act of God in Jesus Christ, for the Jews first, but then also for the Gentiles.

Second, this research applies a narrative approach to Paul's letter.[66] This approach does not necessarily consider Paul's letter as a narrative or even narratives, but it looks at the text as a "reflective discourse" based on a story of God culminated in death and resurrection of Christ, which provides the "narrative substructure" for Paul's theology and which is alluded to in Paul's discourse.[67] A narrative approach helps to look beyond the literary markers, and behind all the literary patterns and conventional speeches of the letter to the Romans to see Paul's essential teaching on Christ's obedience within the bigger picture of God's relationship with his children. The inner logic of Paul's thought helps the reader to follow the arguments of the letter.

The narrative approach should be also applied to Paul's usage of the scripture. As Matlock puts it, "a 'narrative' reading of Paul is both a type of approach and a type of argument."[68] In other words, when Paul refers to or echoes scripture he "derives coherence from their common relation to the scriptural story of God's righteousness. Though the quotations appear eclectic and scattered, they usually must be understood as allusive

---

63. Cousar, "Continuity," 210.

64. Hays, *The Conversion*, ix. This approach to Paul's usage of the Jewish scriptures has become especially prominent since the discoveries of a similar phenomenon in Qumran. Stendahl, *The School of Saint Matthew*, 194–201, was one of first ones to point out that the eschatological conviction explains the freedom in relation to the text in both Qumran *pesharim* and the NT. Ellis appropriated the term for that technique, *midrash pesher*, in *Paul's Use*. Stanley, *Paul*, 29, develops a further careful approach suggesting that Paul adapted the biblical quotations to communicate his own understanding of the passage.

65. See Watson, *Paul*, 16–17.

66. Hays, *The Faith*; Witherington III, *Paul's Narrative*; Dunn, *The New Perspective* and *The Theology of Paul*; B. Longenecker, ed., *Narrative Dynamics*.

67. Hays, *The Faith*, 28.

68. Matlock, "The Arrow and the Web," 53.

recollections of the wider narrative setting from which they are taken."[69] Paul does not even always indicate quotations (e.g., Hab 2:4 in Rom 1:17), attributing them to the wider context of the scripture as a whole.[70] Paul reads the scripture narratively as the story of God's election and redemption of his people that has been fulfilled in Christ.[71] Even through the lens of Christ Paul's gospel stands in coherent continuity with the witness of Israel's scripture[72] to the faithfulness of God to Israel, not only for the sake of Israel but also for the sake of all people.

Third, the actual underlying argument of the letter needs also to be considered within the wider worldview and belief system on which Paul draws. N. T. Wright holds that all societies have a "worldview" that serves as "the grid through which reality is perceived and experienced."[73] For him such fundamental perspectives form a matrix of thought that must be understood in order to interpret the thinker. So, to understand Paul and his thinking one must place him within the symbolic world of second temple Judaism that includes Jewish writings, traditions and practice.[74] In these frameworks, chapter 2 explores Jewish texts[75] where God is referred to as the Father in relation and actions to the people of Israel.

Fourth, P. Alexander posits a heuristic approach that considers later information as shedding light on first-century texts.[76] The function of the later data "would be to act as a possible model with which we explore" Paul's writing. Applying this approach "we can plausibly fill in some of the gaps in our knowledge by disciplined historical imagination based on comparative models."[77] This approach helps to show the potentiality of the text and is applied in chapter 5 on the Aqedah.

---

69. Hays, *Echoes*, 157–58.
70. Watson, *Paul*, 45.
71. Hays, *The Conversion*, xvi.
72. Hays, *Echoes*, 157.
73. N. T. Wright, "Romans and the Theology of Paul," 32.
74. N. T. Wright, *The New Testament*, 145–338.
75. This category includes both OT and other Jewish texts of 2TP. Although there is a distinction between biblical texts and other Jewish literature in terms of authoritative status, together they constitute a valuable reference source for Paul's Jewish background. They all are 2TP literature that form Paul's worldview. See further Crawford, *Rewriting Scripture*; Brooke, "The Rewritten Law, 31–40.
76. Alexander, "The Qumran Songs," 349–72.
77. Alexander, "Orality," 183.

Outline

For Paul the good news of the gospel of God is precisely concerning his Son (1:3, 9), who is obedient to the Father (5:19) and in whom ancient promises and claims of God's intervention and redemption were reaffirmed (3:21–26). Accordingly, to understand Paul's message of redemption adequately, this study examines the OT and 2TP texts where the language of God as Father and Redeemer is viewed in relation to Israel and those within Israel. The chapter concludes that God as Father is redeemingly involved in the whole story of Israel. It highlights both the importance of the obedience of the people of God so that the name of God will be proclaimed in all the earth and the failure of God's son Israel to remain obedient to God the Father and, thus, to be a light to the nations. Despite this fact, God as Father and Redeemer is expected to act in the life of his people on behalf of his righteousness/faithfulness to them. There are expectations that God as Father and Redeemer will act through a messianic figure to accomplish his promises.

On the basis of this background chapter 3 deals with Paul's teaching on redemption as the act of the Father accomplished in the Son. Paul develops the idea that in Christ God's dealing with Israel continues but it continues in such a way that Christ becomes the key for the interpretation of God's purposes derived from the Jewish scriptures. This retrospective reading of Israel's story in the light of Christ enables Paul to reconsider the idea of God the Father and Redeemer of Israel as the Father of Christ and of all who are in Christ. It also enables him to redefine the family of God universally in relation to both Jews and Gentiles.

The main focus of chapter 4 is the extent to which Paul reflects the idea of God the Father who redeems in terms of God's own covenantal faithfulness/righteousness revealed in Christ's faithfulness. This chapter is a part of overall debate concerning πίστις Χριστοῦ. This thesis contributes further to the subjective understanding of it as a part of Paul's bigger theme of the divine initiative and redemptive purposes accomplished through Christ's obedience.

Chapter 5 refers to the story of Abraham in Romans and presents an array of arguments of how Abraham's faith helps Paul to unfold the narrative of God's redemption through Christ's faithfulness. The second part of the chapter explores Abraham's obedience within the Aqedah tradition and Paul's reflection on the Aqedah motif for the story of God's redemption in Christ. It argues that Paul shifts the significance of human obedience in Abraham's story to God's righteousness/faithfulness, mercy and love for the whole of humanity. He reinterprets the Aqedah in the light of the divine redemption that came about through Christ's obedience.

In Romans 5:12–21 Paul's discussion on obedience becomes an explicit explanation of Christ's own faithfulness as the fulfillment of God's purposes for the world. Chapter 6 brings to the forefront Paul's contrast between Adam and Christ. This contrast allows Paul to illuminate the superiority of Christ, who being like Adam did not sin, but obeyed God till death and condemned sin, thus reconciling humanity to God. This chapter includes Paul's overall conclusive claims about Christ who has not only accomplished the redemptive work of Israel but who has also reversed the fall of Adam.

Chapter 7 draws together the main conclusions of the research indicating its contributions in the area of Pauline interpretation.

Chapter II

God the Father in Jewish Tradition

1. Introduction

TRADITIONAL OT SCHOLARS SUCH AS Eichrodt and Childs understand the fatherhood of God in connection with other imagery known in the scriptures (King, Shepherd, and Redeemer). They consider these names as God's self-communication to his covenantal people.[1] In such a systematic approach, however, the idea of God's fatherhood itself does not receive an adequate treatment. David Tasker emphasising the significance of the study of the fatherhood of God in the OT writes, "Very little exegesis of the explicit 'God is a Father' texts found in the OT has been undertaken by biblical scholars to date."[2] His research on God's fatherhood in the OT is useful for this research in terms of linguistic and contextual analysis of OT texts passages where God is referred to as Father.

Moreover, the idea of God's fatherhood in Jewish scripture and tradition has been undermined in the past. In 1892 W. Bousset wrote that "the later Judaism [i.e., that of Jesus' time] had neither in name nor in fact the faith of the Father-God."[3] Both Bultmann and Jeremias continued to espouse Bousset's view.[4] Other scholars recognize and emphasize the idea of God the Father in Judaism.[5] However, no thorough research has been done in this area.

---

1. Childs, *Old Testament*, 40; Eichrodt, *Theology*, 69.
2. Tasker, *Ancient*, 4.
3. Bousset, *Jesu Predigt*, 242.
4. Jeremias, *Prayers of Jesus*; Bultmann, "The Significance," 11; Kittel, "ἀββᾶ," 6.
5. Wicks and Charles, *The Doctrine of God*, 344; Zeller, "God as Father," 119; M. Thompson, *The Promise*, 48–53.

W. Nunnally greatly contributes to the concept of God's fatherhood in his research on the Qumran scrolls. He is persuaded that the idea of God the Father is prominent in Jewish texts in relation to Israel. Moreover, "the sectarian literature of Qumran appears to be part of a movement toward an intensification and greater personification of the Father-son relationship."[6] This is a valuable claim that reappraises the view laid by Bousset and others and shows that God as Father is addressed corporately and personally in relation to the righteous ones of Israel. He also emphasizes the significance of the obedience of the son(s), which is, according to him, in balance with the love of the Father. Both aspects are "prerequisites of equal gravity to the maintenance of the Father-son relationship."[7] Nunnally's view is helpful in the development of the idea of the fatherhood of God in 2TP.

In Jewish tradition there are various texts that both characterize and invoke God the Father. The purpose of this chapter is not so much to contribute to OT theology as to study both OT and 2TP texts as potential background for Paul and to see contextually how the idea of God's fatherhood is related to his redemptive purposes. This research will be essential for understanding Paul's concept of the Father who redeems through Christ.

2. Evidence in the OT

There are only eighteen instances where God is designated as Father in the OT (Deut 32:5; 2 Sam 7:14; 1 Chr 17:13; 22:10; 28:6; 29:10; Ps 68:5; 89:26; 103:13; Prov 3:12; Jer 3:4–5, 7–8; 31:9; Isa 63:16 (twice); 64:8; Mal 1:6; 2:10).[8] However, the number of references alone can obscure the prominence of the idea. Other passages consider the relationship between God and Israel as a father-son relationship in which God acts as a loving father (for example, Exod 4:22; Deut 14:1; Isa 45:11; Jer 31:9; Hos 11:1). The idea of God being the Father also emerges in the personal names of the Israelites (e.g., 1 Sam 8:2; 2 Sam 8:16).[9] The concept of God's fatherhood is a broad category; however in the OT it is closely related to

---

6. Nunnally, "The Fatherhood," 236.
7. Ibid., 237.
8. Tasker, *Ancient*, 6.
9. Although acknowledged, the study of the personal names is not part of this research. See C. Wright, *Knowing God*, 24–25.

Israel. When God calls Israel out of slavery he acts like a father to it; Israel is his son (Exod 4:22). God liberates his son Israel, rescuing the people from their woes, thus being their Father and Redeemer (Isa 63:16).[10]

2.1. Father as Redeemer of Israel

C. Wright notes the concept of God being the Father of his people Israel is far from lacking in the theological repertoire of the OT.[11] God is described as the Father of the whole nation Israel. In Exodus 4 God calls Israel his son with the intention of redeeming Israel out of Egypt. In his instruction to Moses God says, "Then you shall say to Pharaoh, 'Thus says the LORD: Israel is my firstborn son. I said to you, "Let my son go that he may worship me"'" (Exod 4:22–23). This implicit reference to God as Father occurs in the context of the particular historical event of exodus, the deliverance of Israel from Egypt. John Durham puts it vividly saying that in God's request to let his son go to worship his divine Father there is a "glimmer of the exodus itself."[12] Although the whole earth belongs to God (Exod 19:5), God has chosen Israel to be in a special relationship; Israel belongs to God as his son whom he rescues from slavery.[13] His redeeming activity is based on the distinctive relationship with Israel. God's redemption out of Egypt remains an important subject throughout Exodus (Exod 6:5–6; 15:12–13; 19:4; 20:2; 33:1). It is sealed by the covenant into which God has entered with Israel as his children (Exod 6:5; 19–24).

The same idea appears in Deuteronomy where God is also depicted as the Father who redeems and carries his son Israel in the wilderness (Deut 1:31; cf. Hos 11:1). Although the verse literally says, "as a man carries his son," the parental image of God is implicit.[14] The exodus motif is present

---

10. גאל (redeemer) is the heart of the exodus motif, the heart of the covenantal relationship, a description of God's intent to be Israel's protector, to help and rescue those who have fallen in need, to be faithful to their election, Grisanti, "גאל," 883.

11. C. Wright, *Knowing God*, 77.

12. Durham, *Exodus*, 56.

13. Within the context Israel as God's firstborn son is contrasted against Pharaoh and his firstborn son, Childs, *Exodus*, 102. The use of the "firstborn son" for Israel is serious and concrete. Israel is God's beloved community. "To misidentify them as Pharaoh has done inevitably leads to mistreatment" (Brueggemann, "The Book of Exodus," 717).

14. See Craigie, *The Book of Deuteronomy*, 103. For Hosea see further Stuart, *Hosea-Jonah*, 177ff.

in Deut 32 when Moses describes God implicitly as the Father who cares for his people in the desert (Deut 32:10) and leads them out (Deut 32:12).[15]

Psalm 68 is parental investment in terms of provision and defense of the needy; the language in this description is the explicit reference to God as father and the language of exodus (Ps 68:5).[16] God leads out (יצא is often used in the exodus) his people (Ps 68:4–6). The psalm also mentions wilderness (Ps 68:7–8; cf. Deut 32:10), Sinai, the possession of the land and the heritage recalling the exodus (cf. Deut 32:6, 9).[17] In this setting the needy ones are the Israelites; they are orphans without God, and the provision God made for his people is his care for them in the wilderness. This idea of God being the Father here is once again implicitly connected with the exodus motif. He takes care of his people.

Prior to the exodus, the Israelites cried out to God because of their slavery (Exod 2:23). The word for service or slavery is the same as the word for service and worship to God (*ābad*).[18] When God releases Israel, he points out that their destiny is to be out of slavery for the service of God who is implicitly their Father. God redeems Israel and calls his people to worship and serve himself (Deut 10:20). They are to be devoted to their God. They are the redeemed ones of God (cf. Lev 25:38, 42–43, 55; Ps 107:2; Isa 62:12). Accordingly, this redemption implies more than just the redemption of slaves from Egypt. This redemption is more like "emancipation and restoration of the enslaved to wholeness in relation to God"[19] who is implicitly the Father of Israel. If prior to the exodus they are described as God's people, they are also slaves in Egypt, or aliens (Deut 10:18–19), the exodus event is important to confirm Israel as God's son or God's sons in Israel's history (Deut 14:1–2; Isa 1:2) with the purpose of serving him. In something like "a formula of adoption,"[20] Israel becomes as the firstborn son of God; no longer a slave. God's redemption of Israel sets the parameters for Israel's identity in relationship to God who becomes their Father.

God's redeeming activity toward his son Israel is also linked to creation language. In Deuteronomy, Moses reminds Israel that God has

---

15. God is explicitly named as Father earlier in Deut 32:6, Tasker, *Ancient*, 83, 86.
16. McCann, "The Book of Psalms," 945. Also Anderson, *The Book of Psalms*, 485.
17. McCann, "The Book of Psalms," 945.
18. C. Wright, *The Mission of God*, 270.
19. Green, *Salvation*, 69.
20. Brueggemann, "The Book of Exodus," 717.

redeemed his people but they have acted corruptly toward Him; they are not acting like his children, "Is not he your father, who created you, who made you and established you?"(Deut 32:5–6; cf. Mal 2:10). Israel belongs to God the Father because God created and established Israel. The language of creation and establishing of Israel is not meant to be taken in any physical or natural sense. God is not progenitor but the establisher of Israel as a nation and their liberator.[21] The idea is grounded in divine election or calling his people out, making them his or adopting them for a purpose to serve the Lord. He is the initiator of the relationship with them.

A similar idea is present in Isa 64:7–8. Israel is the work of God's hands. As their Father, Redeemer (cf. Isa 63:16) and potter, literally the one forming—יֹצְרִי (the same root as God forming Adam in Gen 2:7),[22] God has the right and is able to shape Israel's destiny and not to remember their sins. The creation language broadens the scope of God's fatherhood and his redeeming activity. Tasker believes that both the legitimacy and the capability for God's fatherhood arise from his being Creator.[23] One can conclude that God's redeeming activity is both creative in nature and founded upon the fact that he created Israel.

When God redeems Israel, he names it his firstborn son (Exod 4:22; Jer 31:9). Regardless of whether this means that other nations are God's sons too,[24] the emphasis is on Israel being God's firstborn son.[25] As the firstborn, Israel is dear to God.[26] Israel has a clear family relationship with God who takes care of it, leading it out of slavery. Moreover, Israel's identity as the firstborn son is also connected with the idea of the nation being God's inheritance. Israel as God's inheritance and his special portion is affirmed in Deuteronomy, "You are children of the LORD your God. You must not lacerate yourselves or shave your forelocks for the dead. For you are a people holy to the LORD your God; it is you the LORD has chosen

---

21. Tasker, *Ancient*, 83. Also Verhoef, *The Book of Haggai*, 266.
22. Tasker, *Ancient*, 150.
23. Ibid., 87, 205.
24. Caragounis, "בֵּן," 676, allows this implication.
25. Scholars notice that the whole focus in Exod 4:22–23 is the contrast of God and his firstborn against Pharaoh and his firstborn. From the beginning and as the story unfolds God is in full command of the situation. The Pharaoh is "nothing more than a shadow player opposite" God, Houtman, *Exodus*, 432; Brueggemann, "The Book of Exodus," 717.
26. Kugel, "4Q369 'Prayer of Enosh,'" 127.

out of all the peoples on earth to be his people, his treasured possession" (Deut 14:1–2; 32:9).

In both Exodus and Deuteronomy Israel, as God's inheritance, is contrasted to the other nations of the earth, underscoring the prerogatives that God grants to the people of Israel (Deut 9:5; cf. Exod 19:5–6). The Deuteronomist expands the idea of God's affection and his call for Israel, "It is not because of your righteousness or your uprightness of your heart that you are going in to occupy their land; but because of the wickedness of those nations that the LORD your God is dispossessing them before you, in order to fulfill the promise that the LORD made an oath to your ancestors to Abraham, Isaac and Jacob" (Deut 9:5; cf. 7:9).

The land that is in view is the land of Canaan (Deut 1:38; 4:21; 4:38; 12:10; 16:20; 25:19—26:1). The land is also the goal of the exodus redemption tradition. God wants to accomplish what he has already promised to the patriarchs.

Although Israel holds possession of the land, the nation is only an alien or tenant in it (Lev 25:23; Jer 2:7; Hos 9:3; cf. Gen 17:8). The prophets warned and even promised that Israel's unfaithfulness to God would lead to exile and the loss of the land (Jer 7:1–15; Amos 3:11; 7:11). The land continues to be Yahweh's and he could take it back if people become faithless. It is not the land itself but its theological significance as God's promise and as an expression of the continuing relationship between God the Father and his people that has the greater significance for this discussion. This explains why the tribe of Levi has no share in the land, for their inheritance is the Lord himself (Deut 10:9; 12:12; Num 18:20–24).

The relationship between God and Israel as one between Father and son is built by God's initiative and for God's purpose so that they serve and obey God. The important issue in this relationship is Israel's obedience to God (Exod 19:4–6). God's chosen son is entrusted with certain responsibilities as the proper response to God and as their part of covenant responsibility to God (Exod 19:4–6). Obedience is the major part of the covenant between God and his people in Deuteronomy. The Deuteronomist speaks also about true obedience to God as circumcision of their hearts (Deut 10:16; 30:10); which is a metaphor that describes a requirement to "a wholehearted commitment in love, from which all other proper behaviour stemmed."[27]

---

27. Craigie, *The Book of Deuteronomy*, 206.

Israel is also to manifest God's steadfast love to those who respond properly to God by loving him and obeying his commandments (Exod 20:6; cf. Deut 5:10). In Exodus there is a combination of imperative of how Israel must behave and the promise of what Israel will be among the rest of the nations.[28] God reminds them to follow his way and all of his commandments in order to extend the experience of God's redeeming activity toward aliens and strangers. After all, they themselves were once aliens and strangers throughout the earth (Deut 10:19; 24:19–22; cf. Lev 19:34). God's desire is that his name will be proclaimed in all the earth (Exod 9:16; Deut 10:19; 24:19–22; cf. Lev 19:34). In Deuteronomy God wants them to be a model for other nations so that they may see the greatness and nearness of God in them (Deut 4:6–8; cf. Gen 12:1–3).

In Isaiah God's faithfulness toward Israel is a demonstration of God's redeeming plans before all the nations, "The Lord has bared his holy arm before the eyes of all the nations; and all the ends of the earth shall see the salvation of our God" (52:10; cf. Isa 19:24–25; 51:4–5). Isaiah recalls that God's purpose in making Israel his chosen son is not for the sake of Israel only. Israel is to be "a light to the Gentiles" (42:6). There is a universal implication in the role given to Israel.

If the Israelites do not obey or if they act corruptly toward God, they are not his faithful sons (Deut 32:5–6). God is, however, still their faithful Father. Israel's unfaithfulness cannot eliminate God's faithfulness (cf. Deut 32:35–42). Ps 103:9–13 declares, "He will not always accuse . . . great is his steadfast love towards those who fear him; as far as the east is from the west, so far he removes our transgressions from us. As a father has compassion on his children, so the LORD has compassion for those who fear him. For he knows how we are made." The psalm knows that the compassion of God is like that of a father and there is unwillingness in God to remain forever angry at his people who commit sins. God is gracious and compassionate, slow to anger, abounding in love (Ps 103:8); which recalls Exod 34:6–7.[29] The psalm depicts a loving and forgiving God (who takes care of his people) through an allusion to the exodus when God carried Israel like a father (Deut 1:31). In spite of Israel's transgressions (cf. Exod 32–34) God continually shows his steadfast love and righteousness (Ps 103:6, 17). God's fatherly compassion

---

28. C. Wright, *The Mission of God*, 224.
29. McCann, "The Book of Psalms," 1092.

or mercy[30] in forgiving sins is mentioned, though, in connection with those who fear him or those who are obedient to him (Ps 103:18; 30:5; allusions to Deut 1:31; Num 11:11–12). The psalm presents the tension between God who demands righteousness and justice, and yet who is committed to relationship with his people, who loves like a loving father and compassionate mother (cf. Isa 49:15), and who especially loves those who obey him. How exactly God stays faithful to Israel in spite of its faithlessness and how he would bring it back to obedience are questions for further consideration.[31]

2.2. Father of the King and His Offspring

While the major event of the exodus relates God's fatherhood and redemption to Israel as a nation, God as Father also continues to relate to certain individuals within the nation of Israel, especially to King David and his offspring (2 Sam 7:14; 1 Chr 17:13; 22:10; 28:6; Ps 2; 89:26–27; Pr 3:11–12). The relationship between God and the king is described as the relationship between father and son. In Second Samuel 7:14 the Lord declares, referring to King David's offspring, "I will be a father to him, and he shall be a son to me . . . I will not take my steadfast love from him" (2 Sam 7:14–15). In 1 Chronicles 17:10–14 the idea of 2 Sam 7 is recapitulated with divine purpose for David and his offspring. Solomon stands alongside David as elected by God (1 Chr 22:8–10). In Psalm 89:26–27 God as Father to the king and his descendants is named again in a cry, "You are my Father" (Ps 89:26).

In this analogy David's designation as God's son and firstborn (2 Sam 7:14; cf. Ps 2:6–7; 89:27) legitimizes him as Israel's representative; as the embodiment of God's covenant people, who is also called his "son" and "firstborn" (Exod 4:22). When Israel becomes a monarchy wrongly motivated by a desire to be like other nations God appoints them a king (1 Sam 8:5). But their king exercises a different sort of kingship compared with the surrounding nations. Their king is "limited by the character of God as revealed in his law."[32] So, when the king disobeys the commandment of God, God rejects him from his role as a king (1 Sam 13:13–14).

---

30. Hebrew roots suggest motherly compassion that God has revealed and enacted to his people. See McCann, "The Book of Psalms," 778, 1092.

31. See the sections below.

32. Coppedge, *Portraits of God*, 101.

"From God's perspective a king in Israel is the representative of God and not his replacement."[33]

The king and the people under him must follow the Lord their God (1 Sam 12:14-15) and be obedient to God (1 Chr 28:21). He is to represent God's lordship (1 Chr 28:5) and to carry out his commands (1 Chr 28:7). The king, as the whole nation, has the responsibility to obey God. C. Wright assumes in this regard that the king of Israel is not "a *super-Israelite*" but "a *model Israelite*" who sets an example of what it means to be an obedient son of God.[34] The king in addition to the whole nation under his dominion must serve God with the implication that they will be a "visible model to other nations" (Deut 4:6-8).[35]

The same idea appears in Ps 2 where God has a father-son relationship with the king, defeats his enemies, makes him a great king in the world, and thus a witness to God's purpose. J. Goldingay also sees here a form of fulfillment of God's promise to Abraham that is expressed in blessings for Abraham and "all people who covet such blessings and in curses who would belittle him" (Gen 12:1-2).[36]

Although the application of "son" to the king seems to shift the focus from God as the Father of all Israel to God as the Father of one individual, the corporate element of God's fatherhood remains, insofar as the king serves as the head and representative of a people.[37] The idea of God the Father of Israel is also retained because God continues to take care of them and to have covenant relationship with all Israel even through their king (Ps 89:3-4).

Although Saul was the first king, God adopts and marks out King David as his son (2 Sam 7:14), his special agent, and a shepherd of God's people, "I have set the crown on the one who is mighty; I have exalted one chosen from the people. I have found my servant David; with my holy oil I have anointed him" (Ps 89:19-20; cf. Ezek 34:1-10). God may chastise his son David but, unlike Saul, he will never cast him off (2 Sam 7: 14-15; cf. Pr 3:11-12). In Ps 2:7 the king is addressed as "my son" and this refers to God's "begetting" the king. The language of "begetting" is likely used in the same way as for the whole nation (Deut 32:6). God makes him as king

---

33. Ibid., 102.
34. C. Wright, *Knowing God*, 92.
35. Ibid., 93.
36. Goldingay, *Psalms*, 95.
37. Also, M. Thompson, *The Promise*, 47.

and enters into the family relationship with him so that God can continuously work with him and through him with the whole nation. Perhaps the significance of the Davidic kings as God's chosen ones was aimed "at those circles which may have questioned the dynastic succession as well as the legitimacy of the house of David."[38] However, ultimately, Nathan's oracles that the Davidic kingdom will endure forever before God (2 Sam 7:15–16) retain their relevance for future generations.[39] Jeremiah says that God will raise up to David a righteous Branch, a king who will reign wisely and do what is just and right in the land (Jer 23:5–6). The Davidic dynasty has particular significance in God's relationship with his people. God promises an everlasting dynasty extending from David to secure a future of promise to Israel (2 Sam 7:5–16; 1 Chr 17:13).

The emphasis in Ps 89 is on the eternity of God's promise (Ps 89:28–29; 36–37). It explicitly names God's promise as covenant (Ps 89:3, 28, 34, 39). It mentions God's steadfast love (that occurs in 2 Sam 7) and his faithfulness (which is Deuteronomic language) in reference to the Davidic dynasty that underlines God's enduring rule through this line.[40] In Psalm 2 God affirms this ongoing relationship with the implication to have dominion over nations (Ps 2:8–9).

Psalm 89 as well as Psalm 2, according to C. Wright, may have had messianic overtones even within the OT pointing to the one like the son of David, who would fulfill the expectations of reigning in justice and peace not only over Israel but over other nations.[41] God will continue acting through his son, the king of Israel (cf. Jer 23:5). Goldingay doubts the eschatological understanding of Ps 89. However, outside the Psalter, he sees affirmation of God's commitment to the Davidic line (Jer 23:5–6; Isa 55:3–5).[42] In any case, the psalms as well as other passages (Jer 23:5–6; Isa 55:3–5), point to God's commitment to the Davidic dynasty and Israel and to God's reigning in the world. The impression is that God the Father will provide the glorious future through the descendants of David. The prophetic writings may bring further insight to the idea of God the Father and his redeeming purpose.

---

38. Anderson, *2 Samuel*, 123.
39. Ibid.
40. McCann, "The Book of Psalms," 1036.
41. C. Wright, *Knowing God*, 95.
42. Goldingay, *Psalms*, 691–92.

2.3. God as a Faithful Father in Renewal

The idea of God being the Father of Israel and of the Davidic kings, as sketched above, is very important in the OT. The concept of God being the Father who redeems the king does not appear, but the language of God's electing, adopting the king and keeping covenant relationship with him and through him as a representative of Israel with the whole people (Ps 2, 89) is present. God the Father who redeems Israel continues to take care of his people appointing the king who would have to lead Israel in obedience to God.

In the prophetic writings Isaiah explicitly connects the idea of God "our Father" with "our Redeemer" (Isa 63:16). Earlier in Isa 51:10 the prophet mentions that Israel has been delivered from Egypt. In Isa 43:1 the author uses the language of creation of Israel and naming Israel "mine," which implies a parent-child relationship. "But now thus says the LORD, he who created you, O Jacob, he who formed you, O Israel: Do not fear, for I have redeemed you; I have called you by name, you are mine" (cf. Deut 32:6). Isaiah 63 is more explicit in referring to God as the Father. The prophet lists God's actions in the past history of Israel. The precise events are not specified. They can be both Exodus and the events of Sinai.[43] The important point is how God acts in the life of people. God dealt with Israel with kindness, compassion and with steadfast love (Isa 63:7). Isaiah uses the language of redemption when God by his love and pity redeemed, lifted and carried Israel (Isa 63:9), when he became their savior (Isa 63:8), and when he led them in the wilderness (Isa 64:13-14). He also implies God's fatherhood when he calls them God's children and his people (Isa 63:8, 11). Finally, in 63:16 Isaiah summarizes who God is for Israel: he is the Father and Redeemer.

Jeremiah, as did Isaiah, recalls the time when God delivered Israel out of Egypt, when he cared for it (Jer 31:1-6). Jeremiah implies that the appeal to God the Father for mercy reflects Israel's tradition and history that constantly illustrates God's election and redemption of Israel out of Egypt (Jer 31:1ff.).

Hosea also recalls the exodus when God brought Israel out of Egypt treating it like a child (Hos 11:1). Hosea uses a beautiful picture of a "father" treating his "child" with love that represents a God-Israel relationship (Hos 11:1-3).[44]

---

43. Watts, *Isaiah 34-66*, 332.
44. In Hosea 11:4 God "bent down to them and fed them," which is a function

The Father Who Redeems and the Son Who Obeys

Some texts refer to God the Father who redeemed Israel and to Israel as God's son who disobeyed the Father. Israel's disobedience is a major theme in Deuteronomy. Moses accuses Israel of having forgotten the fact that God is the faithful one who cares for his children (Deut 32:4–5). He is their Father who created or formed them (Deut 32:6), which recalls the language of God becoming their Father and Redeemer. Yet, they behave so corruptly that they can no longer be called his children (Deut 32:5). In the opinion of R. Clements, Deut 32, even if composed later than the rest of the book, "rests on its suitability as further warning to Israel against continued disobedience and apostasy."[45]

Jeremiah declares that in spite of the fact that Israel was elected and placed among the sons of God, given an inheritance and patrimony among the nations, and came to call God "Father," these privileged sons committed apostasy and became faithless (Jer 3:3, 19–20). Instead of addressing God the Father who established them and redeemed them out of Egypt (cf. Deut 32), they mischievously call objects as their father and worship Canaanite idols.[46] "They say to wood, 'You are my father,' and to stone, 'You gave me birth.' They have turned their backs to me and not their faces; yet when they are in trouble, they say, 'Come and save us!' Where then are the gods you made for yourselves? Let them come if they can save you when you are in trouble! For you have as many gods as you have towns, O Judah. 'Why do you bring charges against me?'" (Jer 2:27–29).

In a similar vein, in Malachi God is presented as a Father who merits honor, obedience, and ongoing response but does not receive them, "A son honours his father, and servants their master. If then I am a father, where is the honour due me? And if I am a master, where is the respect due me?" (Mal 1:6). Malachi's narrative discusses Israel's unfaithfulness to God, reminding them that God establishes Israel. "Have we not all one father? Has not one God created us? Why then are we faithless to one another, profaning the covenant of our ancestors?" (Mal 2:10; cf. Deut 32:6; Isa 64:8). In his narrative Malachi condemns Israelites' marriages with foreign women who do not have the same Father/Creator.[47] This is

---

performed by the mother. Deuteronomy 1:31; 8:5, Num 11:11–12, Isa 49:15; 66:10–13 designate God as mother. Hosea uses other images for God (as a lover, husband, parent) to show God's faithfulness and care for Israel.

45. Clements, "The Book of Deuteronomy," 527.

46. J. A. Thompson, *The Book of Jeremiah*, 180.

47. Verhoef, *The Book of Haggai*, 265ff. See the connection between God's redeeming activity and creation language in section 2.1 above.

a breakdown of mutuality within the community that leads to idolatry. Malachi interprets being faithless with one another in terms of being faithless to God the Father.

In spite of Israel's disobedience there is a certain hope for restoration and new life if people would return to God their Father. Deuteronomy brings assurance of God's care for Israel and of Israel's triumph among the nations (Deut 32:36ff.). Malachi, Isaiah, Jeremiah, Ezekiel all attest to a future beyond the end of Israel's disobedience and punishment.

Eschatological expectations in Malachi are expressed in family terms, "They shall be mine, says the LORD of hosts, my special possession on the day when I act, and I will spare them as parents spare their children who serve them. Then once again you shall see the difference between the righteous and the wicked, between one who serves God and one who does not serve" (Mal 3:17–18).

The Deuteronomic language here operates on a different level. "They will be mine," and "my special possession" will be applied, not to all Israel, but only to the righteous segment who continue serving God (cf. Mic 7:18; Isa 10:20–22; Hos 2:23). They will be his special possession (the language of inheritance that is applied to the whole Israel as well in Deut 14:1–2; 32:9). God will renew his promise to those who fear him and who value his name.[48]

Isaiah understands the release from Babylonian captivity as a new exodus and he uses the concept of God the Redeemer to describe it (for example, Isa 41:14; 43:14; 44:6, 24; 48:20–21; 49:7; 59:20). The exiles call upon God as Father in their present distress and hope for a new redemption and return to the land (Isa 63:16). Isaiah conveys the idea that redemption has to do with restoring the relationship between God and Israel (Isa 43:1ff). Isaiah connects God's redeeming action in the return from exile with the forgiveness of Israel's sin and from the effects of Israel's sinfulness (Isa 43:25; 40:1–11).

On the basis of God being the Father (Isa 64:8) his people ask God not to remember sins (Isa 64:9). The Father who created them is taking care of them. Isaiah 64:7–8 uses the metaphor of Israel being the clay, the work of his hands, presumably in a sense of historical reminiscence when he calls them out, gives his covenant, and leads them out of slavery to the

---

48. The difference between the righteous and the wicked occurs only here in Malachi, however, the contrast of these two groups is a major motif in psalms (1:37), proverbs (10), and the prophets (Hab 1:4). See R. Smith, *Micah-Malachi*, 339.

promised land.[49] The emphasis is on God's saving character. His people call upon God's mercy and forgiveness of the Father. Like Jeremiah, Isaiah pictures Israel's rescue from punishment with the image of a father's forgiving love (Isa 64:1ff.; cf. Jer 31:8–9). Thus, in Isaiah God is not only "our Father" but his name is inseparably tied to God being "our Redeemer" from the ancient times. This is God who has been known to Israel.[50]

God cannot afford to let his son go unredeemed, or be held in a bondage of sin and unrighteousness. In Isaiah there is a future hope for the restoration of Israel. It might not be the whole Israel, but the remnant of the righteous within Israel, the survivors of the house of Jacob (Isa 10:20–22; cf. 1 Kgs 19:10–18; Jer 31:7).

God's faithfulness toward Israel in Isaiah is a demonstration of God's redeeming plans before all the nations, "The Lord has bared his holy arm before the eyes of all the nations; and all the ends of the earth shall see the salvation of our God" (Isa 52:10; cf. Isa 19:24–25; 51:4–5). Isaiah recalls that God's purpose for making Israel his chosen son is not for the sake of Israel only. Israel is to be "a light to the Gentiles" (Isa 42:6).

Moreover, the idea of God gathering others who are not his is clearly in the writer's mind (Isa 56:1–8; cf. Deut 32:21; Mal 1:11). Isaiah also says that God will bless other nations (Isa 19:25). Isaiah 65:1 may reinforce the same idea saying that God would reveal himself to those who did not seek him or call on his name before (Isa 65:1). The overall context though, suggests that God actively offered himself to his people but they constantly disobeyed him. Their problems are not the result of God's listening to them but of their rebellion.[51] Isaiah shows God's initiative in calling his people and his continuous concern and expectation for his people to come back to him who is the Father (Isa 65:1–8). He concludes that God will be revealed to the nations through his redeemed people (Isa 66:18–24). Thus far one can conclude that references to God as Father and Redeemer are connected in Isaiah with the history of Israel, starting with God's redeeming them out of Egypt and then Babylon, its disobedience, and God's persistent calling to repentance. Other connected ideas are that of the remnant and of Israel being a light to other nations, and, finally, God's revelation to the nations through his redeemed people.

---

49. Tasker, *Ancient*, 150.
50. See also Oswalt, *The Book of Isaiah*, 613.
51. Ibid., 636–37.

In Jeremiah 3:19, while the prophet laments the people's idolatry in the name of God and expresses God's disappointment about his children's unfaithfulness, he also describes God's desire to restore the people into the intimate relationship. This relationship is suggested by a familiar image of a father and a son, "I thought how I would set you among my children, and give you a pleasant land, the most beautiful heritage of all the nations. And I thought you would call me, My Father, and would not turn from following me."

Jeremiah develops the theme of God's restoration as another glorious exodus similar to Isaiah's new exodus motif (Isa 35; 40:3–5; 41:18–20; 42:16). Jeremiah expects the new covenant describing Israel's restoration as the act of God the Father that transcends the exodus from Egypt in every way but also is reminiscent of Deutero-Isaiah, where the return from captivity in Babylon is depicted.[52] "With weeping they shall come, and with consolations I will lead them back, I will let them walk by brooks of water, in a straight path in which they shall not stumble; for I have become a father to Israel, and Ephraim is my firstborn" (Jer 31:9; cf. Exod 4:22–23).

The idea of Israel's firstborn son and God the Father is important here. This is reminiscent of God leading Israel, his son, in the time of exodus. Now, he will renew with Israel "the same fatherly love he displayed in centuries past."[53]

A similar theme can be found in Hosea. Although Hosea does not explicitly speak of God as Father, the prophet does speak of Israel as God's child who, in spite of all God's compassion, love, and mercy, refused to obey God (Hos 11:1–8). Hosea continues to articulate the merciful God of Israel who redeemed them out of slavery (Hos 11:1), and protected them in the wilderness (Hos 9:10; 11:3–4). Hosea especially claims that God will renew his relationship with his people. He writes that God would address "not my people" as "you are my people." They will say, "You are my God" (Hos 2:23; cf. Isa 65:1). The Deuteronomic language of God's special relationship to Israel ("they will be mine" and "my special possession") reappears in Hosea (Hos 1:10; 2:23) where it applies to the Israelites scattered within the world of pagan religions and influenced by them.[54] Hosea condemns the people's idolatry proclaiming

---

52. J. A. Thompson, *The Book of Jeremiah*, 569.

53. Ibid.

54. Macinthosh notices that Hosea's message is concerned with the Northern kingdom and may be with the exiled from it. However, already in 2:1 the vision of the author is transferred to the covenant people and "becomes proleptically a paradigm

God's covenantal love for Israel and summoning the people to repentance and return to God (Hos 2:8, 18–19). Hosea writes the message of hope that God will renew the covenant that was broken by Israel's infidelity. They will become children of the living God (Hos 1:7, 10).

3. Evidence in Second Temple Period Literature

3.1. God the Father of Israel

The understanding of God being the Father of Israel in later Jewish literature is diverse.

God is referred to as Father of the nation of Israel scattered among the Gentiles. Tobit praises God for both righteousness in punishment and mercy offered specifically to the exiled Israel. He emphasizes God's presence and care for Israel even when they are scattered, and urges Israel to acknowledge him as the Lord God and Father at the same time. "Acknowledge him before the nations, O children of Israel; for he has scattered you among them. He has shown you his greatness even there. Exalt him in the presence of every living being, because he is our Lord and he is our God; he is our Father and he is God forever"[55] (Tob 13:3–4; cf. Wis 2:16; Sir 23:1, 4; 51: 10; *3 Macc.* 6:3; *Jub.* 19:29). God as the Lord and Father of Israel both chastises and has mercy, exiles and gathers, but Israel can hope for his mercy only by turning to God,

> If you turn to him with all your heart and with all your soul, to do what is true before him, then he will turn to you and will no longer hide his face from you. So now see what he has done for you; acknowledge him at the top of your voice. Bless the Lord of righteousness, and exalt the King of the ages. In the land of my exile I acknowledge him, and show his power and majesty to a nation of sinners: Turn back, you sinners, and do what is right before him; perhaps he may look with favour upon you and show you mercy. (Tob 13:6)

---

of blessings" (Macintosh, *Hosea*, 28, 37). Yee observes that although Hosea is a northern prophet, v. 1 gives priority to the southern kings of Judah, whose reign extended beyond the kings mentioned in v. 1. His word may be to his later Judean audience as well. Hos 3:1 emphasizes especially the eventual unity of God's people, Yee, "The Book of Hosea," 217.

55. The English translation of Tobit, Sirach and The Wisdom of Solomon comes from *New Revised Standard Version*. All the other translations of the 2TP literature (excluding DSS) come from Charlesworth, ed., *Pseudepigrapha*.

Tobit pronounces Israel as a sinful nation, where Tobit is an example to them (cf. Tob 1:3). However, if Israel turns to God and acts in truth before him, God will have mercy upon them. In this prayer God is addressed as Father, Lord, and King. Tobit acknowledges God who rules over all times and places but also God who is like a father, who has mercy toward his children and will act on this basis. Tobit's appeal emphasizes the importance of obedience in relation to God described in terms of turning back to God the Father and acting righteously before him.

In *Jubilees* the name "father" for God appears several times. God describes to Moses the apostasy and the ultimate restoration of his people who will cleave to their Father again,

> And the Lord said unto Moses: "I know their contrariness and their thoughts and their stubbornness. And they will not obey until they acknowledge their sin and the sins of their fathers. But after this they will return to me in all uprightness and with all of (their) heart and soul. And I shall cut off the foreskin of their heart and the foreskin of the heart of their descendants. And I shall create for them a holy spirit, and I shall purify them so that they will not turn away from following me from that day and forever. And their souls will cleave to me and to all my commandments. And they will do my commandments. And I shall be a father to them and they will be sons to me. And they will all be called 'sons of the living God.' And every angel and spirit will know and acknowledge that they are my sons, and I am their father in uprightness and righteousness. And I shall love them." (*Jub.* 1:22-26)

This language is closely tied to Deuteronomy where Israel's restoration depends on repentance of the nation.[56] Moreover, God has to change Israel after the people return to him: circumcise their hearts, create a new spirit, and purify (cf. Deut 4:29-31; 30:1-10; 10:16; 14:1). Then the process of full restoration may be complete according to *Jubilees*, and the relationships between God and Israel will be as between father and sons, as God intended to be when he chose Israel (cf. Deut 32:6ff.). The allusion of "sons of the living God" to Hos 1:10 is to the restoration motif between Israel and God. The writer of *Jubilees* expects his readers to share a common view of God the Father derived from the OT where God called forth a people to serve him in righteousness. He also reminds the reader that God's people disobeyed and turned away from God. In *Jubilees* God

---

56. Vanderkam, "Recent Scholarship on the Book of Jubilees," 405-31.

knows what is to be the future. The restoration of Israel is certain. The author of *Jubilees* sees redemption differently from Isaiah though (Isa 42:6 where Israel is "a light to the nations"). The Gentiles are enemies for the Jews (*Jub.* 1:19). Redemption and restoration in *Jubilees* are for the people of Israel only. This redemption is also connected with the renewal of loyalty to God's commandments (*Jub.* 1:24) that takes a central place in *Jubilees*.

In *Third Maccabees* 7:6, a pagan king Ptolomy Philopator, concedes that the "God of heaven surely defends the Jews, always taking their part as a father does for his children." The text shows that even a Gentile king testifies that God is wholly involved in the life of his people Israel as a father. He continues to take care of them.

The *Apocryphon of Ezekiel* has been preserved in four fragments only found in secondary Christian sources.[57] Fragment 2 is in Clement of Alexandria and it contains an interesting remark, "Repent, house of Israel, from your lawlessness. I say to the children of my people, if your sins reach from the earth to heaven, and if they are redder than scarlet or blacker than sackcloth, and you turn back to me with a whole heart and say, 'Father,' I will heed you as a holy people."

It is impossible to reconstruct the whole narrative of this text. However, the fragment alludes to OT texts (Ezek. 3:16–21; 18:31; 39:22; Isa 1:18; Jer 3:19) and refers to Israel's need to repent before God the Father in order to come back to him and to become a holy people again.

In the "Prayer concerning God and Israel" (4Q369 1 II, 6) Israel is referred to as God's firstborn son. The text lists God's beneficial acts on Israel's behalf (lines 1–9) including giving Israel righteous laws "as a father to his son" (line 10).[58] Kugel points out that this prayer presumes a people of Israel corporately still as a single entity.[59] As such, this is another key text that considers God the Father in relation to the whole Israel, his care and ongoing involvement. The text juxtaposes God's fatherly disciplining of Israel with the gift of God's love, which includes giving Israel the Torah.[60]

---

57. Charlesworth, ed., *Pseudepigrapha*, 1:487.

58. The English translation of the DSS is from Martinez and Tigchelaar, *The Dead Sea Scrolls*.

59. Kugel, "4Q369 'Prayer of Enosh," 148.

60. See further ibid., 119–48.

3.2 God the Father of the Faithful Ones within Israel

In the majority of 2TP texts God is referred as Father and the eschatological Redeemer of the faithful ones within Israel. *Jubilees* stresses the importance of Jacob's dynasty in relationship to God the Father. In 19:15–31 Abraham blesses Jacob in whom he recognizes his seed and the one whom God chooses for himself. Jacob is identified as Israel and the ancestor of all the children of Israel (*Jub.* 19:18; 23:23; 31:15). Abraham offers a prayer for his grandson, "May the Lord God be for you and for the people a father always and may you be a first-born son" (*Jub.* 19:29). The name of the son given to Israel (Exod 4:22) and to the king of Israel (2 Sam 7:14) is applied to Jacob and then to the people of Israel. In 1:28 the author explicitly says that God is the Father of all children of Jacob. God will always be the Father for Jacob and for his descendants who will be his sons and will fill all the earth (*Jub.* 19:19–29).

In *Third Maccabees* God-as-Father imagery is grounded in the special election of Israel by God both in relation to the exodus story and in relation to Abraham and Jacob. The author recalls Israel's history and God's active participation in it, "Look upon the seed of Abraham, upon the children of Jacob, whom you sanctified . . . you destroyed in the depths of the sea his [the Pharaoh's] proud host, Father, causing the light of your mercy to shine upon the people of Israel" (3 *Macc.* 6:3–4). In his prayer the elderly Eleazar appeals to God the Father. He names God as the Father who redeemed and rescued his people in the past. Now he asks God to help and to rescue those Jews in Egypt who are persecuted by the unbelieving Gentiles, "When Jonah was pining away unpitied in the belly of the monster of the deep, you, Father, restored him uninjured to all his household. So, now, you who hate insolence, full of mercy, protector of all, manifest yourself swiftly to those of the people of Israel who are outrageously treated by the abominable and lawless heathen" (3 *Macc.* 6:8–9).

The idea of God being the Father is tied to God's acting in the past on Israel's behalf and in the life of individuals. He is the Father who redeems, restores, protects, and has mercy. On this basis he is asked to act further in the life of the Israelites who are in distress and persecuted by the Gentiles.

For Sirach the son of God is described in different terms than in *Jub.* and 3 *Macc.* Sirach points out that the righteous person is to show mercy toward the needy to the degree of being able to rescue them from the oppressors (Sir 4:9) and as a redeemer for the needy. In this case he is like a father to orphans and like a husband to their mother (Sir 4:10a). Then, according to Sirach, "You will then be like a son of the Most High, and he will love you more than does your mother" (Sir 4:10). Sirach especially emphasizes compassion and a willingness to rescue the needy ones as virtues that characterizes a person as being like a son of the Most High, loved, and blessed by God (Sir 4:10–16). Sirach pictures God as a parent who will love more than a mother does (cf. Isa 66:13), or as the Hebrew text says, one who will rescue you from the pit.[61]

In 23:1, 4 Sirach addresses God as Father in the prayer asking for his assistance, protections, and power to stand against the lustful cravings and desires, "O Lord, Father and Master of my life, do not abandon me to their designs, and do not let me fall because of them! . . . O Lord, Father and God of my life, do not give me haughty eyes, and remove evil desire from me." Sirach personalizes the address of God as "my Father." It is a prayer of a righteous Jew to God his Father. Also in addressing God as Father and Master/God of life Sirach combines the idea of God as the parent and as the sovereign ruler.[62] Sirach asks God not to forsake him. The context of Sirach implies that God would listen and act on behalf of the supplicant because God already had acted and rescued him before (cf. Sir 51:11–12).[63] Thus, in Sirach the idea of God the Father is connected with the righteous Jews or even the righteous Jew. Just as God redeems and cares for the needy, the righteous one must do the same. Doing so, the person acts as God's son.

In Wisdom the idea of God the Father is also expressed in relation to the righteous one. In the beginning of the book there is the speech of the wicked whose actions and presumption would be proved wrong and ultimately bring death upon themselves (Wis 1:16–24). Within the reasoning of the wicked the author includes the righteous one who opposes the actions of the wicked (Wis 2:12). The righteous one professes to have knowledge of God, calls himself a child or servant of God (Wis 2:13), and boasts that God is his Father (Wis 2:16). The righteous one identifies himself as a child of God and relies on God whom he considers Father. The wicked deride him for that and decide to put him to death as a test to prove whether his claims are true (Wis 2:17). They say, "If the

---

61. Collins, *Ecclesiasticus*, 673.

62. There is one more possible reference to God the Father in Sirach, however, the case is very ambiguous. Greek manuscript 51:10 reads, "Lord, father of my Lord." The Hebrew of Sir 51:1 could be interpreted as "God, my father," or "God of my father." See ibid., 697.

63. In this sense God acts as Redeemer.

righteous man is God's child, he will help him, and will deliver him from the hand of his adversaries" (Wis 2:18). The implied suffering and death of the righteous one is particularly close to the suffering servant motif of Isaiah (Isa 52:13—53:12), however, in Isaiah the sufferings of the servant are vicarious. Here the wicked are judged and accused by the author for the false judgment on human life (Wis 2:21–24).[64]

In *Psalms of Solomon* the idea of the fatherhood of God is implied when God disciplines the righteous ones within the nation (*Pss. Sol.* 13:8–10) or all Israel (*Pss. Sol.* 18:4) as a beloved and firstborn son.[65] Yet, the Psalms distinguish sharply between the righteous ones and the sinners (even among the Jews) who do harm to the righteous (ch. 4). The situation for the righteous will be resolved, if not now, then in the future, because God has mercy and delivers them (*Pss. Sol.* 2:34ff.). The sinners will be destroyed (*Pss. Sol.* 2:31, 34; 15:12).

Israel as a nation is still remembered as "the portion and inheritance of God" (*Pss. Sol.* 14:5). Although for their sins they are scattered, God will raise up a king, the son of David, who will eject the sinners and purge Jerusalem. He will gather the people together (*Pss. Sol.* 17:23–25). He will know all the sons of their God (*Pss. Sol.* 17: 17–30).

The king will also destroy the godless nations whom God uses as an instrument of his anger against Israel (*Pss. Sol.* 8:7ff.). The Gentiles will be subjugated to Israel's king (*Pss. Sol.* 17:30–31).

In *Testament of Job* Job relies on God and affirms a certain otherworldliness when he refers to the Father above all in prayers, "My throne is in the upper world, and its splendour and majesty come from the right hand of the Father" (*T. Job* 33:3, cf. *T. Job* 33:9; 40:2–3; 47:11; 50:3). The address "Father" appears in one of the Greek manuscripts. Others have "God" and "Saviour," "Father in the heavens."[66] In 33:9 "the chariots of the Father" appears in all manuscripts.[67] In each case, though, Job associates his "splendor" and "majesty" with the "Father" supposing that God the Father will assist him and that his kingdom "is forever and ever" "in the chariots of the Father" (*T. Job* 33:9).[68] God as Father is used here in relation to the righteous individual (cf. Sir 23:1, 4).

64. Kolarcik, "The Book of Wisdom," 462

65. The idea of the father's discipline is present in 2 Sam 7:17 in relation to the Davidic king with the promise that his kingdom will be established forever.

66. Charlesworth, ed., *Pseudepigrapha* 1: 855.

67. Charlesworth, ed., *Pseudepigrapha* 1:856.

68. In psalms (145:10–12) the glorious splendor of God are linked with the

In more recently published scrolls there are additional references to God as Father, and these references include direct, personal address to God in prayer. There is, for example, a prayer attributed to Joseph, asking God the Father for protection from the persecuting Gentiles (4Q372 1 16). Whether the document is anti-Samaritan[69] or the Samaritans function as a reminder to the southern tribes (Levi, Judah, and Benjamin) that the exile of Israel (Joseph) is not over,[70] the author encourages his readers to call out to God, in the words of Joseph: "My father and my God, do not abandon me in the hands of the gentiles, do me justice . . . your mercies are great and great is your compassion for those who seek you" (4Q372 1 16–19). The hope of God's restoration of Israel, or at least the hope of some tribes within Israel, is associated with the plea to God the Father.

Schuller refers to another prayer to God in personal terms from Qumran (4Q460 5 I, 5), which seems to close with the address, "my father and my lord."[71] The context of the fragment, although difficult to establish with certainty because of lacunae, suggests that Israel and Ephraim are blamed for the guilty deeds before God. The prayer addresses God as Father, affirming that he has not forsaken his servant, whoever he is (a single individual or representative of the faithful remnant), but he considers himself to be serving God and relying on his help against the evil plans.

In 1QH XVII, 35–36 God is referred to as Father "to all the [son]s of your truth. You rejoice in them, like her who loves her child." In 4Q504 1–2 III, 1–21 אבי (my father) appears by itself at the beginning of the fragment followed by a number of lacunae. Although it is uncertain whether the reference "my father" refers to God, the context of the rest of the fragment suggests allusions to the OT where the language of God being the Father of Israel occurs. "You have established us as your sons in the sight of all the peoples" (line 5; cf. Deut, 32:6, 9). "For you called [I]srael "my son, my first-born" (line 6; cf. Exod 4:22) "and have corrected us as one corrects his son" (line 7; cf. 2 Sam 7:14). Thus, it is most likely that the fragment recalls the covenant relationship between God and Israel and the address "my father" refers to God as an address from the lips of those who consider themselves God's children.

---

universal praise.

69. Schuller, "4Q372 1," 371.
70. Thiessen, "4Q372 1," 395.
71. Schuller, "The Psalm of 4Q372 1," 72–75.

3.3 God the Father of the Future Messiah

The idea of God the Father of the future messiah appears in the *T. 12 Patr.* The testaments are considered largely messianic.[72] There is a vision in the *T. Levi* about a gradual decline of the priesthood. While the first person to be anointed to the priesthood will be great, he shall speak to God as father, and his priesthood shall be fully satisfactory to the Lord (*T. Levi* 17:2), in the seventh there shall be pollution (*T. Levi* 17:8), and then the priesthood will lapse (*T. Levi* 18:1). Chapter 18 announces the arrival of a new priest, sent by God, who introduces a new era. Levi, predicting this arrival in very special terms, tells that he will share in the joy about his coming, together with Abraham, Isaac, and Jacob (*T. Levi* 18:14). The spirit of holiness (*T. Levi* 18:11) will come upon him with a fatherly voice, as from Abraham to Isaac (*T. Levi* 18:6). He will redeem the righteous (*T. Levi* 18:9). He will be the agent of God's redemption and the instrument of universal divine blessing (*T. Levi* 18:1–11).[73]

In *Testament of Judah* the spirit will be poured out on the messianic figure "as a blessing of the holy Father" (*T. Jud.* 24:3). "This is the Shoot of God Most High; this is the fountain for the life of all humanity" (*T. Jud.* 24:3–6). This language is closely related to the idea of the eschatological king in the Old Testament and the descendant of David (Num 24:17; cf. Isa 11:1; Jer 23:5; 33:15; Zech 3:8).

At Qumran, in 4QFlor 1 I, 10–12, 2 Sam 7:11–16 is interpreted messianically. The point of interest here is that the language of God being the Father is used in the reference to the Qumran Messiah who will arise from the Shoot of David (close to *Pss. Sol.* 17:26–32) and save Israel. He will arise with the Interpreter of the Torah to rule in Zion at the end of

---

72. Charlesworth, ed., *Pseudepigrapha* 1:777. De Jonge supposes that the Levi-Judah passages in particular belong to a later stage in the history of the Testaments and they have been redacted in several ways to serve Christian interests. De Jonge, "Christian Influence in the Book of the Twelve Patriachs," 229. Agreeing with de Jonge, Kugler nevertheless emphasizes that the text offers "proof of God's undying will to secure Israel's fate," and that "God will provide another chance at salvation through the return of the saviour" (Kugler, *The Testament of the Twelve Patriarchs*, 56).

73. It is interesting that in *Pss. Sol.* 17:26–32 the author unfolds the idea of the Messiah, the anointed son of David, who brings together for God a holy people, the righteous ones who are all children of God. The idea is that God will raise up the king, the son of David over Israel. He will destroy the godless nations and will restore the relationship with his righteous people on the basis of his faithfulness and promise toward them (*Pss. Sol.* 17:21, 30). He will rely on God and lead the flock of the Lord faithfully and righteously (*Pss. Sol.* 17:44).

time.⁷⁴ This means that at least in some Jewish texts the idea of the "son of God" from the Davidic line has messianic overtones.

3.4 God the Father Who Adopts Gentiles

The idea of God the Father who adopts Gentiles appears in *Joseph and Aseneth*. This text unfolds the OT story of Joseph's marriage to Aseneth, daughter of an idolatrous priest (Gen 41:45), describing Aseneth's conversion to Judaism. God is a loving father who is ready to receive those who repent honestly (*Jos. As.* 11:7-14; 12:8). Aseneth prays to God and asks him to be her father, replacing the father and mother who rejected her because of her conversion to Judaism. "I am now an orphan . . . because you are the father of the orphans, and a protector of the persecuted and the helper of the afflicted" (*Jos. As.* 12:12-14). God is described as a sweet, good, and gentle Father, quick in mercy (*Jos. As.* 12:15).

In this text it is possible for those who seek him to know God because God is "the father of Repentance" (*Jos. As.* 15:7-11). At the same time, it is not clear what the general picture of the Gentiles' adoption is other than following Jewish ways of living. Burchard puts it well, saying that "Gentile's conversion is welcomed but not sought," and "depends on God's mercy and the presence of Judaism in general."⁷⁵

Some texts underline the idea of God being the Father in the universal sense. In Wisdom 14:3 God is evoked directly as Father by the author in relation to God's providence, "But it is your providence, O Father, that steers its [the ship's] course, because you have given it a path in the sea." The author praises God the Father for the wonders of creation and for his providential care in the universe.

The idea of the universality of God the Father is seen explicitly by Philo and Josephus who were influenced by Greek ideas and philosophy. For Josephus God is the Father of all (*Ant.* 1:230; 2:152) and universal Father (*Ant.* 1:20). Philo depicts God the Father as the Maker of the universe (*Decal.* 51, 61). In these texts the idea of God's fatherhood is described in relation to the creation of the world rather than in any salvific or redeeming terms.

---

74. VanderKam, *The Dead Sea Scrolls Today*, 70-71; Brooke, *Exegesis at Qumran*, 197-205.

75. See theological discussion by Burchard, "Joseph and Aseneth," in Charlesworth, ed., *Pseudepigrapha* 2:188-94.

Although the direct language of God's fatherhood is missing, the Isaianic idea of Israel being the light to the nations is found in *T. 12 Patr.* (*T. Levi* 14:3–4; *T. Levi* 18:3; cf. *T. Naph.* 8:3–4; *T. Jud.* 24:6).

There are several references in the 2TP to God in relation to all men expressed in terms of begetting. In the Sibylline Oracles God is the one who has begotten all (*Sib. Or.* 3:550), "the immortal begetter of all men" (*Sib. Or.* 3:604; cf. 3:295).

4. Conclusions

The idea of God being the Father is present and more pervasive in Jewish tradition than usually acknowledged. There are several implications of this analysis that are important for understanding the development of the concept further in Paul.

First, the OT idea of God being the Father is developed with reference to his redeeming activity in the deliverance of Israel from Egypt when God elects and lifts Israel to the status of "son" (Exod 4:22). He is the Father and Redeemer of Israel in the exodus and the intervening centuries (Isa 63:16). This relationship between Israel and God is sealed by the covenant into which God has entered with Israel as his children (Exod 19–24). The Father's redeeming activity is creative in nature and grounded in the fact that he formed Israel as a nation (Isa 64:7–8, Deut 32:6–7, Mal 2:19).

Second, God as Father and Redeemer is understood in terms of his own righteousness (Deut 32:4ff.). God's special relation to Israel and his promise is given not because of Israel's righteousness but because of God's righteousness (Deut 9). He acts with mercy and protection toward his children Israel even in the times of punishment (Tob, *3 Macc., Pss. Sol.*).

Third, God's purpose for Israel, for making it a special, holy nation, like his son, is far reaching: his son Israel is to be obedient to God, to serve him, to be a light to the nation, and to proclaim his name in all the earth (Exod 9:16). The OT elevates the idea that God's faithfulness toward Israel is a demonstration of God's redeeming plans in front of all nations (Ps 2, 103) to whom they are supposed to be a light (Isa 42:6). In some texts God is evoked directly as Father in a universal manner (Wis; *Sib. Or.; Ant.*). However, God's work in the world is complicated. God can adopt the Gentiles but not on a universal scale (*Jos. As.*). God will be revealed to all nations among whom Israel is a light (*T. 12 Patr.*). But the special relationship of God is with the patriarchs and the special blessings are on Judah and Levi. Some texts underline that the Gentiles are to be excluded and not to be mingled with the Jews (*Pss. Sol.*, *3 Macc.*). In *Jubilees* all Gentiles are rejected. God also uses Gentiles to punish Israel for disobedience (*Pss. Sol.*).

Fourth, despite Israel's disobedience the OT writers express hope for the future fulfillment of the promised restoration between God and his people and address God as Father in prayers for deliverance (Isa 63:16; 64:8). God as Father will have mercy and bring his son Israel home from exile. He will renew his relationship with people (Isa 64:1ff.; cf. Jer 31:8-9; Ps 103:6-14). Psalms and prophets connect God's redeeming action from exile with God's forgiveness of Israel's sin and from the effects of its sinfulness. Some texts emphasize that God as Father will renew his promise to those who fear him and who value his name (Mic 7:18; Isa 10:20-22; Hos 2:23). In *Jubilees* God as Father is expected to restore a relationship with his people if they turn back to him and keep God's commandments (*Jub.*; 4Q369 1 II, 6). The restoration is thought of in relation to the whole of Israel (*Tob, Jub., Apoc. Ezek.*); righteous ones within Israel or righteous Israel (Sir 23:1, 4; Wis 14:3; 3 Macc. 6:8-9; *T. Job* 33:3; 4Q372); or particular dynasties such as Jacob and his descendants (*Jub.*, *3 Macc.*), or his children (whoever they are in 4Q369 1 II, 6).

Fifth, God as Father is described not only as the Father of Israel as the whole nation but also of the king David and his offspring. Although the idea of God being the Father who redeems the king does not appear, the language of God's electing, adopting the king and keeping covenant relationship with him and through him as a representative of Israel with the whole people is retained. The importance is that God the Father who redeems Israel continues to take care of his people by appointing the king who would have to lead Israel in obedience to God. Some texts point out that God as Father will continue acting through his son, the Davidic king, his anointed one (Ps 2, 89; Jer 23:5-6; Isa 55:3-5). The idea of the "son of God" from the Davidic line has messianic overtones. He will introduce a new era in the relationship between God and Israel (*Pss. Sol., T. 12 Patr.*, 4QFlor).

Chapter III

God the Father Revealed in Christ

1. Introduction

CHAPTER 2 HAS SHOWN that the idea of God as Father is understood in Judaism in relation to Israel. This idea is tied to the redeeming activity of God in the deliverance of Israel from Egypt (Exod 4:22–23; 6:6; Deut 7:8) and from Babylon (Isa 51:11; 63:16ff.). God is known as the Father who redeems Israel (Isa 63:16). The references to God as Father and Redeemer are related to God's covenant relationship with Israel. Israel, as God's son is to be obedient to the Father and to proclaim his name before other nations.

The prophets write, however, that God's name is profaned in the world because of Israel who does not display his holiness before the eyes of other nations and does not serve as a light to other nations (Ezek 32–36). God's people disobey their Father (cf. Deut 32). His people fail to do their part; God, on the other hand, will act through Israel and he will show his holiness (Ezek 36:22–23). God the Father will renew his relationship with people (Isa 64:1ff.; cf. Jer 31:8–9; Ps 103:6–14). This was an expectation of the Jews of the 2TP, as the previous chapter shows.

This antecedent is thought of in terms of God's righteousness and faithfulness. The OT presents us with the contrast of God's continuing faithfulness to and compassion for his son and Israel's disobedience and faithlessness. God is expected to act in Israel's life in the future on the same basis of his righteousness and faithfulness to Israel whom he chose to be his son. This is the background for understanding Paul who seeks "to ground his exposition of the gospel in Israel's sacred texts."[1]

For Paul, God's redemption (ἀπολυτρώσις) has already taken place (3:24). Paul claims that God's righteousness is now revealed (1:16-17; 3:21). However, it is revealed in a new light: apart from the law even though the law and the prophets testified about it (3:21). Righteousness is revealed through the faithful obedience of Christ (3:22; 5:12-21). Both aspects of the Jewish expectation find expression in Paul: God's redemption has taken place and true obedience is offered in Christ. God, who is known in the OT as the Father who redeems, has acted as such in Christ, his Son. The Jewish scriptures make complete sense for Paul as he looks at them retrospectively through the prism of God's revelation in Christ and interprets them in the light of Christ. In Christ Paul has something more to say to the Jewish expectation of his time but also to the whole world.

2. Redefining God's Fatherhood

2.1 Father of Christ

Paul mentions God as Father four times in Romans. While the OT and later Jewish writers refer to God the Father who redeems and cares for his son Israel, the king of Israel and the faithful ones within Israel, for Paul God is, the Father of Jesus Christ (6:4; 15:6) and he is "our Father" (1:7; 8:15). The second address clearly involves both Jews and Gentiles, and even the whole created order as it waits to be brought into the glorious freedom of the children of God (8:21). While the corporate address of God as "our Father" will be considered later, let us explore Paul's language of God the Father of Christ and its significance in God's redemptive story.

The idea of God being the Father of Christ in Romans emphasizes the close relationship between the two: the Father and the Son. The distinctive relationship between them is clear from the way that Paul repeatedly brackets God and Jesus together, as in 1:7, "Grace to you and peace from God our Father and the Lord Jesus Christ."[2] This suggests an equal level of the two as the source of blessing for the believers.[3] L. Hurtado points out that Jesus "is not reverenced as another deity of any

---

1. Hays, *Echoes*, 34.
2. D. Wenham, *Follower of Jesus*, 117.
3. Jewett, *Romans*, 116.

independent origin or significance; instead, his divine significance is characteristically expressed in terms of his relationship to the one God."[4] Moreover, it is God who has exalted Jesus to "the position of reverence"[5] (6:4). This is evident through Christ's death and resurrection. God has given his Son over to redemptive death (8:3, 32) and has reconciled humanity to himself through Christ's death (5:10). He raised him to life (8:34)! Paul says that Christ was raised from the dead through the glory of the Father. In this formula of Christ's resurrection (6:4; cf. 4:24; 8:11; 10:9) God is not only described as the Father in relation to Christ but also his glory becomes visible in Christ's resurrection. In 1:4 God is implicitly described as the Father of Christ who is declared to be the Son of God with power by his resurrection from the dead (1:4). Clearly, the idea of God's fatherhood is linked with what has happened on the cross; and it is illuminated through Christ's resurrection (cf. 1:1–5). God's involvement in and through Christ and the close involvement of Jesus in the praise of God the Father (1:7; 15:6) enables Hurtado to call this unity "binitarian"[6] and to affirm "the connection between Jesus' death and divine purposes."[7]

Paul not only underlines the unique relationship between God the Father and Christ but also describes God's action in and through Christ as having a certain effect on the believers, including Paul (he uses first person plural). Paul explains that we were reconciled to God through Christ's death (5:10). We have peace with God given by Christ (5:2). We are God's children in Christ (8:14–17). Furthermore, the believers are to conform to the likeness of the Son; they are co-heirs with him and thus, are God's larger family, his children (8:14–17, 29). The OT status of Israel before God Paul claims for himself and his readers. In the light of the gospel this indicates that "the people of God are to be seen as siblings of the firstborn son (8:29)."[8] The language points to the unity of the believers as the people of God and to the belonging to the family of God in Christ. Presumably, Paul expands the idea of God's family that is now formed in Christ.

---

4. Hurtado, *Lord Jesus Christ*, 52.
5. Ibid., 52, 104.
6. Ibid., 134–52.
7. Hurtado, "Jesus' Divine Sonship," 229.
8. N. T. Wright, "The Letter to the Romans," 421.

Paul explains that in Christ's burial (6:4), death and resurrection (6:5) there is a participation in Christ for all believers.[9] This is the newness of life for the believers (6:4) so that they are not slaves to sin anymore but slaves of righteousness (6:15ff.). This idea of setting free from slavery and becoming slaves to God (cf. 6:22) recalls the exodus language. The Israelites were set free from Egypt to serve their God and Father (Ex 2:22–23). N. T. Wright, recognizing the exodus language here, writes that sin takes "the role of Egypt and/or Pharaoh"; righteousness is, suggestively, "a periphrasis" for God.[10] Paul clearly evokes the exodus story but in his description exodus has taken place in, because, and through Christ. Everyone who has died with Christ has been freed from sin (6:7).

It appears that Paul unfolds God's redemptive story of the new exodus in Christ. Second, God's redemption is for all in Christ, both Jews and Gentiles. It reflects Paul's earlier argument as he states the purpose of his mission and explains the gospel of God concerning his Son. In Christ and for his name's sake people from all nations are called into obedience of faith (1:5). All believers are empowered to live a new life because Christ has been raised from the dead. In both instances, where Paul uses "Father" in relation to Christ (in 6:4 and 15:6) he refers to the believers' unity and participation in Christ. They are to follow Christ so that they can glorify God the Father of Christ (15:5–6). They are to belong to God the Father as children because of Christ (8:15). In Jesus God's redemption becomes effective for the Jews and for the Gentiles who now receive the Spirit of sonship.

Although how and why both Jews and Gentiles enter into God's family through Christ is not clear yet, the ground for this explanation lies in the close and unique relationship between God the Father and Christ Jesus whom God has raised from the dead.

Despite the fact that God is described explicitly as the Father of Jesus Christ twice in Romans, the idea of Jesus' sonship certainly contributes further to the discussion about the fatherhood of God. Traditionally, Jesus' sonship points to his divinity.[11] However, M. Hengel already notices that Paul uses Jesus' sonship language deliberately with

---

9. Although Christian burial with Christ in 6:4 is introduced in baptismal symbolism and is important for the discussion of this rite, the focus of Rom 6 is not on baptism as a ritual or sacrament but as an event through which the believers participate in Christ. See further D. Moo, *Romans*, 361–67.

10. N. T. Wright, "New Exodus," 28–29.

11. Bultman, *Theology of the New Testament*, 1:128–29.

connections to particular themes and emphases.¹² L. Hurtado specifies Paul's use of divine sonship language for Jesus as significant in reference and relationship to God.¹³ He writes that this language carries not only honorific overtones of Jesus but also a strongly theocentric force. This emphasizes God's involvement in Jesus and links the salvation of the elect with the status of Jesus.¹⁴ In this sense, Jesus' status as God's Son does not so much function to indicate Jesus' divinity but it connotes Jesus' special relationship to God and his unique significance in God's plan.¹⁵ Hurtado's suggestions deserve special attention because in Romans Paul especially connects the language of Jesus as God's Son with God's redeeming activity (1:3–4, 9; 5:10; 8:3, 29, 32; cf. Gal 2:20; 4:4–5).

The questions for this thesis are: 1) how does Jesus' sonship language help Paul to unfold the idea of God the Father who redeems, 2) how does the Father fulfill his promises in his Son, and 3) who are the recipients of God's redeeming activity in Christ?

2.2 Father Who Fulfills His Promises in His Son

In Romans 1:1–7 Paul argues that the OT anticipates the coming of God's Son. The Son has to do with the disclosure and fulfillment of God's promises: the gospel of God promised beforehand in the holy scriptures concerns his Son, Jesus Christ (1:3–4). Paul connects Jesus' divine sonship language with his adherence to Israel through the Davidic line (1:1–3) as well as with the idea of calling the Gentiles into obedience of faith (1:5). By that Paul emphasizes God's faithfulness to Israel and "God's great generosity in annexing Gentiles into the company of the redeemed, making them sons of God, even though the privileges of Israel (9:1–5) are not theirs by natural rights."¹⁶

Paul identifies Jesus Christ as the Son of God of Davidic descent according to the flesh, κατὰ σάρκα (1:3). By κατὰ σάρκα Paul stresses the humanity of Jesus and the identification with all humanity as the second Adam (the theme that Paul develops in ch. 5).¹⁷ Jesus is sent in

---

12. Hengel, *The Son of God*, 7.
13. Hurtado, "Jesus' Divine Sonship," 233; Hurtado, *Lord Jesus Christ*, 101–8.
14. Hurtado, "Jesus' Divine Sonship," 223.
15. Hurtado, *Lord Jesus Christ*, 107.
16. Hurtado, "Jesus' Divine Sonship," 233.
17. The idea is traditionally explored by many commentators as a contrast to Jesus'

the likeness of sinful flesh, σαρκὸς ἁμαρτίας, to carry out the work of redemption entrusted him by the Father (8:3). Although he is in the flesh just like Adam and fully representative of the human race he does not disobey God, instead, he remains obedient to God (5:12–21). His "fleshly" humanity is "the place where he does for Adamic humanity that which Adamic humanity could not do for itself."[18] Jesus accepts and fulfills the purpose of his sending: he deals with sin, ἁμαρτία, for all people. The gospel of God concerning his Son according to the flesh, κατὰ σάρκα, has universal implications for Paul.

Moreover, Jesus is God's Son from the Davidic dynasty. This reference recalls the OT imagery, particularly Ps 2, where the Israelite king, the seed of David is named as God's son (Ps 2:7; cf. 1 Sam 7:14; 1 Chr 17:13; Ps 89:26–27) and described as God's anointed one, τοῦ χριστοῦ αὐτοῦ (Ps 2:2). In Second Samuel 7:13–14 God promises to be his Father and to establish his eternal reign, "I will establish the throne of his kingdom forever. I will be a father to him, and he shall be a son to me." The rule of the Lord's anointed one will extend as far as the rule of God himself. All the nations will be his inheritance and the ends of the earth his possession (Ps 2:7–9). Keeping in mind that the king is the representative of the whole people of Israel, God's promises to the king involve his people.

The establishment of the Davidic kingdom includes messianic expectation in the OT as, for example, in Jer 23:5–6, "The days are surely coming, says the LORD, when I will raise up for David a righteous Branch, and he shall reign as king and deal wisely, and shall execute justice and righteousness in the land" (cf. Isa 1:1, 10; Ezek 34:23–24). The Messiah will manifest the characteristics of the great king in Israel, like Jesse, David's father (Isa 11:1, 10) or David himself (Isa 9:2–7). He will bring safety and salvation to Israel and Judah, his name will be "the Lord our righteousness" (Jer 23:6; cf. Ps 89; Jer 23:5–6; Isa 55:3–5; *Pss. Sol.* 17:21–32; *T. 12 Patr.*). In the Qumran text that alludes to 2 Sam 7:11–16, the Messiah will arise from the Shoot of David and save Israel (4QFlor; 4Q 246).

Describing Christ as God's Son of Davidic descent Paul recognizes Jesus' special relationship and place in God's plan, as well as his messianic function. The coming of Christ signifies the fulfillment of the Jewish messianic expectation (cf. 15:12). For Paul, God's anointed One is

---

divine nature κατὰ πνεῦμα. See discussion in N. T. Wright, "The Letter to the Romans," 418; D. Moo, *Romans*, 47; Dunn, *Romans 1–8*, 13; Jewett, *Romans*, 106. See chapter 6 on this.

18. N. T. Wright, "The Letter to the Romans," 418.

Jesus, in whom God's righteousness has been revealed (3:21–22). In him people have been set free from sin and have become slaves of righteousness (6:18ff.). The language of God's deliverance and the new exodus idea in Romans 6:4–23, as stated earlier, is clearly related to Christ and to his messianic fulfillment. In referring to Jesus as the Son of God of a Davidic descendant Paul points to "the one in whom Israel's destiny is summed up and brought to proper fulfilment."[19]

For Paul, Christ Jesus is God's designated Son (τοῦ ὁρισθέντος υἱοῦ θεοῦ) with power by resurrection (1:4). While the precise meaning of this passage is in dispute, most recent scholars argue that Paul's emphasis is placed on the assertion that Jesus is already described as God's Son even before he is God's Son with power by resurrection.[20] By resurrection from

---

19. Ibid., 419.

20. Dunn argues that Paul did not view Jesus as a pre-existent divine figure who became "incarnate" at his birth. For him, Paul's Jesus was a man in whom God's pre-existent wisdom and power were embodied, and who, through his obedience to the call and commission of God, was raised and exalted to become Lord. According to Dunn, this whole passage (1:1–7) is best read in the light of its parallels with the story of Adam in Gen 1–3: both Adam and Jesus were made in God's image or form, yet while Adam reached out to become like God (Gen 3:5, 22), Jesus willingly took the role of humble obedience, even to the point of death on the cross. Because of his obedience, he accomplished the restoration of what Adam had ruined, and was exalted by God to the position of Lord, from where he will receive the acclamation due to God himself (cf. Isa 45.23). See Dunn, *Christology in the Making*, 114–21. In the same way, Ziesler points out that the divine promises fulfilled in Christ were pre-existent but it is not necessary that Christ himself was. For Ziesler the main point here is the language of Son's commissioning, obedience, and special relationship to God that makes possible the sonship of those who believe in him (Ziesler, *Pauline Christianity*, 43).

The majority of other scholars disagree with that. Fitzmyer suggests that "with power" modifies the title "Son of God" and not the verb ὁρισθέντος. In this reading the Son of God was already the Son but was designated the Son of God in power by resurrection. Jesus is both the Son of God in weakness and the designated Son of God in power. See Fitzmyer, *Romans*, 235; and Cranfield, *Romans*, 2:62. N. T. Wright points further to the tautological nature of the statement in verses 3–4: it is his Son who is "appointed" Son. So, Jesus is already Son but now he is a Son with different status or function. By virtue of his obedience to the will of the Father Jesus did not first become God's Son at resurrection, but rather he entered into a higher rank of sonship at that event. The pre-existent Son entered into human experience as the promised Messiah and "was publicly designated Messiah through that event" (N. T. Wright, *The Challenges of Jesus*, 108).

Moreover, the argument of the pre-existence of Christ corresponds with Paul's fundamental identity between God himself and his Son. The pre-existence of Christ reflects the key convictions: Jesus' agency in creation and redemption and, consequently, his significance and unity of divine purpose (that he fulfils for humanity as the second Adam and for Israel in particular as its Messiah and representative). See

the dead and after Jesus' total obedience to the will of the Father even up to death (cf. Phil 2:5–12) he is declared the exalted Son with power. The relationship between Jesus and God remains; the status has changed: Christ is God's Son with power because he is the obedient Son.

Thus, the notion "with power" already identifies Christ as the obedient Son, an idea that Paul will unfold further in the letter (3:22; 5:12–21). As son of David, Jesus Christ not only belongs to Israel (cf. 2 Sam 19—20:2; 1 Kgs 12:16; 2 Chr 10:16) but being son of David and the obedient Son he is the true representative and the embodiment of Israel. Jesus accomplished what God has always intended for Israel: to be obedient and to be a light to the nation. As an obedient Son he does not only reverse Adam's disobedience (5:12–21) but offers the true obedient faithfulness (3:22) that Israel has failed to demonstrate (3:2–3). As the obedient son of David, he fulfills God's purposes for Israel and all the nations calling them into obedience of faith (1:5). Wright argues that "it is by bringing Israel's history to its climax that God, through the Messiah, has opened the way of mercy to all the nations."[21] In Keck's language, Christ rectifies Israel's past.[22] In him Israel's destiny is indeed "brought to proper fulfilment."[23]

The connection of Rom 1:4 with Ps 2 enhances the notion of God's Son further. In this psalm the designation of God's son and king is related to God's vindication and promise to make the nations into king's inheritance (Ps 2:8). If Paul alludes to the psalm applying it to Jesus, he sees it in the light of the Easter event.[24] Paul's statement that Christ "was declared to be Son of God with power" refers to God's supreme acts of vindication Jesus and to his empowerment in a new and exalted status as Lord by resurrection after Jesus demonstrated complete obedience to the Father (1:4). Jesus has always been God's Son but after his complete faithfulness to God the Father, even death on the cross, God exalts him

---

Hurtado, *Lord Jesus Christ*, 118–26.

21. N. T. Wright, "The Letter to the Romans," 747. See also N. T. Wright, *The Climax*, 34–40.

22. Leander Keck, "'Jesus' in Romans," 448.

23. N. T. Wright, "The Letter to the Romans," 419.

24. In Luke's account Paul speaks these words in Antioch alluding to Ps 2 (Acts 13:32–33), "And we bring you the good news that what God promised to our ancestors he has fulfilled for us, their children, by raising Jesus; as also it is written in the second psalm, 'You are my Son; today I have begotten you." The psalm is applied in terms of the fulfillment of God's promises at the resurrection of Jesus. It is very likely that here Paul implies the same.

God the Father Revealed in Christ

as the Lord because of his obedience. He is God's true Son and the King of Israel. Moreover, the nations are called into the obedience of faith through him and for his name's sake (1:5). In the Son and through his obedience Paul sees the fulfillment of the OT prophesies that concern Israel and all the nations.

The declaration of God's Son with power is done through the spirit of holiness according to Paul. "The spirit of holiness" has no parallels in the NT but appears infrequently in the HB (Isa 63:11; Ps 51:11) and more often in 2TP.[25] In both cases in the HB this spirit is associated with the presence and guidance of the LORD. The psalmist asks God to be present with him, to renew him inwardly, and not to remove the spirit of holiness from him. In 2TP the spirit of holiness denotes a whole range of ideas: the means of prophetic inspiration (1QS 8.16), the means of obtaining spiritual knowledge otherwise inaccessible to human beings (Wis 9:17; 1QH 20:11–12), as well as, a very distinctive expression of "a new spiritual disposition imparted by God to individual Jews," which B. Smith defines this as "an eschatological principle of obedience" (*Jub.* 1.21; 4Q504; 1QS 4.18–21; 2.19–13.12; 9.3–4; 1QSb).[26] In the latter sense the spirit of holiness occurs in the context of the restoration motif that God will work out among the Jews renewing and bringing them back to the right relationship (cf. Ps 51:9–10; Deut 30:1–10). An intriguing example of the "spirit of holiness" in relation to both the anointed one and to the restoration motif comes from the *T. Levi*.

In the messianic vision of Levi a king will arise from Judah. He will found a new priesthood that will concern all nations (*T. Levi* 8:14). The new priest will be the agent of God's redemption (*T. Levi* 18:1–11). The heavens will be opened, and from the temple of glory sanctification will come upon him with a fatherly voice (*T. Levi* 18:6). The righteous ones shall find rest in him and the spirit of holiness shall be upon them (*T. Levi* 18:9, 11). The important observation is that the "spirit of holiness" is associated with the eschatological restoration of relationship of God's people with God. God will establish a new priesthood through the anointed one (*T. Levi* 18:2) when sin shall cease (*T. Levi* 18:9). All nations will be illuminated by the grace of the Lord (*T. Levi* 18:9); and all the saints will be clothed in righteousness (*T. Levi* 18:14). Thus, the significance of the spirit of holiness is the idea of bringing people back to relationship with

---

25. B. Smith, "Spirit of Holiness," 76.
26. Ibid.

God and the illumination of all nations by the grace of the Lord. This implication opens a new point of departure for understanding Paul.

If for Paul as for some 2TP writers "the spirit of holiness" is associated with the future Messiah and the eschatological call to the renewal relationship with God, Paul declares the fulfillment and restoration of this relationship because of Christ's resurrection. The future is already realized in Christ's obedience. In him and because of his obedience till death, Jewish expectations are fulfilled. "A new spiritual disposition"[27] became a reality with the possibility to have minds set on the Spirit (8:5–11). In him the new era of redemptive story has begun.

Moreover, in Christ and through him, other nations are called into the obedience of faith (1:5). Only through him will the many be righteous (5:19). God sent him to deal with sin so that all (Jews and Gentiles) may live according to the Spirit in the righteousness of God bringing people into a right relationship with himself provided by Christ.[28] God has given his Son for the sake of sinful humans providing assurance that they will not be condemned or separated from him (8:32). Although Jesus has a primacy and uniqueness as Son (πρωτότοκον, τὸν ἑαυτοῦ υἱὸν, 8:3, 29), Christians are seen as his many siblings, ἐν πολλοῖς ἀδελφοῖς: he is the firstborn among a larger family of believers (8:29).[29] Others are co-heirs with Christ and to be conformed to the likeness of God's Son (8:29). In Christ God can be our Father (8:15). For Paul, the result of God's restoration foretold in the scripture, is the reality of "the spirit" or the reality of obedience not only for Israel, but also for other nations made possible by God's obedient Son (1:1–5; ch. 8). The believers are set free to live not according to the flesh but according to the life-giving Spirit of Christ. The result is the formation of the new community, new family of God (8:14–17) that can be obedient because of Christ. The implication is that God the Father, for Paul, is the universal Redeemer because of the Son who obeys.

---

27. B. Smith's language in ibid.

28. The Spirit is another major concept that unites the work of the Father and the Son (8:1–17). Paul's explicit interchange of "the Spirit," "the Spirit of God," "the Spirit of Christ," "the Spirit of him who raised Jesus from the dead" and "the Spirit of adoption" certainly points to that (ch. 8). I will return to this theme later.

29. See on the unique sonship Hurtado, "Jesus' Divine Sonship," 217–33.

3. Redefining God's Family

The idea of God's fatherhood is further revealed by Paul in the references to God as "our Father" (1:7) and "Abba-Father" (8:15), which define those who belong to him as his family.

3.1 Holy People of God, Jews and Gentiles

Paul's greeting from God "our Father" belongs to all God's beloved, called saints, who are in Rome (1:7). The terms "our Father," "beloved," "saints" (holy ones) evoke corporate implications of all those who belong to God the Father through Christ.[30]

The corporative reference to God as Father recalls OT passages where God is the Father of Israel, of the whole people (Exod 4:22; Deut 32:5–6). In the 2TP there is already a shift from a national to a more personal (whether a single individual or representative of the faithful remnant) relationship between God and people. God is referred to in personal terms as Father from the lips of the righteous Jews (Sir. 51:10; Wis 2:16; 4Q372).[31] Both OT and 2TP literature emphasize the idea of God the Father who will redeem or restore either the whole of Israel (Isa 64:1ff.; cf. Jer 31:8–9; Ps 103:6–14; *Apoc. Ezek.*) or righteous ones within Israel or righteous Israel (Mic 7:18; Isa 10:20–22; Hos 2:23; Tob 13:6, *Jub.*; Sir 23:1, 4; Wis 14:3; *3 Macc.* 6:8–9; *T. Job* 33:3; 4Q372).

In the same way the language of a "holy people" in the OT is referred to Israel in a sense that God has chosen them out of all the people to belong to him, "For you are a people holy to the LORD your God; the LORD your God has chosen you out of all the peoples on earth to be his people, his treasured possession" (Deut 7:6). In Exodus also the choice of Israel, as God's sons, is given to be a kingdom of priests and a holy nation (Exod 19:6). This relationship is sealed by the covenant into which God has entered with Israel.

In the 2TP literature God elects and loves Abraham (*1 En.* 44:10; CD III, 2–3), Joseph (*Jos. Asen.* 23:10), or the people of Israel (*Jub.* 2:20; *4 Ezra* 6:58). "The saints" and "beloved ones" are the righteous ones within Israel upon whom the spirit of holiness will rest (*T. Levi* 18:9–11). Thus,

---

30. Thompson also recognizes the corporate terminology here, however she does not examine "saints" in her context and does not use intertextuality in her approach (M. Thompson, "Mercy upon All," 208).

31. See chapter 2 above.

the idea of God's beloved, chosen and holy people firmly belongs to the description of Israel and the righteous ones within Israel in Jewish texts.

Paul readdresses the language of "God's beloved, called saints" to all (πᾶσιν) in Christ (1:7a), a word that Paul uses extensively in the letter. Paul lists his implied audience, which is predominantly Gentile but also Jewish, among the holy ones (8:27; 16:2, 15). They are those who belong to Christ, are loved by God and also address God as Father. As W. Greathouse states, "They were no longer simply Gentiles or Jews; they had been called to belong to Jesus Christ (1:6). God had claimed them for himself."[32] God claims them his own just as he claims Israel his own. They all, Jews and Gentiles, are God's own people now. As saints and beloved ones they are the righteous ones. Paul develops a significant theme that God pours out his love for those who do not merit it (5:5-8; 8:31-39; 9:13), on both Jews (11:28) and Gentiles (8:35; 9:25-26). Jewett describes the formula "all God's beloved" as "explicitly inclusive," suggesting the impartiality of God's love and including all "recipients of God's boundless love flowing from the Christ event."[33]

In this light those who call God "Father" are his people but this time both Jews and Gentiles are like God's Israel. Yet, as Esler recognizes, nowhere in Romans does Paul call the new entity Israel, "keeping a more benign attitude to Israel than elsewhere."[34] In Romans Paul is reticent about this, unlike Galatians 6:16, where he explicitly names the Israel of God in reference to those in Christ, the former Jews and former Gentiles. Esler points out that, perhaps, because of Paul's previous experience in Galatia, where he had taken a tough line on the Jews and "may not have won the day," here he avoids calling a new entity Israel.[35]

Paul's benign attitude in Romans to the Jews does not prevent him from referring to Israel in 11:26. Paul subsumes Israel within the notion of being in Christ but does not remove the ethnic category of Jew and Gentile. In his usage of the metaphor of the olive tree, believing Gentiles are grafted into a good olive tree that represents Israel. They become children of Abraham and share common lineage as God's people in Christ. Although the unbelieving Jews are broken off as branches, the faithful remnant has been saved (11:1-10), which includes Paul himself and his fellow Jewish believers in Jesus the Messiah. Moreover, God is able to

---

32. Greathouse, *Romans 1–8*, 45.
33. Jewett, *Romans*, 113.
34. Esler, *Conflict*, 307.
35. Ibid., 360.

God the Father Revealed in Christ

bring the broken off Jews back into the tree if they do not continue in the unbelief. Paul speaks in terms of salvation for both Jews and Gentiles: the fullness of the Gentiles (11:25) and of the fullness of the Jews (11:12). In his view, all are part of the people of God through Christ. Their full number is for Paul all Israel. It is the true Israel.[36]

Conceivably, Paul is reticent to use the term "Israel" for those in Christ in Romans because he wants to avoid the misunderstanding that the newly formed community in Christ is the replacement of Israel. For Paul it appears very important to display that Christ comes as the fulfillment of God's promises to the Jews given in the scripture (1:2; 3:21; 15:8) so that the Gentiles also may glorify God (15:8) and be called into obedience of faith through him (1:5; 16:26). For Paul all who are led by the Spirit are God's children and heirs, co-heirs with Christ (8:14–17). This family is no replacement of Judaism or Jewish ethnicity but invariably it is "a melding of new and old"[37] because of God's act in Christ. This family welcomes both ethnic groups and this new identity includes both.

Paul informs the reader that God shows no favoritism (2:11; cf. 2:1) and, as such, he does not favor the Jews over and above the Gentiles or the other way around. God wants and intends to save Israel as much he wants to save the whole creation. Although Paul considers himself the apostle to the Gentiles, his mission purpose does not exclude bringing the Jews to salvation. Rather it is on his agenda that some of them be saved (11:13). Paul invites the Roman church to join him in this mission not only to the Gentiles but also to Jews in every aspect even in ministering through material things (15:27).

In agreement with Wenham, we must remember that Paul "does not see Jesus just as Saviour of the world in general, but also as the Messiah of Israel in particular ('to the Jews first,' Rom 1:16), as is clear from all his letters, especially Rom 9–11."[38] Again, recognizing that Paul does not emphasize the superiority of one group over the other; rather he unfolds God's purposes through Christ for both groups.

Throughout Romans Paul declares God's redemptive purposes for the Jews and the Gentiles are fulfilled through Christ. Both Jews and Gentiles are enabled to call God Father or Abba through Christ, which makes them like a renewed people, the holy remnant, or, in the context of Romans, it makes them God's renewed family. This is why the terms

---

36. See further Bell, *Provoked to Jealousy*, 121ff.
37. Campbell, *The Deliverance*, 1032n107.
38. D. Wenham, *Follower of Jesus*, 121.

that were previously applied to Israel as God's beloved and holy people are being reapplied by Paul not only to the Jews but also to the Gentiles in Christ (9:24ff.; 10:14–18; 11:28–32; 12:1–2). They both are God's people living as one body (ch. 12). In Christ Paul redefines God's family. His explanation of that in 8:14–17 deserves special attention.

3.2 Shared Sonship in Abba-family

A new family of God for Paul is formed by the Spirit of sonship where the children of God share their sonship with Christ and address God as Abba, Father (8:14–17). Paul's idea of the new Abba-family needs further unpacking. First, is there importance in Paul's reference to God as Abba and how does it contribute to identifying those who belong to Abba? What is the role of the Spirit in leading the children of God? Finally, how does the concept of sonship/adoption help Paul to define God's family?

Paul's usage of the Aramaic address "Abba" in Rom 8:15 (as well as in Gal 4:6) recalls Jesus' own usage of the term in addressing God in Mark 14:36. In his well-known research Joachim Jeremias considers the novelty and uniqueness of Jesus' address to God as *Abba* in prayer. For Jeremias, familiarity between God and his people became possible only because of Jesus. He argues that the word *Abba* as an address to God, was taken from children's speech, and is something like "Daddy" in English. Jesus addressed God like this all the time and taught his disciples so to speak.[39]

The problem with trying to explain the term *Abba* is that no equivalents of the Aramaic "Abba" are found in other instances of the NT and Jewish literature.[40] On the other hand, the Hebrew equivalent אב (ab) of Aramaic *Abba* frequently appears in prayers to God at Qumran. Joseph addresses God as "my Father and my God" (4Q372 1 16). Another reference "my Father and my Lord" is found in the text from Qumran

---

39. Jeremias, *Prayers of Jesus*, 53–54, 57. Among the contemporary scholars supporting this view, see L. Johnson, *Reading Romans*, 124.

40. There is an example of "abba" used in reference to God in the literature of Rabbinic Judaism of the Babylonian Talmud (*Taanith* 23b) where Rabbi Hanan ha-Nehba takes the children's cry of "Abba" in order to appeal to God's fatherly mercy to give rain while he himself uses the invocation "Master of the world, the Holy One," *Babylonian Talmud*, 7:120. From this example it would be rather difficult to suggest that God was addressed as "Abba" in personal terms either from the lips of children or adults in Judaism especially before or during the time of Jesus. Also, *Targ. Ps.*89:27; *Targ. Mal.* 2:10. Vermes, *Jesus the Jew*, 210–11.

(4Q460).⁴¹ In 4Q369 1 II, 6–10 God is described as having a special relationship with Israel as father to a son.⁴² In 1QH XVII, 35–36 God is referred to as Father "to all the [son]s of your truth." In 4Q504 1–2 III, 1–21 the address "my father" refers most likely to God as an address of his people.⁴³ In the light of these discoveries it is plausible to assume that *Abba* was a term used not only by small children to address their fathers, but it was also a term that adults used in address to God. *Abba* is clearly better understood as the equivalent of "Father" rather than "Daddy."⁴⁴ At the same time, the term implies an intimate relationship and personal invocation. The Aramaic term might be distinct but not unique in reference to God.

Jeremias might be mistaken about Jesus' childish language and that the term may not be known as a personal address to God before Christ. However, his emphasis that the reverence and familiarity of Jesus' address conveys a special relationship to God still stands.⁴⁵ Marianne Thompson picks this up in her research showing that by his relationship with the Father Jesus granted to his disciples a share in his own relationship with God.⁴⁶

Paul is citing the address in Aramaic in both instances, which is consistent with the Markan account of Jesus addressing God as *Abba*. Paul writes to Christian communities, which already have had some contact with the Jesus story. That could plausibly include the "Abba" tradition—as represented in the (later) Gospel of Mark. Paul's usage of this address in practice in the community and its consistency with Markan account for Jesus addressing God as *Abba* shows Jesus' close relationship with God.⁴⁷ It seems best to assume that traditions about Jesus' distinct relationship with God the Father whom he called "Abba" were known and were influential in shaping the view of sharing Son's sonship that God's Spirit grants to his children. The early church used it as an evidence of their relationship with the Father based on Jesus' relationship with the

---

41. Schuller, "4Q372 1," 362–63.
42. See further Kugel, "4Q369 'Prayer of Enosh,'" 119–48.
43. See research on that in chapter 2 above.
44. Barr, "Abba," 46.
45. Jeremias, *Prayers of Jesus*, 11–12.
46. M. Thompson, "Mercy upon All," 205.
47. D. Wenham, *Paul and Jesus*, 64.

Father. It is quite plausible that the "Abba"-exclamation communicated the union with Christ and through him with God the Father.

The term that is used by the Markan Jesus is certainly used in the Greek-speaking Pauline churches. It is not unique but it shows a distinct and special or familiar relationship with the Father through Christ. This address, then, does not embody a radically new concept. God as Father was portrayed in the Old Testament and Judaism with the hope that somehow the relationship between God the Father and his people will become more prominent and will be restored (Deut 30:6; Jer 31:9; *Jub.* 1:22–26). In Christ this relationship becomes realized and restored. It is not so much that God is now thought of as Father, but that Jesus reveals the heart of the Father for Jews, Gentiles, and all created order (8:15–27).

Paul further explains this in relation to the Spirit. First, for Paul the Spirit signifies the unity between God and Christ since he often uses the Spirit of God and Christ interchangeably (ch. 8). This enables Paul to draw on all that he said about the gospel of God concerning his Son Christ Jesus up to this point. God is the Redeemer for both Jews and Gentiles and he acts as such as the Father through his obedient Son and Jewish Messiah. The Spirit is apparently the same "spirit of holiness" (1:4) according to which Jesus is appointed as God's obedient Son and through whom all the nations are called into obedience of faith.[48] Now, God himself through Christ in the Holy Spirit may live in the believers.

Secondly, the reality of belonging to God's family and calling him "Abba" is brought about through Christ by the Spirit. In other words, this reality has been accomplished in Christ; and the Spirit brings to and assures the believers of this reality (8:16). For Paul possession of the Spirit marks belonging to Christ (8:9). Believers are shaped by the Spirit and are conformed to the likeness of the Son (8:29). Moreover, by the Spirit, through Christ and with Christ believers belong to God's family (8:14). Campbell puts it succinctly, "The Spirit enables Christian participation in the mind of Christ, and hence a new relationship with God the Father."[49] Thus, the Spirit for Paul "identifies the people of God over against those who still live according to the present age,"[50] or over against those, who do not participate in Christ and are not God's family.

---

48. See the discussion earlier in 2.2.

49. Campbell, *The Quest*, 200.

50. Fee, *God's Empowering Presence*, 538.

Paul's description of the role of the Spirit may be a further logical connection to the past. In 8:14 the image "led by the Spirit" recalls the "leading imagery" of the exodus when God led Israel (Exod 40:34–38; Deut 1:33; Num 9:15–23; 1 Kgs 8:10–11; Ps 77, 104),[51] including by the pillar of cloud and fire (Exod 13:21–22).[52] This is the time when God redeems Israel, he acts as Israel's Father, and Israel is described as God's son.[53] The exodus event is the ground for future hope of God's presence and restoration of Israel based on God's continued faithfulness. God will act as Father and Redeemer in spite of Israel's failure to obey him (Isa 63–64; cf. Isa 43:25; 40:1–11). If Paul has the language of God's deliverance out of Egypt in mind he reinterprets it. First, in universal terms, "all who are led by the Spirit of God are children of God" (8:14). Second, the Spirit has come about through Jesus upon Jew and Gentiles alike marking a new exodus and new redemption, and forming a new family of God. For Paul God the Father, who acted in Israel's history, now has acted in his obedient Son, the Jewish Messiah, and has poured out his love into our hearts by the Holy Spirit (5:5). Now he adopts all those in whom the Spirit dwells.[54]

Paul echoes redemption out of slavery again when he says, "For you did not receive the spirit of slavery to fall back into fear" (8:15a). The Israelites cried out to God because of their slavery (Exod 2:23). When God releases Israel, he points out that their destiny is to be out of slavery to worship and serve him. They are redeemed slaves of God (cf. Lev 25:38, 42–43, 55). Accordingly, this redemption implies more than just redemption of slaves from Egypt. The redemption is more like "emancipation and restoration of the enslaved to wholeness in relation to God"[55] who is implicitly the Father of Israel. Israel is marked as the son of God and not a slave anymore. God's redemption of Israel sets the parameters for Israel's identity in relationship to God who is their Father and who redeems out of slavery.

Paul applies the language of redemption out of slavery to those who are led by the Spirit of God. They are not to go back to slavery but are God's children by adoption (8:14–15). Paul reinterprets the idea of slavery, though. It is no longer enslavement in Egypt. The idea implies sin, obedience to sin, the mind set on the things of the flesh, disobedience

---

51. Keesmaat, *Paul and His Story*, 55–59.
52. N. T. Wright, "The Letter to the Romans," 593.
53. As shown in chapter 2 above.
54. Ibid.
55. Green, *Salvation*, 69. See chapter 2 above.

to God, and broken relationship with him (chs. 5–8). The work of God through Christ and by the Spirit offers restoration of the broken relationship. The restoration is for the Jews with their "sorry litany of unfaithfulness and rebellion"[56] (2:17–28) and for the Gentiles, who were aliens and wicked (1:18–32 that echoes Deuteronomic language) but now called into obedience and into God's family. The fact that all the believers may say "Abba" is because sin is condemned and righteousness is alive. Christ has dealt with sin, and the Spirit now "effects the 'righteousness' that the Torah aimed at but could not produce."[57] Paul presses home the idea that the fulfillment of promises and expectations of Judaism come in and through Christ by the Spirit but it comes for all who believe, forming a new family of God.

Furthermore, Paul explains the idea of redemption and belonging to the Father in terms of sonship/adoption (υἱοθεσία). The suggestion has been made before that the practice of adoption was a legal practice in the Greco-Roman world.[58] If so, then the idea was familiar to Paul's Gentile audience. However, the background of this metaphor is certainly Jewish. The idea of bringing up somebody's child and treating it as one's own is known in the OT (Exod 2:10; Esth 2:7). Moreover, the whole idea of God's fatherhood is connected with the idea of Israel (and the king of Israel) becoming God's son (Exod 4:22; 2 Sam 7:14).[59] The term refers to Israel's prerogative of election to be God's people. Paul is using it in this sense in Rom 9:5. This idea of divine adoption of Gentiles finds some development in the 2TP, as noticed in chapter 2. Aseneth, the daughter of the pagan priest, prays to God and asks him to be her Father, replacing the father and mother who rejected her because of her conversion to Judaism (*Jos. As.* 12:14–15). Aseneth's conversion is her adopting Jewish ways of living. From the text it is not clear how God can adopt Gentiles on a universal scale; only, by adopting the Jewish way of living. Other 2TP texts exclude Gentiles from the idea of God's salvation (3 *Macc.*; *Pss. Sol.*; *Jub.*).[60] Paul, however, rethinks the whole idea of adoption.

---

56. Westerholm, *Understanding Paul*, 117.

57. Fee, *God's Empowering Presence*, 538.

58. The evidence, though, is very circumstantial. The divine adoption plays even lesser role in Greco-Roman sources. Scott, "Adoption, Sonship," 16. Cranfield, *Romans*, 1:397. Graystone, *Romans*, 69. Esler, *Conflict*, 247.

59. See chapter 2 above.

60. See chapter 2 above.

Paul places the adoption of both Jews and Gentiles into God's family on the same level when he states that those who live according to the Spirit of Christ belong to God the Father. It is a radical claim that Jews need to be adopted into the family of God through Christ just as Gentiles. Although theirs is the adoption as sons, as well as the covenants, the law, the temple worship (9:5), still not all of them are true Israelites or children of Abraham or of God for that matter (9:6–7). Their staying in God's promises depends on God's call and faith in God's promises (4:13–14; ch. 9). For Paul, God has fulfilled his promises in Christ; and he has called not only from the Jews but also from the Gentiles (1:1–5; 9:24–29; 15:8–12). Jesus Christ is the firstborn among many brothers and sisters who are to be conformed to him (8:28–29). So, those who are in Christ are the family of God, according to Paul. Through belonging to Christ and by the Spirit "we," including both Jews and Gentiles, call God "Abba, Father." In Christ through the Spirit a new family of God has been formed that has renewed relationship with God the Father. In a formula of adoption Jews and Gentiles alike become God's children, like a new Israel with the provision to address God as Father and to become God's heirs and co-heirs with his own Son.

Since Jesus Christ is the obedient Son, Jews and Gentiles conforming to him, conform to his obedience and to God. The new way of living conforming to the likeness of God's Son (8:29) and sharing in his sonship signals the restored relationship with God and the fulfillment of God's promises. It also points to a future time of fulfillment and restoration of all creation, which will follow as a direct consequence of the resurrection of those in Christ (8:18–27). Yates points out that "Paul has not forgotten the promise to Abraham, that the whole cosmos will be blessed through his seed (cf. Rom 4:13)," however, it "must await the full glorification of the children of God at the resurrection before experiencing the renewal for which it longs."[61] The important implication, though, is the effect of what has already happened in Christ for the glorious future. The new family has been formed and redemption is now taking place. Jews and Gentiles already participate in Christ, conform to him, and share everything with him, including future glory and complete redemption.

In sum, for Paul, the Jews and Gentiles in Christ who are led by the Spirit of Christ share sonship in the family of God and have relationship with God the Father. In this way Paul sees the fulfillment of God's

---

61. Yates, *The Spirit and Creation*, 153–54.

promises to restore relationship with Israel and to bless and bring in other nations to whom they were called to be a light. This is the fulfillment that concerns the whole creation that will be liberated from its bondage and brought into the glorious freedom of the children of God.

4. Redefining the Faithfulness of the Father

4.1 Covenantal Righteousness/Faithfulness

In Romans God reveals himself through the Son as Father of both Jews and Gentiles (1:2-3; 6:4) and as Redeemer (3:24). God's redemption is a part of his righteousness to which the scripture testifies beforehand (3:21-25). Just as God has been righteous and faithful in the past leading Israel out of Egypt and Babylon, God is righteous and faithful in the present setting his children free from sin (6:18), adopting them into his family (8:12-17), and sending his Son as a sin offering (8:3). For Paul God's redemption is consistent with God's faithful and righteous character that now has been revealed through redemption in Christ for everyone (1:17; 3:21) and awaits future glory of the whole created order (8:18-27).

Three particular traits in regard to redemption are intrinsically distinctive in Paul: God's redemption is in Christ; it is for everyone; and it is based on God's own righteousness that is known in the scriptures. Such perspectives raise a number of questions. If God's righteousness comes through the faith of Christ to all who believe, where does Jewish particularism fit? In a similar vein, if God's righteousness is grounded in divine covenantal faithfulness and promises of redemption toward Israel, how does Paul explain the inclusion of the Gentiles? If God's redemption is all God's work in Christ, are people passive recipients of that?

Much of Protestant exegesis from Luther onwards has taken the expression "the righteousness of God" to refer to a status of righteousness imputed by God to believers in Jesus Christ, failing to draw parallels to the notion of God's righteousness from the OT (3:21).[62] Ernst Käsemann notices that while God's righteousness as a gift to the believers is not excluded, the primary sense of it in Paul lies in relation to God's own righteousness as it is attested by the scripture.[63] Although Käsemann refers to God's righteousness known in the OT, he concludes that in Paul's

---

62. D. Moo, *Encountering*, 80–83.
63. Käsemann, "The Righteousness of God," 177.

view God's righteousness is not his covenantal faithfulness to Israel but his faithfulness to the whole world.[64]

The majority of contemporary scholars observe not only the interplay between God's righteousness/faithfulness in Paul that can be traced in Jewish texts but also recognize the overlap of God's righteousness with his faithfulness to Israel.[65] M. Gorman insists on a close connection between God's "faithfulness," God's "truthfulness," and God's "righteousness" in Romans (3:3, 5, 7; 15:8), which seems to refer to one of the most prominent divine characteristics in the Bible—God's covenant fidelity to Israel that is "demonstrated in saving power."[66] According to Moo, God's righteousness in Paul includes divine intervention to deliver his people in "fulfilment of his promises."[67] Witherington also connects the language of God's righteousness directly with people's redemption.[68] In a similar way, Sam Williams writes that God's righteousness brings to mind ideas of deliverance or salvation and is consistent in Romans with God's faithfulness to his promises.[69] Hays goes further to say that God's dealing with humanity is a manifestation of his righteousness and "not arbitrary dissolution of his promises to Israel."[70]

Paul announces in Romans that God's righteousness has been revealed just as the scripture promised (1:18; 3:21). By that very fact Paul's explanation about God's righteousness at the present time is a direct consequence of God's righteousness/faithfulness to Israel. If God's righteousness has been revealed now, it means that God is proved to be true to himself and to his own purposes to deliver his covenant people. Even Jewish unfaithfulness could not nullify his faithfulness according to Paul (3:2). God remains true even if everyone is a liar (3:4).

If God acts on behalf of his righteousness/faithfulness what is then the advantage of being a Jew (3:1)? Or what is the value of circumcision (3:1). In the case of Abraham the circumcision is a seal of the righteousness, the outcome of his faith in God's promises (4:11). In 2:29 Paul echoes the Deuteronomy and Jeremiah thought of the circumcision of the heart

---

64. Ibid., 177–78.
65. See Dunn, *The Theology of Paul*, 340–46. Also, Dunn, *Romans, 1–8*, 133.
66. Gorman, *Apostle of the Crucified Lord*, 350.
67. D. Moo, *Romans*, 222.
68. Witherington III, *Paul's Narrative*, 256.
69. Williams, "The 'Righteousness of God' in Romans," 262, 271.
70. Hays, *The Faith*, 283.

(Deut 30:6; Jer 4:4), the real circumcision, which is a matter of heart, spiritual and not literal. Thus, the sign of the covenant and belonging to God their Father through the covenant relationship has an undeniable importance to Israel (cf. 9:4–5) because they point to God's faithful character and involvement with his people. But physical circumcision as such does not confer any ethical or eschatological advantages, as Campbell rightly argues. Circumcision is of value if the Jews obey the law, if not, as the scripture testifies, "the circumcision has become uncircumcision."[71]

If circumcision is of no value, are the oracles of God the Jewish advantage (3:2)? Τὰ λόγια, (the oracles) refers to the words of God to his people (Deut 33:9; Ps 17:31; 118:148; 147:19–20) or to the OT and the divine message of salvation elsewhere in the NT (Acts 7:38; Heb 5:12; 1 Pet 4:11). Paul connects the advantages of the Jews with the fact that God has spoken to them and has entered into a special relationship with them elevating them into the status of his son, taking care of them and promising redemption. Τὰ λόγια may be Paul's shorthand for the privileges of Israel that he enumerates in 9:4–5.[72] But more importantly, they include God's promises and God's faithfulness that are recorded in the scripture (3:3ff.; 9:4–5). It means that the Jews are privileged to be familiar with scriptures that tell about God's grace and his actual redemptive action toward them throughout their history. They are privileged to know God's faithfulness that can overcome Jewish and all human unfaithfulness. The scripture that is entrusted to the Jews carries incontestable witnesses to that (3:4ff.).

Paul's language echoes Deuteronomy in which he has a special interest as he uses it several times throughout the letter (Deut 7:7; 10:6–9; 11:8; 13:8–10; 32 in 10:19; 12:19; 15:10). In the Song of Moses (Deut 32) Moses scolds Israel for its faithlessness to God reminding it that God is still their Father and God of faithfulness, righteous and upright. "A faithful God, without deceit, just and upright is he; yet his degenerate children have dealt falsely with him, a perverse and crooked generation. Do you thus repay the LORD, O foolish and senseless people? Is not he your father, who created you, who made you and established you?" (Deut 32:4).

Deuteronomy indicates that Israel belongs to God the Father because God created it or established Israel as his people. Somehow before that in Egypt the children of Israel were aliens themselves (Deut 10:18–19). When God delivered them out of Egypt, he acted like a Father to

---

71. Campbell, *The Deliverance*, 575, 589.
72. D. Moo, *Romans*, 183.

them. God as Redeemer elects and lifts his people to the status of "son" and promised to lead them into the promised land. The most significant aspect here is why God is acting this way: "It is not because of your righteousness or the uprightness of your heart that you are going in to occupy the land; but because of the wickedness of these nations the LORD your God is dispossessing them before you, in order to fulfill the promise that the LORD made on oath to your ancestors, to Abraham, to Isaac, and to Jacob" (Deut 9:5). The idea of God's acting in the life of Israel is tied with God's faithful and righteous character. God manifests his faithfulness through his active faith-keeping. He keeps his covenant intact in spite of Israel's unfaithfulness.

This is exactly what Paul takes from the OT. If the Jews fail to keep their part of the covenant (2:17–29), God's faithfulness in making promises and keeping them is not invalidated (3:4). God remains true to his obligations and promises that include his people (3:1–8). In 3:3–7, to human ἡ ἀπιστία, ψεύστης, ἡ ἀδικία, τό ψεῦσμα (faithlessness, liar, injustice, falsehood) Paul contrasts ἡ πίστις τοῦ θεοῦ, ἡ ἀλήθεια τοῦ θεου, ἡ δικαιοσύνη θεοῦ (God's faithfulness, God's truthfulness, and God's righteousness). Just as Moses' Song (Deut 32) served as a witness to the people of Israel of what God has done for them (cf. Deut 31:19) Paul writes this letter to confirm that the very words of God are still entrusted to Israel (3:2). They should know what God has done and how God stands committed to the covenant he has made. Together with Moses Paul celebrates God's faithful character in spite of Israel's infidelity, even in spite of universal human sinfulness (3:10–20).

The advantage of the Jews (3:2), however, turns out not to be so much an advantage. Campbell's alternative explanation of Rom 3:2 in this respect makes perfect sense. He suggests that the question in 3:1 is Paul's and the answer in 3:2 belongs to his opponents.[73] If this is so, then in the following verses Paul elicits the correct response from his interlocutors that in fact they are no better at all (3:9). In 3:3 Paul asks the interlocutor whether God's standards of judgment will be relaxed in the face of Jewish transgressions. The answer (3:4) is of course not: God's judgment will not

---

73. Most scholars explain this otherwise: the question is asked by Paul's opponent (3:1). See ibid., 177–83. However, even if this is Paul's opponent who asks the question, Paul's answer carefully points to the heart of the matter that everyone is in sinful position before God (3:9). If the question is Paul's and the answer belongs to his opponents, as Campbell believes, Paul reorients the discussion toward God helping the interlocutors realize that that there are no advantages in salvific terms for anyone. See Campbell, *The Deliverance*, 573ff.

tolerate such behavior. Paul directs the conversation further: Is it not unjust of God to pour out wrath on us (3:5)? Absolutely not: How will God judge the world then (3:6)? But if by means of my falsehood the truthfulness of God overflows to God's glory, why then am I still condemned as a sinner (3:7)? The interlocutor is convinced: the judgment of such people is positively deserved (3:8). Now, Paul repeats again the question about the advantage (3:8). The interlocutor replies to this (Campbell imagines the state of the interlocutor now as "presumably a little shamefacedly"[74]): not in every respect. Thus, Paul reorients the discussion toward God helping the interlocutors realize that there are no advantages in salvific terms for anyone, including a Jew.

God's past dealing with his people is important for Paul (9:4–5). God remains true to his obligations to the people he has chosen as his own (3:1–8). If God is not faithful to Israel, he could be not trustworthy at all. In the overall context Paul avows that God has not rejected his people (11:1, 11) and that finally "all Israel will be saved" (11:25–26). Although the phrase "all Israel" divides Pauline scholars in their opinions,[75] it certainly shows that God remains faithful to his promises of redemption which include Jews (15:8). How God is going to do that and who God's people really are, are the questions of the role of Christ and God's purposes for the Jews and the Gentiles from the very beginning that we are still to uncover in this research.

Paul emphasizes that Jewish failure does not mean that God's faithfulness will shine more brightly if God acts for good (3:7–8). The problem of Israel's unbelief still remains (9:1–5) and Paul addresses this in chs. 9–11. More importantly, if Paul's letter is written mostly to the Gentiles with his focus on bringing the Gentiles into the obedience of faith (1:1, 5; 15:15–18) Paul still recognizes the significant place of Israel in the purpose of God. If there is any view among the Gentile Christians that God has rejected the Jews for their unbelief, Paul insists that God is faithful to Israel just as it is written in the scriptures. Israel remains beloved for the sake of the ancestors (11:28). Moreover, he stresses that the Gentiles owe gratitude to the Jews because they share spiritual blessings (15:27). God has chosen them to bless all nations. Christ himself comes from them (9:5); he is the obedient Son (1:1–5) and, thus, a light to the nations. He fulfills Israel's function.

74. Campbell, *The Deliverance*, 576.

75. For a summary of views, see Fitzmyer *Romans*, 619–20; Cranfield, *Romans*, 576.

Paul shows that God of Israel is the same God who keeps his righteousness/faithfulness to his people of old. Paul's gospel does not start from nowhere. It has a deep and solid background in the Jewish tradition and takes into account God's people of old in a very direct way. Paul apparently presupposes that his readers are familiar with God's righteousness/faithfulness from scripture. God as Redeemer is trustworthy because he has been faithful to his people. God has kept his own promises and purposes to Israel despite its unfaithfulness. However, it is not yet the whole picture of God's redemption. Paul is concerned in a particular way with the promises to Israel as he reads them through the lens of Christ in such a way as to show how they encompass Israel and the entire created order.

4.2 Faithfulness and God's Bigger Purposes

In pursuing the idea of God's covenantal faithfulness to Israel Donaldson goes as far to say that the salvation of the Gentiles for Paul, is a result of Christ's ministry but not part of God's faithfulness to the patriarchal promises. Paul reads his convictions that Christ has accomplished salvation for all into the scripture that he is citing rather than coming to this conviction from the scripture. Although the salvation of the Gentiles, is not part of God's faithfulness to the covenantal promises, Paul appeals to the scriptural texts in support of his gospel to the Gentiles with such conviction in mind.[76]

Donaldson's theory sounds appealing, but it needs to be nuanced. First, Paul may read his conviction into the scriptural texts; however, for Paul God's redemptive plan is consistent with his promises and purposes for his chosen people of old (11:1–2; 15:10) and also for those who were not his people from the very beginning (9:25–26; 15:8–12). Paul starts with his conviction that God has acted in Christ; this enables him to read scripture in this way. So, Paul has a retrospective reading of scripture in the light of Christ. It is often not the most obvious reading, but that is because Paul is reading it through his lens of Jesus. God's righteousness to Israel in this reading is God's righteousness to redeem Israel and through Israel the whole world.

Second, Paul's conviction about God's faithfulness to Israel and his seeking for other nations is supported in the OT. God acts in the life of his people and other nations on the basis of his own righteousness (cf.

---

76. Donaldson, *Paul and the Gentiles*, 99–101.

Deut 7, 9, 32). He wants his name to be proclaimed in all the earth (Exod 9:16). God's redemption in the OT as, for example, in Isaiah that "the Lord has bared his holy arm before the eyes of all the nations; and all the ends of the earth shall see the salvation of our God" (Isa 52:10; cf. 51:4–5) finds its realized expression in Paul's fulfillment of the gospel for all the nations (1:1–5; 3:21). In Isaiah, it could be argued that this is a demonstration of God's deliverance of Israel before all the nations to whom they are called to be a light so that the nations may be in awe of the God of Israel (Isa 42:6) and so that God's name will not be profaned. However, the idea of God gathering others who are not his and who are foreigners is also clearly in the writer's mind (Isa 56:1–8; cf. Deut 32:21; Mal 1:11).

Although OT and 2TP provide some examples of the Gentiles joining the people of God (Ruth, Aseneth), the picture of bringing the Gentiles into the people of God is not complete and quite complicated. God can adopt Gentiles but not on a universal scale (*Jos. As.*). In Testament of Twelve Patriarchs God will be revealed to all the nations among whom Israel is a light (*T. Levi* 14:3–4). There are other references to the future salvation of the Gentiles (*T. Levi* 18:3; cf. *T. Naph.* 8:3–4; *T. Jud.* 24:6). Gentiles are to be excluded and not to mingle with the Jews (*Jub.*). God also uses Gentiles to punish Israel for disobedience (*Pss. Sol.*).[77]

For Paul, Gentiles do not only see the salvation of God, they are called to the obedience of faith (1:5; 16:26). The power of God is demonstrated for salvation to everyone (1:16). The overarching emphasis of Paul's gospel is for both Jews and Gentiles because of God's righteousness (1:16–17; 3:22; 4:11; 10:4, 11–13).

Paul explains the inclusion of the Gentiles negatively and positively.

First, negatively, Paul places both Jews and Gentiles on the same level of sinfulness before God. Paul develops the theme of Gentiles and Jews being under sin from the beginning of Romans (1:18—2:29). Both Gentiles and Jews are in a great need for God's intervention. Both Jews and Gentiles are in the same position of untruthfulness. Only God is true and righteous (2:5); and he does not show any favoritism (2:11). In 3:4 Paul exclaims, "Let God be true and everyone be a liar." The first part of the saying seems to "demonstrate the link between divine reliability and the validity of prophetic oracles."[78] For Paul God of Israel revealed in the scriptures is the same God who is true to his word. The second part of

---

77. See chapter 2 above.
78. Jewett, *Romans*, 246.

this saying echoes Ps 116:11 (115:2 LXX). While the psalmist assumes the distinction between the righteous and the wicked, and the expression that everyone is a liar comes from the lips of the one who walks before God in faith (Ps 116:9), Paul generalizes the fact that everyone is a liar. All people are "shown to be chronically suppressing the truth and exchanging truth for lies" (cf. 1:18–32).[79]

Paul establishes the charge that Jews and Gentiles alike are under sin (3:9) further (3:10–20). This time he refers to the scripture adducing multiple evidences from the OT.

Paul embraces all people into the category of the unrighteous declaring that there is no one who is righteous, not even one (3:10) and there is no one who shows kindness, not even one (3:12). Paul's citations come from both Eccl 7:20 and Ps 14:1, 3 (LXX 13:1, 3). While Ecclesiastes mentions that there is no one on earth so righteous as to do good, the psalm simply says that there is no one who does good. Both texts agree that there is no one who does good. Then Paul adds, no one seeks and understands God (3:11); all turned aside and became worthless (3:12). Paul almost verbatim repeats Ps 14:3 (LXX 13:2) where God looks down from heaven to see if there are any who seek after God and sees that they have all gone astray, they are all alike perverse.

Psalm 14:1–3 and its almost identical Psalm 53:1–3 (LXX 52:1–3) describe those who become corrupt, do not seek God, and do not do any good. However, the psalms distinguish between "the evildoers" and "the righteous." The righteous are God's people among whom God is present and whom God will restore (Ps 14:4–7).[80] Both psalms underline hope and restoration that could come only from God (Ps 14:7; 53:6). Paul eliminates the distinction between the wicked and the righteous and argues for the universal human corruption. This way he aggravates the need for hope and restoration for all.

Ecclesiastes 7 also unfolds the ways of the righteous and of the wicked. Then the author adds that there is no one on earth so righteous as to do good without ever sinning (Eccl 7:20). This phrase could relate to the rulers of the earth or even to all people in the context of Eccl 7:21. There is no righteous one among them. However, when Solomon prays at the dedication of the Temple he says that "there is no one who does not sin" (1 Kgs 8:46). He addresses Israel and recognizes that all Israelites

---

79. Ibid.
80. The idea is present in the later period as well, *Pss. Sol.* 17:15, 19; 1 QH 12:38.

sinned against God; they did wrong and acted wickedly. He asks God for forgiveness. Although there is a possibility for Israel to come back to God because the king asks for forgiveness, the fact that Israel acted wrongly before God and needed forgiveness remains. Paul uses the scripture to support his claim about the universal human sinfulness: it concerns Israel as well all the Gentiles. All acted wrongly before God including Israel.

In Romans 3:13 Paul combines the message of Ps 5:9 (LXX Ps 5:10) and 140:3 (LXX 139:4). In 3:14 Paul refers to Ps 10:7 (LXX Ps 9:28). In 3:18 there is a citation from Ps 36:1 (LXX Ps 35:2). All the quoted psalms again make a distinction between the righteous and the wicked. Ps 36:1 is quite harsh in describing the wicked: they have no fear of God. The absence of fear before God is a common expression in the OT and 2TP for impiety (cf. Ps 5; Ps 15; Pr 14:2).[81] The righteous, on the contrary, do fear and honor God (Exod 18:21; Deut 6:2; Ps 11:10; *T. Sim.* 3:4). Paul drops the distinction between the righteous and the wicked. There is only one category for him. He includes the Jews along with the Gentiles in the category of the wicked who have no fear for God (3:18). He places them on the same level as enemies of God.[82]

In 3:15–17 Paul cites Isa 59:7–8. Here Paul finds a negative description of Israel. Isaiah pronounces God's indictment on his people whose massive sinfulness separates them from God.

Paul conflates Isaiah's message about Israel with other aforementioned scriptural references that describe the sin of the wicked making his point clear that the scripture contains evidence of sin and unrighteousness of both Jews and Gentiles. All are in the same degree of condemnation before God.

In 3:19–20 Paul makes sure that all those who follow the law understand that no one is declared righteous in God's sight by observing the law; rather, through the law people become conscious of sin. Since the scripture testifies to universal sinfulness no one, especially those who are within the law,[83] or, those who are entrusted and guided by the scripture, could raise any objections against such solid evidence (3:19). The whole world is accountable, ὑπόδικος (under indictment)[84] before God (3:19).

---

81. Jewett, *Romans*, 263.

82. Watson, *Paul*, 128–30.

83. The law here is most likely used in the inclusive sense of all scripture (cf. Isa 1:10), Jewett, *Romans*, 264.

84. Ibid., 256.

The phrase "No human being will be justified in his [God's] sight" in 3:20 alludes to Ps 143:2 (LXX Ps 142:2).[85] The psalm affirms the universal unrighteousness: no one living is righteous before God. Paul makes a particular emphasis on those who follow the law: no one will be justified before God by deeds of the law (3:20). Once again, Paul builds up a case of universal human sinfulness, of both Jews and Gentiles. So, when the scriptures speak to human unrighteousness before God, this includes the Jews. All those who are guided by the scripture, i.e., Jews, are found unrighteous before God, because the scripture itself testifies to the universal sinfulness.

At the same time Ps 143 (cf. Ps 14, 53) anticipates God's redeeming activity that will be effective because of his faithfulness and righteousness and that, according to Paul, has been finally revealed through Christ's faithfulness (3:21ff.). Paul's whole development of human indictment anticipates God's redemption that will concern the whole world. Moreover, the whole idea of redemption is placed by Paul into the category and possibility of God's involvement through Christ (3:22).

Positively, God's inclusion of the Gentiles is a part of his bigger purposes from the very beginning (1:1–7; 3:21–26). The power of God for salvation is for everyone, first for the Jew, then for the Gentile (1:17; cf. 3:29; 10:12). God has been faithful to Israel not only for the sake of Israel but for the sake of all people so that God's universal purposes would be fulfilled (10:11–13).

Paul's most supportive argument for inclusion of the Gentiles into God's big purposes is his discussion on Abraham in ch. 4. The Abraham discussion in Romans 4 a multi-faceted argument. We will return to Abraham's example later to put more light on the idea of faithfulness. At this point it is important to stress that Abraham is seen to be a model of God's acceptance of the Gentiles. Abraham is the paradigmatic proselyte, converted from Gentiles (4:10) who was found righteous through faith before circumcision. On the basis of faith he is the father of all who believe but have not been circumcised (4:11). He is also the father of all circumcised who walk in his faith (4:12). Accordingly, the Gentiles, like the Jews, are descended from Abraham, the forefather of all people. Paul clearly doesn't think that Abraham is the physical progenitor of all, but this is not the only place where his argument of descent is not necessarily biological descent.

---

85. Hays, "Psalm 143," 114.

In chapter 9 Paul further explains the concept of the true children of Abraham. Here he makes the opposite point. Not all Abraham's physical descendants are his children, consequently not all are Israel, and not all are children of God. Only those who share Abraham's faith (4:11–12) are the children of God's promises and grace, and his descendants (9:8). In other words, the election of God's people has always depended on God's gracious election and mercy (9:6–13). This way Paul denies God's rejection of Israel and includes the extension of the salvation to the Gentiles for God has mercy on all (11:32). God is faithful to Israel in Christ but he also extends his mercy toward the Gentiles adopting them into his family. The true children are led by the Spirit and heirs with Christ. Although not all the Jews by birth find reconciliation with God through Christ, Paul expresses the hope that they will do (11:14). In the meanwhile the believing Gentiles make their way into the family of God. God has mercy on all.

In 9:23–29 Paul presents the faithfulness of God to Israel as being worked out through inclusion of the Gentiles using a catena of scripture references.

First, Paul cites Hosea 2:23; 1:10 (LXX 2:25, 1), where the prophet delivers God's message of hope to Israel. God will renew his relationship with them in spite of their infidelity; they will become children of the living God again. Hosea points to God who actively calls out estranged people back to himself. Paul extends Hosea's call of Israel to the Gentiles and includes them with the covenantal formula "my people" and "children of the living God" into the exalted status of the children of God and, accordingly, into the promise of God who wants to restore the relationship with them. Wagner is helpful in shedding more light on Paul's usage of Hosea. He writes that Paul reads the scripture as a testimony to the reversal wrought by "God's grace, in which those apparently outside the scope of God's mercy are included among the people God has redeemed for himself." This way Paul refocuses Hosea into a "prophecy of the 'riches of God's glory' now showered upon *Gentile* 'vessels of mercy.'" Paul does not erase the distinction between Israel and outsiders but redefines "the basis in which Jew and Gentile come to be a part of God's people." Hosea's vision has become a reality for Paul in the community that already consists of Jews and Gentiles that God has called into being.[86]

Second, Paul adds some important observations in regard to Israel itself: God's promise and election has also not failed for his people

---

86. Wagner, *Heralds*, 83, 85.

(9:27–29; cf. 9:1–6). They would not be like Sodom and Gomorrah (9:29). The remnant will be saved (9:27). Paul cites Isa 10:22, conflating with Hos 1:10, Isa 10:23; 1:9 (9:27–29). In their context both Isaiah and Hosea pronounce judgment against Israel. As a whole, however, they bring good news of reconciliation to all Israelites scattered around in the world (Hosea) or to a remnant of Israel (Isaiah). Both prophets proclaim God's covenantal love for Israel. They summon the people to repentance and return to God (Hos 2:8, 18–19). The Lord stops the total destruction leaving some survivors, the seed (Isa 1:9). The righteous ones within the nation who truly rely on the Lord will be the remnant that returns to God (Isa 10:23).

The Isaianic prophecies of "remnant" and "seed" function together in Paul as a reminder of God's faithfulness to the promises given to Israel.[87] Based on these promises Israel has a hope for restoration in spite of the present disobedience (11:26–32). Now, the "remnant" in Pauline context is the "seed" that is the true children of God promised to Abraham (9:7–8), not all Israel, but both Jews and Gentiles whom he prepared in advance for glory (9:23–24).

Paul clearly reads the Gentiles into the texts of the OT that originally address Israel or the faithful ones within Israel and, thus, he redefines Israel by including the Gentiles. God's redemption is an equally necessary and fulfilled act for all new people of God who are now able to orient themselves toward God conforming to his Son (8:29).

Furthermore, Paul places God's redemption into an eschatological context when the full revelation of the children of God and the redemption of our bodies will take place (8:19–25). This event will be the release from the bondage of the whole creation as well.[88] Since the creation is inevitably related to the children of God who already can enact "their rightful belonging to God's family and to contribute to the ultimate restoration of the creation,"[89] then it means that also in the present age creation can gain "glimpses of its longed-for-hope of freedom."[90] The accomplishments of Christ on the cross are effective now and for the future of the whole creation (3:21–26; 5:9–10; 6:1–11).

---

87. Ibid., 116.

88. Paul's cosmic concern as interwoven into the human drama of salvation becomes especially lucid in the light of Isa 24–27 or Ezek 36–37. See Yates, *The Spirit and Creation*, 153–54.

89. Jewett, *Romans*, 519.

90. J. Moo, "Romans 8.19–22," 89.

In its particular expression the gospel, although Jewish in origin and character, reaches beyond the Jewish national boundaries to include people from among all the nations. This particular expression is a part of a larger theological claim about the solidarity of sin and God's provision for redemption of all. When Paul refers to the OT scriptures for the grounds of his arguments he re-interprets them in the light of the fulfilled prophecies for both Jews and Gentiles. God's deliverance that is known in the scriptures and promised for the future is active now for the Jews and for the whole world just as God intended it from the very beginning.

4.3 God's Faithfulness in Christ

For Paul, Christ provides the key for interpreting the story of God and God's dealing with Israel in order to bless them, other nations and the whole world. The gospel of God for Paul is concerning his Son, Jesus Christ (1:1–3). Christ confirms Jewish promises as he has become a servant of circumcision on behalf of God's truth so that the Gentiles may glorify God (15:8–9). On the one hand, one might see Paul's gospel as highly Christological. On the other hand, Christ does not act apart from God or apart from promises that were given in the OT. On the contrary, God has redeemed through Christ's faithfulness (3:21–22) just as the law and the prophets testified. That which the law could not do, God did by sending his Son (8:3). Christ is the fulfillment, the goal of the law (10:4).[91] The same God that has worked in the life of Israel is acting through his Son in the life of all who believe. Paul's gospel is still thoroughly theocentric. Keck goes further to say that Christ is referred to in Romans "'adverbially'—to specify and qualify God's act."[92] The point of this argument rightly points toward the unity of the redemptive work of God through Christ. However, to describe Christ's role "adverbially" is to undermine Paul's high Christology to some extent. Paul's gospel is theocentric and

---

91. τέλος is understood by most modern scholars as the aim of the law in contrast to the older tradition that Christ is the termination of the law. It makes a better sense in Paul's context when he says that the law and the prophets testify about God's righteousness (3:21), that Paul's gospel confirms and fulfills rather than determines the law (3:31), see N. T. Wright, "The Letter to the Romans," 655–58; Hays, *Echoes*, 75–83; D. Moo, *Romans*, 641. Wagner is helpful in this discussion as he adds that the Torah points to the total submission to God's righteousness that is now totally revealed in Christ. See Wagner, *Heralds*, 119.

92. Keck, "'Jesus' in Romans," 449.

Christological at the same time. Christ reveals and fulfills the character and the purposes of God.

Christ is the revelation of God's faithfulness/righteousness (3:21–25; 10:3–4; 15:8). Paul's further interpretation of the Old Testament in 15:8–13 confirms that he sees Christ as the one who perfectly fulfills the law's demands and thus makes salvation and glorification of God's name possible for all the nations.

In 15:8–9 Paul explicitly states that Christ confirms the promises made to the patriarchs. It means that this act confirms God's righteousness/faithfulness to Israel. Paul puts it this way: Christ appears to be the means of demonstrating God's covenant faithfulness to Israel so that the Gentiles may glorify God for his mercy (15:9). That is, "the purpose and result of this process has always been the praise of the God of Israel by the nations of the world (15:9–12)."[93] This is such an important declaration for Paul that to prove his point he refers to multiple scripture quotations.

In 15:9 he says, "Therefore I will confess you among the Gentiles, and sing praises to your name," alluding to Ps 18:49 (LXX 17:50), "For this I will extol you, O LORD, among the nations, and sing praises to your name." The psalm repeats with some minor textual differences 2 Sam 22:50 and so rehearses and celebrates God's deliverance of the king. The important part is that this psalm keeps testifying to God's steadfast love in the post-exilic era and his sovereignty over nations. It reinforces the eschatological dimension that God will bring deliverance for the house of David in the future, "Great triumphs he gives to his king, and shows steadfast love to his anointed, to David and his descendants forever" (Ps 18:50). God's deliverance has universal proportions as the king becomes "the head of the nations" (Ps 18:43) and praises God among the nations (Ps 18:49). Referring to the psalm Paul proclaims that the eschatological expectations have been realized. Christ as the Davidic descendant has redeemed the Jews according with the scriptures and the Gentiles have an opportunity not only to see it but actually because of him and through him are called into the obedience of faith and into the family of God (1:1–3; 8:15). The Gentiles can indeed glorify God for that. In the light of the psalm Christ has become "the head of the nations," the promised Messiah that has brought about the redemption so that now all the nations may glorify the God of Israel for his mercy upon all.

---

93. B. Longenecker, *The Triumph of Abraham's God*, 101.

Verse 15:10 "Rejoice, O gentiles, with his people" echoes Deut 32:43 (LXX). Deuteronomy 32 is the Song of Moses where he warns Israel against continued disobedience and apostasy, and the consequent judgment on Israel. However, the Song includes the message of hope as well. In spite of unfaithfulness Israel will be vindicated by God. All the enemies would be removed from the land and Israel's relationship with God would be restored. The doxological conclusion itself in verse 43 reads differently. The MT reads, "Praise his people, O nations," or possibly, "O, nations, make his people sing out of joy" (הַרְנִינוּ גוֹיִם עַמּוֹ).[94] Paul uses the LXX, "Rejoice, O nations, together with his people" (εὐφράνθητε, ἔθνη, μετὰ τοῦ λαοῦ αὐτοῦ).[95] Paul's choice of the LXX reflects a more positive attitude towards the Gentiles. Wagner points out that Paul's choice of the LXX here enables him to tie Deuteronomic language with his previous discussion on God's faithfulness to Israel and Gentile's inclusion (9–11) and to emphasize that God is praised by all nations for his actions on behalf of Israel and through Israel to the whole world.[96]

In 15:11 Paul's phrase "Praise the Lord, all you Gentiles, and let all the peoples praise him" recalls Ps 117:1 (116:1 LXX), "Praise the LORD, all you nations! Extol him, all you peoples!" The LXX evidence places all the nations, πάντα τὰ ἔθνη, after the Lord, τὸν κύριον, in the psalm.[97] In Paul, πάντα τὰ ἔθνη precedes τὸν κύριον, which, in the light of the Gentile catena in 15:8–12 could be Paul's emphasis on the Gentiles praising the Lord.

Paul's choice of this particular psalm is striking. The psalm itself invites not only Israel or Judah but a universal audience, πάντα τὰ ἔθνη, to praise the Lord. N. T. Wright concludes that the message of the universal praise implies that the God of Israel was the Creator of the whole world, and "that therefore the other nations, though presently stuck in idolatry, ought eventually to come to recognize and worship the same God that Israel worshiped."[98] The universality of the invitation in the psalm, though, is based not on the idea of God's creation of the whole world but on God's love and faithfulness and his desire to redeem his people. "Praise the LORD, all you nations; extol him, all you peoples. For great

---

94. See more in Wagner, *Heralds*, 216.
95. See more in Ciampa, "Deuteronomy in Galatians and Romans," 114.
96. Wagner, *Heralds*, 317.
97. Stanley, *Paul*, 181.
98. N. T. Wright, "The Letter to the Romans," 748.

is his steadfast love toward us, and the faithfulness of the LORD endures forever. Praise the LORD!" (Ps 117:1–2). The language recalls the exodus where God reveals to Moses his very essence of love, faithfulness, and of forgiving sins, which does not exclude the judgment of sin, "The LORD, the LORD, a God merciful and gracious, slow to anger, and abounding in steadfast love and faithfulness, keeping steadfast love for the thousandth generation, forgiving iniquity and transgression and sin" (Exod 34:6–7).

In this light God's universal purposes are unfolded in two stages. First, God keeps his faithfulness and steadfast love to Israel. Secondly, even though God has chosen Israel he reveals his love and faithfulness to them so that it is to be known to all the nations. The implication is that God's purposes embrace not only Israel but all the nations to whom Israel was supposed to be a light. Since Paul claims that God's righteousness/faithfulness is revealed and in Jesus the Jews and all the nations can restore their relationship with God, the universal praise of God becomes a reality. Referring to this psalm Paul once again unites all the Gentiles (πάντα τὰ ἔθνη) and all his peoples (πάντες οἱ λαοί), most likely referring to Israel, into a community that can worship God together.[99]

Now in 15:12 Paul comes to the focal point of his discussion to show that scripture prophesies the inclusion of the Gentiles in the worshiping community as a result of God's redeeming activity in Christ. Paul writes, "The root of Jesse shall come, the one who rises to rule the Gentiles; in him the Gentiles shall hope." This phrase alludes to Isa 11:10, "On that day the root of Jesse shall stand as a signal to the peoples; the nations shall inquire of him, and his dwelling shall be glorious." Within the broader context (Isa 10–12) Isaiah talks about the return of a remnant of both Israel and Judah and God's purpose to renew the whole created order. Isaiah announces the coming of God's agent, the descendant of Davidic line, the stump of Jesse who will gather the scattered people of Judah and Israel. God's name will be exalted among the nations. When Paul refers to the scripture he does not only emphasize that this agent will rule over nations but also that the Gentiles will have hope in him.

Since both Jews and Gentiles can worship God, Paul's reference to Isaiah is read as fulfilled prophecy. The promised Messiah from the root of Jesse or from the Davidic descendant (1:1–3) is none other than Jesus Christ. God's Son has come as fulfillment of Israel's hope and promises. Paul already quoted Isaiah to affirm God's promises to preserve the remnant of

---

99. Wagner, *Heralds*, 315.

his people (9:29). Here Paul stresses that Jesus has also come to rule over the Gentiles and to become their hope. The Davidic Jewish Messiah Jesus Christ is hope not only for the Jews but for the Gentiles as well. Isaiah's remnant includes then all Jews and Gentiles in Christ.

Paul reinterprets the OT passages to make his point clear. In Christ OT hopes and promises to Israel and to the whole word have been fulfilled. Both Jews and Gentiles can not only praise God or rejoice together, they also can put their hope in Christ. Paul concludes the section with the imperative that both groups may abound in hope (15:13). If there are any cultural and ethnical differences in Paul's communities (chs. 12–15) they are obliterated by the common eschatological hope. Paul assures that God keeps his promises (15:8). God has sent his Son, the Messiah, to redeem the world and he has raised him from the dead. Christ is the Lord. All the nations may glorify God for that.

Also God is still the God of hope (15:13). Paul places the present work of God in Christ and the hope of the community into an eschatological framework. Jesus would be seen and acknowledged as Lord of all and every knee will bow at his name (14:11; 15:12; cf. Phil 2:10–11) when God's full glory will be revealed (8:18–21). The community needs to live its present life in this faith that God has already acted in his Son (15:13) with the expectations of God's final fulfillment of his promises in the future when the hope will overflow. The community needs to live in the power of the Holy Spirit as co-heirs with Christ, conforming to him now (cf. 8:14–17, 29) with the prospect of the final redemption in the future (cf. 8:22–25).

For Paul Christ is the means of demonstrating God's covenantal faithfulness to Israel. God's faithfulness to Israel is not only for the sake of Israel but for the sake of the Gentiles so that the Gentiles may also glorify God for his mercy. For Paul the story of Israel and God's faithfulness to them are closely connected with the inclusion of the Gentiles. God's ancient project was brought into completion in the ministry of his Son. In Christ God as Redeemer is fully understood.

5. Conclusions

God's persistent redeeming activity in the story of Israel is central to Paul's narrative substructure. It forms the foundation of his whole picture of redemption that rests upon God's faithfulness: God the faithful Father is true to the promises he gave in the scriptures to redeem and restore his people. However, Paul explains this concept universally because of Christ. Jesus Christ, God's Son and Jewish Davidic Messiah is the key for interpreting the story of God's dealing with Israel and God's purposes for the world. In Christ God is the faithful Father who redeems Israel and all the Gentiles. In him God has begun the new era of redemption history of the world, a new stage of his redemption plan that concerns Jews, Gentiles, and the whole created order.

Paul also expands the idea of sonship. He argues that in Christ, God's own Son, God has formed a new family that consists of all in Christ led by the Spirit. But it is far bigger than most expected. This way not only the Gentiles but the Jews are to be adopted into God's family through Christ. Both Jews and Gentiles incorporate into God's family conforming to the character of his Son. How precisely Paul explains the act of Christ as part of God's righteousness and redemption is the question of the next chapter.

Chapter IV

Christ's Faithfulness as Fulfillment of the Father's Faithfulness

1. Introduction

IN ROMANS THE CONCEPT of God being the Father who redeems, as we have sketched it in the previous chapter, is based on the promises of the Jewish scripture. God's redemption is fulfilled in Christ, reinterpreted and therefore is expressed in a new light. In Christ, for Paul, there is redemption for everyone; all can be part of God's family. While OT and 2TP passages refer to God the Father of Israel and/or of the faithful ones within Israel, Paul uses the address of God the Father of Christ and through Christ of both Jews and Gentiles. Both Jews and Gentiles are enabled to call God "Father" through Christ, which makes them like a new Israel that includes both ethnic Israel who are in Christ and Gentiles in Christ. In this light God as Father is a renewed category in the sense that God is now the Father of all people who are in Christ; his renewed people includes both Jews and Gentiles. The potentiality of God's fatherhood for all, both Jews and Gentiles, is through Christ.

In regard to the new Israel C. Wright notices, "Paul does not hold any other way for Jews to be part of eschatological Israel other than the same way that Gentiles are now joining that community—only through faith in Jesus of Nazareth, the Messiah."[1] C. Wright considers Jews and Gentiles as equal members of God's new people formed through Christ. Throughout his narrative Paul places Jews and Gentiles on the same scale

---

1. C. Wright, *The Mission of God*, 528.

Christ's Faithfulness as Fulfillment of the Father's Faithfulness 83

when he says both of them are under sin (1:18—3:20; 3:23; 5:12–21). At the same time, God's righteousness is revealed for everyone (1:16; 3:21). The possibility to be a part of God's family is for Paul through Christ led by the Spirit of Christ (8:14–17).

This is a major move for Paul that the Jews have to become part of the renewed Israel on the same basis as the Gentiles. If both Jews and Gentiles are joining God through the same means, Christ Jesus, what about the significance of being a Jew or the history of Israel? This is a serious question because it raises another question about God's truthfulness in history. In the last chapter we saw how this question is answered in demonstration of how Paul redefines the family of God. Clearly, the foundation of Paul's answer is laid in Jesus Christ himself, in what he has accomplished, thus fulfilling what the scripture has testified and what God has promised. For Paul, the matter of joining God's family is not only of faith in Christ (3:22b; 4:23-25; 10:9), it is first of all the matter of Christ's own faithfulness, πίστις Χριστοῦ (3:22, 26).[2] God puts his Son forward as an atoning sacrifice for all, effective through Christ's faithfulness, which is probably the correct interpretation of the much-debated πίστις Χριστοῦ (3:21-25).

The questions for this chapter are: how does Paul convey the idea of Christ's faithfulness; what impact does πίστις Χριστοῦ have on Jews and Gentiles according to Paul, or in what way is God's redemption effective through Christ's faithfulness?

---

2. The phrase πίστις Χριστοῦ is difficult to translate at least for two reasons. First, the word πίστις has a broad range of meanings, including not only trust, faith, but also obedience, faithfulness, reliability, and fidelity. Secondly, Χριστοῦ is in the genitive case, which can be rendered as objective or as explicative subjective. The question is what does Paul mean by it? First, Paul connects faith and obedience in ways that make them virtually synonyms (1:5; 16:26). Moo is right that "obedience" and "faith" are mutually interpreting (D. Moo, *Romans*, 52–53). The same is applied to πίστις Χριστοῦ as an act of Christ's faithful obedience to God through which many become righteous (5:19). So, Christ's faith includes the understanding of faithful obedience of the Son to God the Father. Christ's faith is faith in God's faithfulness. Second, the genitive permits co-existing of more than one meaning. Objective and subjunctive ideas are not mutually exclusive in Hebrew and Greek. In this regard Garlington makes a valuable observation, "Paul's Semitic background could easily account for a flexibility in his Greek usage, permitting more than one meaning to reside in his genitival phrases, Garlington, *A "New Perspective,"* 4. Christ's faith is then "not a denial of faith in Christ as a Pauline concept (for the idea is expressed in many of the same contexts, only with the verb πιστεύω rather than the noun), but implies that the object of faith is a worthy object, for he himself is faithful" (Wallace, *Greek Grammar*, 116). The appeal to understand the nuances of faith must be made to context, authorial usage, and the narrative as a whole.

2. The Function of Obedience of Faith in Rom 1:5

God's righteousness is effective by his grace through the redemption of Christ because of his faithful obedience (3:21–26; 5:15–19). Paul develops his teaching in such a way that Christ's faithfulness in the story of redemption in 3:22, 26 does not come as a surprise (cf. 1:5; 1:17).

In 1:5 Paul describes the apostolic mission in terms of calling to the obedience of faith (ὑπακοὴν πίστεως), which forms an *inclusio* of the entire letter (1:5—16:26) and leaves no doubt as to the significance of this phrase for Romans.[3] However, what precisely this significance is, is debatable in modern scholarship. Wilckens believes that "Glaubensgehorsam" (obedience of faith) is a concept where faith determines obedience. It is characterized through πίστις Χριστοῦ (3:21, 26) and means "Glaubensvollzug" (performance of faith).[4] Wilckens' understanding of obedience that consists in faith reflects the view of the majority of commentators.[5]

But Jewett finds it problematic. He thinks that both terms cannot be interchangeable. Faith limits obedience. Paul speaks of a special obedience produced by the gospel. For Jewett ὑπακοὴν πίστεως means acceptance of the message of salvation that would have honored both Jews and Gentiles helping them walk by the Spirit, to relate to, and love each other.[6] Jewett's view is close to Minear's understanding of ὑπακοὴν πίστεως. Minear considers "the obedience of faith" in the light of Paul's discussion about the weak and the strong (chs. 14–15). He believes that Paul reminds both groups how "the gospel of God has destroyed their extreme positions by its inclusion of both Jews and Gentiles." Calling into obedience of faith is calling "to the same life of holiness, a life empowered by the same divine Spirit, and expressed by a welcome as inclusive as God's. Each group was deeply indebted to the other group."[7] Having said that, Minear also believes that "everything which proceeds from faith tends to produce a greater or stronger faith" (which is "Glaubensvollzug" for Wilckens) referring also to Rom 1:17.[8]

Miller, acknowledging the view of mutual acceptance and welcoming "one another in a manner reflecting Christ's own welcoming them,"

---

3. Crafton, "Paul's Rhetorical Vision," 329; .Miller, "Jewish Context," 104.
4. Wilckens, *Der Brief an die Römer*, 66–67.
5. See the list in Jewett, *Romans*, 110.
6. Ibid. This also reflects Miller's view in *The Obedience of Faith*, 59–60.
7. Minear, *The Obedience*, 38.
8. Ibid., 42.

expands the idea of obedience further. He writes that Paul fosters obedience among the Roman Christians that consists of offering themselves to God as an act of worship (12:1). This specifically takes a concrete form in the manner in which they relate to each other (12:3—15:6).[9] Miller relates the idea of the obedience of faith to the relationship of the Jews and the Gentiles in the postresurrection time (1:1–5) as one people of God or as the "eschatological people of God." He also recognizes that the manner of relating to one another is consonant with their identity in Christ.[10] His arguments are important and deserve further considerations in relation to the oneness of God's people and in relation to God's faithfulness/righteousness revealed in Christ.

Although the phrase itself might be unique to the whole pre-Christian Greek literature and Paul himself,[11] the idea behind it is certainly present in the OT. In the OT the notion of faith includes a response to the word of God in faithfulness: faith that consists in obedience. The ὑπακοὴν πίστεως sets a literary marker for Abraham's response to God's command and promise that Paul will develop later (ch.4). Abraham hears and obeys God believing that God will act in his life. This is reckoned to him as righteousness. Without going into detail about Abraham's faith at this point, it is fair to say that the obedience of faith is a key issue in his relationship with God and deeply rooted in the history of Israel.[12]

The concept of hearing obediently is closely related to keeping the covenant. When Israel has heard God's voice and accepted the responsibility to obey his commandments, its obedience resulted in God's blessings (Deut 4:1–14) but failure listen to his voice led to the curse (Deut 11:26–28). Israel as God's chosen son is entrusted with certain responsibilities as to the proper response and obedience as God's people. Obedience is an essential part of the relationship between God and Israel that is stated in Deuteronomy (ch.6). Paul uses the language of Deuteronomy throughout his letter (10:6–8; 11:8; and Deut 32 in 10:19; 12:19; 15:10) asserting the importance of its message for his own purposes.[13] The Deuteronomist speaks about true obedience to God as circumcision of their heart (Deut 10:6–16). This is echoed in Paul when he talks about

---

9. Miller, "Jewish Context," 105–8.

10. Ibid., 111.

11. Jewett, *Romans*, 110.

12. Even the faith of Abraham (Gen 15:6) relates to the future of people of Israel whose forefather he is rather than to his personal destiny.

13. Ciampa, "Deuteronomy in Galatians and Romans," 99–117.

a true Jew who is one inwardly, and real circumcision is a matter of the heart. Paul sees it in a new light though as a matter fulfilled by the Spirit through Christ, not by the written code (2:29; 7:6).

As has been shown above, the central message of Deuteronomy is the history of the Jewish disobedience and rebellion eliciting curse and punishment. Paul also detects this deep sinfulness within Israel and points to Israel's failure of obedience to God (2:17–29). The future in such terms is bleak, as Moses suggested in his last words to Israel (Deut 32). Paul's conclusion, based on his exegesis of the scripture (3:10–19, where he explicitly refers to Psalms and Isaiah), is similar, "No human being (πᾶσα σάρξ) will be justified in his [God's] sight" (3:20). Paul's language is universal, though. He attests Israel's and Gentiles' untruthfulness and affirms that the whole world is accountable to God (3:19). Paul extends the understanding of unrighteousness and disobedience by inclusion of both Jews and Gentiles into the same category of the unrighteous ones before God (3:9). It is as Paul places both Jews and Gentiles under the Deuteronomic curse (1:18–32; 2:9; 3:1–20). This allows Paul to increase the need of both Jews and Gentiles for a redeeming relationship with God.

This quick sketch already points to the obedience of faith as an expected response of the people of God to the covenant relationship with God the Father. The idea of the obedience of faith has a relational aspect. The word ὑπακοή corresponds to the verb ἀκούω (to hear), which is the regular LXX rendering of שׁמע (Shema) in Deut 6:4. N. T. Wright believes that Paul's further reference to the Shema, namely to "God is one" (3:29–30), indicates that Paul has a Deuteronomic train of thought. He concludes, "To bring the nations into 'obedience' would therefore mean to bring them into the family of this one God."[14] Wright's conclusion fits well in Paul's overall narrative. If obedience is related to the covenant relationship, and Paul speaks of calling even the Gentiles into obedience, then his goal is to include all the nations in the covenant relationship with this one God of Israel. For Paul Deuteronomic language takes on a special role for the universal purposes of God.[15] All the nations are called into the covenant relationship with God. They are called to belong to the family of God (since Paul prefers family language, 1:7; 8:14–17).

In Romans ὑπακοή and πίστις refers not only to the relationship to God that should characterize believers (1:5, 8; 4:5, 9, 11–13; 10:16; 16:19,

---

14. N. T. Wright, "The Letter to the Romans," 420.

15. For a recent discussion on the importance of Deuteronomy in the NT, see the collection of essays in Moyise and Menken, *Deuteronomy in the New Testament*.

26) but also to Christ's willing commitment to his destiny (3:22; 5:19). In the contexts of 1:1–5 Paul affirms who Christ is, namely Israel's promised Messiah, a real human being of the Davidic descendant.[16] He is God's Son from the beginning but he becomes his Son with power by the resurrection event after Jesus' total obedience to the will of the Father until death. Christ is described as the obedient Son. The designation of God's son that belonged to Israel and to the righteous ones within Israel is now reserved for Jesus; and through him both Jews and Gentiles are children in God's family. For Paul God's new family of both Jews and Gentiles in Christ is to conform to the likeness of his only Son (8:29). When Paul writes that the Gentiles are now to be called to the obedience of faith he unfolds the theme of Christ's act, namely his obedience as God's fulfillment of OT prophesies concerning all the nations. The call to the obedience of faith has several implications for Paul; all related to Christ. First, this call is into relationship to God through Christ. Second, the call to the obedience of faith is the call to relationship with Christ himself and one another through Christ. In other words, the call to the obedience of faith is consistent with their identity in Christ. This significant argument influences Paul's understanding here in 1:5 and especially later in 1:17.

In 1:5 Paul writes that it is through him and for his name's sake he receives grace and apostleship to call people to the obedience of faith. Christ is the key ingredient for this universal call to the relationship of obedience. The questions are how and why the Gentiles can enter into the obedience of faith through the Jewish Messiah? The explanation comes on at least two levels.

First, it comes when Paul elaborates on the newness of God's acting through his Son (3:21–25; 5:18–19). God's covenantal faithfulness endures and overcomes all human unfaithfulness in Christ through his obedience. Paul explains this in ch. 5.[17] Jesus Christ, the obedient Son, is much more than the disobedient Adam (5:12–21). He is the new Adam who does not commit sin but obeys the will of the Father. Through his obedience God has reconciled humanity to himself (5:11). And through his obedience the many will be made righteous (5:19). The implication of Christ's obedience is the new realm for Christians, the realm of participation in Christ's obedience that can be expressed as entering the sphere or realm of his rule; when the old self dies (6:6) and when they are controlled

---

16. See discussion on the Father of Christ earlier.
17. See chapter 6 below.

by the Spirit of Christ, belong to him, and in him to God in covenantal relationship as God's children (8:14–17).

Second, Christ is the true representative of Israel, the Jewish Messiah, and the obedient Son (1:1–5). As such, he fulfills God's purposes to Israel and through Israel to other nations. The function of being a light to other nations, the one that Israel failed to accomplish in order that the Gentiles may rejoice with Israel (cf. 15:8–13), is fulfilled by Christ, by his obedience. Therefore, in Christ it is possible to call all people to the relationship with God. In Christ, all Jews and Gentiles belong to God, and they are in family relationship with one another (8:14–17; 8:29–30).

Paul's statement to call all the people into the obedience of faith is more than his apostolic mission purpose to all the nations. Paul's gospel is an eschatological fulfillment of God's purposes to Israel and to the whole world (1:1–3; 3:21–22). Paul informs his readers that his gospel is promised through the prophets in the scripture (1:2). In other words, the very writings of the OT presuppose the coming of the global gospel and the inclusion of the Gentiles into obedient relationship with God. Paul refers to the scripture to reveal and explain God's purposes from the very beginning. If Paul claims that the nations are called into the obedience of faith, then he means that this call has been expected from the scripture and now has taken place. The notion of ὑπακοὴν πίστεως has, then, a fulfilled dimension and is directly related to what God has done in Christ. It is an eschatological fulfillment in Christ for the Jews and then the Gentiles as well.

Paul closes his letter (16:26) explaining and affirming this eschatological fulfillment even further. His gospel proclamation of Christ is "the unveiling of God's long-kept secret," the revelation of mystery, or of "the long concealed plan of God" (16:25–26).[18] In other words, in Christ God's long-concealed plan has been made known; the mystery of the divine purpose for the salvation of the humankind has been revealed (cf. Eph 3:3–6). Paul claims once more that Christ came according to the scriptures with the purpose of bringing about the obedience by faith (16:26). Dunn notes in this regard, "That purpose was in full continuity with God's earlier revelation through prophet and scripture. But what had now been made clear, as God had always intended it should, was that God's saving purpose reached out to all nations and that it was entered

---

18. N. T. Wright, "The Letter to the Romans," 768.

into through faith—a faith that was not different from nor opposed to the obedience God has always looked for in his people."[19]

The obedience of faith is people's answer to God's faithfulness that now has been fulfilled in Christ through his faithful obedience. It is their participation in Christ's faithful obedience. Wright notes that generations of theologians worried whether the emphasis on obedience (1:5; 16:26) does not suggest the priority of good works rather than pure faith,[20] translating ὑπακοὴν πίστεως as "commitment of faith" for that purpose.[21] However, their anxiety misses the point. N. T. Wright's response is helpful, "When Paul thinks of Jesus as Lord, he thinks of himself as a slave and of the world as being called to obedience to Jesus' lordship." Paul does not "offer people a new religious option" but "summon[s] them to allegiance to Jesus, which will mean abandoning other loyalties" and responding in obedience.[22]

"Calling into obedience of faith" has a deeper meaning than appears at first. The call is into the covenantal relationship with God available through Christ. The phrase ὑπακοὴν πίστεως describes a particular response to the gospel of God concerning his Son. If now through Christ the Gentiles can enter into the covenant relationship with God, then God has acted in a very powerful way through his Son. Paul alerts the reader from the very beginning that Christ has done something that was not possible before. In him OT promises come true and God's righteousness is revealed (1:17; 3:21; cf. 16:26). When Paul calls nations into the obedience of faith he certainly has in mind that God as Redeemer acts through his Son who demonstrates the total obedience to the will of the Father dying on the cross and dealing with sin (8:3). The implication is that God's redemption in Christ through Christ's faithfulness makes possible our participation in the "obedience of faith."

There are several important concluding points.

Generally, Paul unites faith and obedience making them a convergent concept and conditioning the way of understanding faith and obedience in a correlated order as a frame for the entire letter (1:5, 16:26).

More importantly, the call to ὑπακοὴν πίστεως is related to Christ's faithful obedience to the Father. It is connected to and clearly derives

---

19. Dunn, *Romans 9–16*, 916.
20. N. T. Wright, "The Letter to the Romans," 420.
21. Fitzmyer, *Romans*, 237, 755.
22. N. T. Wright, "The Letter to the Romans," 420.

from the obedient powerful risen Son of God through whom this call came about. This is the call into active participation in Christ's faithful obedience that Paul is still to unfold throughout his letter.

Furthermore, this is the call of both Jews and Gentiles to the covenant relationship with God and each other through Christ. This call reflects the eschatological fulfillment of God's purposes and promises through Christ for all the nations. With this in mind we shall turn to Rom 1:17 where Paul deals with faithfulness for the first time.

3. God's Righteousness and Christ's Faithfulness in Rom 1:17

The theme of God's righteousness/faithfulness, his power for redemption, is so important to Paul that he announces in 1:17 God's righteousness is revealed for the Jews as for the Gentiles. No less important is how it is revealed: from faith to faith, ἐκ πίστεως εἰς πίστιν (1:16-17). Paul believes that it has been revealed just as it is written in the scripture, quoting Hab 2:4.

There are many questions raised in this statement. Whose faith and what faith? How does Paul interpret Habakkuk? The expression "from faith to faith" has been variously interpreted throughout the history of the church and provokes reflections by different commentators:[23] (1) from the faith of OT saints to the faith of NT saints (Origen); (2) from an immature faith to a more mature faith (Calvin); (3) from a law-oriented faith to a gospel-oriented faith (Zahn, Schlatter); (4) from the faith of the preacher to the faith of the hearers (Augustine); (5) from present faith to a future, deeper faith (Cassirer, Phillips); (6) from God's faithfulness to man's faith (Barth), etc. Although all these observations are theologically significant, they fail to deal adequately with the connection of this statement to the following quotation from Habakkuk. Paul clearly indicates that "just as it is written" with the reference to Hab 2:4 is the matrix from which he derives his own assertion,[24] ἐκ πίστεως εἰς πίστιν. Watson asserts that all Paul's formulations about "the faith of Christ" derive from

---

23. Reasoner, *Romans in Full Circle*, 1-9; Cranfield, *Romans*, 99; Fitzmyer, *Romans*, 263. More recently in Quarles, "From Faith to Faith," 1-21; Taylor, "From Faith to Faith," 337-48.

24. Watson, *Paul*, 43.

Hab 2:4.²⁵ Campbell believes that the entire data of using πίστις "bears a significant and presumably generative relation" to Hab 2:4.²⁶

To understand the meaning of "from faith to faith" one should start then with the Habakkuk quotation.²⁷ How does the Habakkuk quotation contribute to Paul's theme of faithfulness? Is Paul in dialogue with the interpretative tradition of Habakkuk as well? A consideration of Hab 2:4 in its Jewish context may show how Paul interprets the quotation in the light of God's revelation in Christ.

3.1 Hab 2:4 in Context

Any interpretation of Hab 2:4 "will be clouded by a certain amount of hypothetical guesswork."²⁸ The text describes God's reply to the prophet's second complaint about the continuing oppression of Judah by the Chaldeans. The prophet is struggling to comprehend the ways of God. Why does a righteous God allow sin to go unpunished (1:13)? The answer comes from God affirming that the wicked one will be punished, and the righteous one shall live by faith (Hab 2:4). It is not clear who is the righteous one in the text. If the wicked one refers to Judah's oppressor, whether an Israelite or a foreigner, then the righteous one most likely refers to Judah.²⁹ It is also possible that the words are applied to Habakkuk since God responds to him. Habakkuk is to live by his faithfulness while waiting for God to act.³⁰ More generally, in the world of oppression the righteous ones are those who are committed to God, who live or survive by faith³¹ in contrast to those who trust in themselves and are not right in relation to God (Hab 2:4a).

The righteous one shall live by faith. The Hebrew word אֱמוּנָה (faith) expresses the key idea of living and can be described as both faith and faithfulness, as "adherence without faltering and obedience with complete

---

25. Ibid.
26. Campbell, "The Faithfulness," 60.
27. Watson, "By Faith (of Christ)," 147.
28. Roberts, *Nahum, Habakkuk*, 111; Hays, *Echoes*, 256; Cranfield, *Romans*, 99; Fitzmyer, *Romans*, 137-38, 253-68; and *To Advance the Gospel*, 236-46; Grieb, *The Story of Romans*, 37.
29. R. Smith, *Micah-Malachi*, 106.
30. Ibid., 107.
31. Moberly, "אמן," 432.

trust."³² It is not clear though whether it refers to the faith/faithfulness of the righteous one (as in the Hebrew manuscript, the righteous one shall live by his faith, וְצַדִּיק בֶּאֱמוּנָתוֹ יִחְיֶה) or God's own faithfulness to Israel that is to be ultimately confirmed (as in the LXX, the righteous one shall live by my faith, ὁ δὲ δίκαιος ἐκ πίστεώς μου ζήσεται). In Roberts' translation, the righteous one shall live by its [the vision's] reliability.³³ He suggests that the antecedent of the third masculine singular suffix in the MT is "vision" from v. 3 (חָזוֹן). Faith, then, would refer to the reliability/fidelity of God's vision and ultimately of God who gives the vision, not to the reliability or the fidelity of the righteous person.³⁴ But the whole context of Habakkuk emphasizes faith as both faithfulness, fidelity and loyalty of the righteous ones while the wicked still triumph and as trust in God's intervention in their lives. There are also manuscripts, as we shall see below, where faith is clearly God's or of the righteous one. If so, then Roberts' interpretation, as much as it is plausible, is too narrow.

Habakkuk's vision is very similar to Isaiah's song about Judah in 26:1–6. For Isaiah God himself would redeem his people from Babylon as he rescued them from Egypt. Even the Gentiles are depicted as either joining in Israel's worship of God and sharing in Israel's blessings (Isa 24:14–16; 25:6–10) or opposing the Lord and suffering his wrath (Isa 24:1–13, 17–22; 25:10–12; 26:11, 21; 41:14). Isaiah's words are similar to Habakkuk's, "We have a strong city; he sets up victory like walls and bulwarks. Open the gates, so that the righteous nation that keeps faith may enter in" (Isa 26:1–2). Isaiah uses a collective noun representing the whole people or the faithful remnant that keeps faith (with no specification of whose faith, which is closer to Paul's usage). In the overall context, though, it is God himself who makes salvation. The righteous nation that keeps faith may enter "God's city." The righteous nation will find its safe place with God because of God's faithfulness and will live if they keep their faithfulness/fidelity as well.

Now, Habakkuk also calls to trust God's assurance and to remain faithful because the hope in God will not disappoint (Hab 2:3). It will surely come and will not delay (Hab 2:3). Prior rightly argues that God's reputation is wrapped up in his promise. He cannot lie (Num 23:19),

---

32. Plaut et al., *The Torah*, 149.
33. Roberts, *Nahum, Habakkuk*, 107.
34. Ibid., 111.

therefore the vision cannot lie.[35] It is difficult, then, to draw a sharp distinction between the vision and the author of the vision. Their reliability is interdependent.[36]

The final triumph of the righteous will take place when "the earth shall be filled with the knowledge of the glory of the Lord, as the waters cover the sea" (Hab 2:14). Habakkuk envisions that God will eventually punish the idolatrous nation (Hab 2:5-20) and bring salvation to the house of Judah (Hab 3:2-19). The righteous one needs to hold on to God, trusting him to fulfill his promise (Hab 2:3). Andersen comments that "the guarantee of life for the righteous is grounded in the reliability of God."[37] God's faithfulness, his reliability, and his faith-keeping are implied in the whole narrative.

This might explain why the Göttingen LXX of Hab 2:4, MSS ℵ, B, Q, V, W* switches into a theocentric perspective: ὁ δὲ δίκαιος ἐκ πίστεώς μου ζήσεται, "but the righteous one on the basis of my faith shall live." It refers to God's own faithfulness/fidelity meaning that the deliverance of Judah lies in the faithfulness of God himself, which reflects the overall trend in Habakkuk.[38]

8HevXII (a first-century Greek scroll of the minor prophets from the eighth cave of Wadi Habra (Naval Hever)), col. 12, reads faith together with the pronoun in the third person masculine singular as in the MT. However, the pronoun cannot refer to the vision anymore because "vision" is feminine in Greek. Moreover, the faith here is placed right after δίκαιος, thus relating closely to the righteous one: literally, the righteous one in his faith shall live ([δί]καιος ἐν πίστει αὐτοῦ ζήσετ[αι]). However, the majority of scholars argue against this translation.[39] The second-century Aquila also reads like 8HevXII: δίκαιος ἐν πίστει αὐτοῦ ζήσεται. But Symmachus had a significant edition of ἑαυτοῦ (his own): δίκαιος τῇ ἑαυτοῦ πίστει ζήσεται.[40] This interpretation emphasizes

---

35. Prior, *The Message of Joel*, 236.

36. Andersen, *Habakkuk*, 214.

37. Ibid., 211.

38. Fitzmyer, *To Advance the Gospel*, 240; Andersen, *Habakkuk*, 211.

39. First, the context suggests relating "faith" to the verb, as argued above. Second, ζήσεται by itself is a weak anticlimax. Third, the connection between δίκαιος and πίστις could be emphasized by a different word order. See D. Moo, *Romans*, 78; Fitzmyer, *Romans*, 264-65.

40. See further analysis Koch, "Der Text von Hab 2:4b," 68-85.

further the necessity of the righteous one to have faith or to be faithful to God: the righteous one shall live by his own faith.

The uncial A inserts "my" (μου) after "the righteous one" linking faith with the gift of righteousness: ὁ δὲ δίκαιος μου ἐκ πίστεως ζήσεται.[41] This is translated as "but my righteous one on the basis of faith shall live."[42]

If the Greek πίστις follows the Hebrew understanding of faith then it must stress both the idea of faithfulness, loyalty, and trust of the righteous one as well as the active idea of God's faithfulness and truthfulness. The context of Habakkuk presupposes this broader notion. The righteous one is to live faithfully in the light of the divine promise that is not yet present. But it is the divine faithfulness that seeks to evoke a human counterpart.[43]

The text on Hab 2:4 is commented on by the author of the *pesher* on Habakkuk from Qumran Cave 1. 1QpHab VII, 17 reads: בֶּאֱמוּנָתוֹ יִחְיֶה וְצַדִּיק, "but the righteous through their steadfast faith will live."[44] The interpretation of it in 1QpHab VIII, 1–3 concerns the observers of the law in the community, whom God shall deliver from the house of judgment because of their struggle and their fidelity to the Teacher of Righteousness. Behind the interpretation lies the conviction that the prophets had spoken more than they knew. In 1QpHab VII, 1 the interpreter declares, "And God told Habakkuk to write the things that would come upon the last generation; but he did not show him the final consummation."

Here, "the righteous" most likely refers to the righteous remnant within the nation. The condition for God's salvation is the continuing observance of the Torah and faith in the Teacher of Righteousness who is the "inspirited interpreter of the prophets."[45] In this context the idea of God's faithfulness and intervention overlaps with the idea of the fidelity and obedience. However, the obedience here is to the law of the righteous ones within Israel. The obedience is their fidelity to the Jewish leader whom God set within the community "to interpret all the words of his servants prophets, through whom God declared everything that was to happen to his people Israel" (1QHab II, 8–10).[46]

41. D. Moo, *Romans*, 77–78.
42. Fitzmyer, *To Advance the Gospel*, 240.
43. Watson, *Paul*, 156.
44. Brownlee, *The Midrash Pesher of Habakkuk*, 125.
45. Watson, *Paul*, 119; Lim, "The Qumran Scrolls, 60.
46. Later Judaism focuses on the strict observance of the commandments referring to Habakkuk as the key principle of them in the whole scripture, *Babylonian Talmud*,

The general conclusion that derives from Habakkuk and its interpretation is that faith implies the faithfulness of God in history as a source for redemption. This is the primary meaning. Faithfulness also expresses the being and life of the righteous one (whether a righteous person or righteous people/community) in a vital divine relationship and obedience (to God first, and in later manuscripts also to his commandments and to the interpreter of the law); and it includes their trust and reliance in God's future act of deliverance, their faith in his faithfulness. In the eschatological sense, Habakkuk's vision is "still panting for fulfilment."[47]

3.2 Hab 2:4 in Paul

Now, referring to Habakkuk, Paul omits any personal pronoun, which detaches him from both the LXX and Hebrew text of Hab 2:4b: the righteous one shall live by faith, ὁ δὲ δίκαιος ἐκ πίστεως ζήσεται.[48] The third person pronominal suffix, however, refers to the "righteous one" making Paul's text not much different from the MT. It is significant though that Paul usually follows the LXX in his quotations, and the omission of the pronoun "may be a deliberate omission to facilitate his application of the verse."[49] For Paul, the OT is a witness for God's gospel that has now been fulfilled in Christ. The implication should be made that when Paul facilitates the application of the verse from the scripture he does so for no other reason than to reinterpret it in the light of Christ as the fulfillment of the prophetic oracles. In other words, if Paul omits any pronoun he really wants his readers to see behind the surface of this omission.

In the light of the announcement of God's righteousness as a present reality and not merely a future hope, Paul refers to Habakkuk as

---

24:173.

47. Prior, *The Message of Joel*, 237.

48. Manuscript C of Rom 1:17 inserts μου after ὁ δὲ δίκαιος leaving the connection between God and the righteous one. To compare: Gal 3:11 quoting Habakkuk omits δε but for the rest is similar to Rom 1:17. Heb 10:38 quoting Habakkuk reads as in MSS A and C of the LXX: ὁ δὲ δίκαιός μου ἐκ πίστεως ζήσεται, "but my righteous one on the basis of faith shall live," where it most likely refers to Jesus Christ himself. See Fitzmyer, *To Advance the Gospel*, 236–46.

49. Fitzmyer, *Romans*, 77. Also, Stanley, *Paul*, 253–64, who concludes that Paul normally quotes loosely from memory, though without straying from the basic sense of the (Hebrew) biblical text; that Paul sometimes "corrected" the wording of his Greek *Vorlage* to accord with his own reading of the Hebrew original; that for his purposes he quotes from Hebrew, Greek and Aramaic texts.

a fulfillment of ancient hope. Paul writes in the time of fulfillment of God's righteousness/faithfulness. Although the full glory is not revealed yet (8:18–21), God's righteousness is revealed already. His righteousness breaks forth bringing salvation to Israel and to all nations (1:5; 1:16–17; 3:21–25). Paul cannot simply repeat the words of Habakkuk implying that God's redemption is still to come. God's redemption has already taken place in Christ for him. The result of God's righteousness through Christ is the gift of righteousness, justification that brings life for all people (5:17–18). Moreover, for Paul the words of Habakkuk are pregnant with all that he means by God's redemption in Christ and by God's promises to all "not just Judah" that are now fulfilled in Christ. Jesus Christ is the righteous One because he remains obedient until the end and is raised by God into life. So, also those who are in Christ are set free for obedience that leads to righteousness and resurrection (6:4, 15–18). In other words, the righteous one shall live not by faith in God who has promised to act, but by faith in God who has already acted as he promised in Christ. For Paul faith and life are a share of the risen life of Christ (6:4, 8). Faith for Paul here is at least faith in the faithfulness of God and of Christ who reveals and fulfills God's faithfulness. Thus, if he really omits the pronoun quoting Hab 2:4, he wants the readers to see this bigger picture of faith that fits his argument in the letter.

There is, however, a different approach to the notion of faith in Rom 1:17. Dunn takes the phrase as an equivalent to "those who believe" (1:16) and defines it by an identical reference to Abraham's believing.[50] The phrase ἐκ πίστεως εἰς πίστιν in 1:17 means "from God's faithfulness (to his covenant promises) to man's response of faith."[51] The meaning of Habakkuk is then, "he who is righteous shall live by faith," in the sense that the person can be righteous before God by his or her faith only and not by the means of the law. Or, in Dunn's words, he who "has been brought into relationship with God . . . by the outreach of God's faithfulness to his own faith, shall experience the fullness of life which God intended for humankind as he lives in the dependence of faith."[52] Fitzmyer believes that the reading of MSS A and C (ὁ δὲ δίκαιός μου ἐκ πίστεως ζήσεται) would be even more congenial to Paul for such understanding.[53]

50. Dunn, "ΕΚ ΠΙΣΤΕΩΣ," 360–61.
51. Dunn, *Romans 1–8*, 48.
52. Ibid., 49.
53. It is not necessary, though. It is interesting that in Hebrew 10:38 the reading of MSS A and C suggests the reference to Christ himself (Fitzmyer, *To Advance the*

This might explain why A and C arise. In this light the previous reading "from faith to faith" accordingly suggests God's act of faithfulness and the faith or trust of individual person or all who believe.

This is a fairly standard reading of Rom 1:16–17 when read through Luther and most Protestants' eyeglasses: Paul's letter is all about God's righteousness and about an individual being justified by trusting not in works of the law but in Christ.[54] Although this is a valid theological statement, it is not primary in Paul's context here.

First, Paul is operating with the corporative terms (Jews, Gentiles, children, heirs) in his letter rather than individual. He is addressing the saints (1:6), the ones, whose faith is being reported all over the world (1:8). It would be right to say that Paul's concern in Romans is not only how a person is justified in the sight of God, but how both Jews and Gentiles, as a new people of God, equally live in obedience of faith as members of covenantal relationship with God. Although the power of God's salvation is παντὶ τῷ πιστεύοντι (for everyone who believes) singular, the corporate aspect is implicit: to the Jew first and then also to the Greek is collective. So, when Paul speaks about righteousness revealed from faith to faith, the corporate aspect of justification of the people of God (Jews and Gentiles) is implied.

Second, Paul's overall idea in Romans is that God acts faithfully despite any human unfaithfulness (3:3–4) and sin (3:22–23). God acts through Christ (5:11). As much as faith in Christ is important and necessary (3:22b), it is not primary for God's fulfillment of his purposes. It is through Christ's obedience many will be made righteous (5:19). To insist on God's faithfulness outreaching to our faith[55] is to miss Paul's Christological focus in his gospel of God.

Furthermore, the question of faith and works of the law is a complicated one in Paul. Paul does not say that the works are useless or that the law is bad. In fact, the law is righteous and good (7:12, 14). And he still affirms that God will give to each person according to what he has done.[56] There will be trouble and distress for both Jews and Gentiles who

---

Gospel, 242).

54. Wilckens, *Der Brief an die Römer*, 1:76; Dunn, *Romans 1–8*, 76; Reasoner, *Romans in Full Circle*, 3–7.

55. Dunn's discussion in *Romans 1–8*, 49.

56. See recent discussion on that in Kyoung-Shik Kim, *God Will Judge Each One According to Works*.

do evil; and there will be glory, honor and peace for everyone who does good (2:6, 9–10). Everyone has to cling to what is good (12:9).

Paul's emphasis on faith in Romans is on faithfulness and it does not contradict good works and the law. In fact, it flows out of the Jewish concept of faith as trust in God, on the one hand, and faithfulness, honesty, fidelity, and integrity in human relationship, on the other. All the nuances complement and supplement each other. Faith upholds the law (3:31). The law points to Christ. Therefore, God sent his Son to do what the law could not do (8:3). Faith and obedience to the will of God are closely related for Paul, but they are related to what Christ has accomplished as a part of God's righteousness (cf. 1:5; 16:26). Paul expects the Spirit of God/Christ to produce all manner of good works in the life of believers (2:6–11; 6:12–13; ch. 8; cf. Gal. 5:13–25). It is not a matter of following the observance of the Mosaic law anymore (3:21), as 1QpHab VII, 17 interprets it. Since for Paul, Christ is the fulfillment of the law (10:4) it is the matter of following Christ. There is a better way to describe it. For Paul, faith as trust, loyalty and faithfulness is in close relationship with what Christ has done. Our faith/faithfulness depends upon Christ's faithfulness to God and is our participation in Christ's faithfulness. In this light Hays' argument, that idiosyncratic interpretation of the text (as "the one who is righteous-through-faith-not-through-works shall live") would be unclear to an unfamiliar congregation in Rome with no further explanation,[57] sounds more convincing. This argument might not only be unfamiliar to the audience but also misleading at this point.[58]

Finally, together with Habakkuk Paul includes in his understanding of faith God's faithfulness to his people and the reliability of his promises. The idea of his people though is not limited by Judah and not even by the whole of Israel. Paul applies Habakkuk's vision to the Jews first but then also to the Gentiles. These promises are now fulfilled for Paul in Christ. When Paul refers to faith (πίστις) it is colored by God's faithfulness already accomplished in Christ for all, the new family of God in Christ.

---

57. Hays, "The Righteous One," 209. Reprinted in Hays, *The Conversion*, 140.

58. Of course, the theme of "faith vs. works" runs throughout the epistle culminating in ch. 4 where Abraham's pure faith matters for God. However, even there Paul's point is that our faith should be directed toward the same God of Abraham who now raised Jesus from the dead (4:24). For Paul, justification is indeed possible by faith but not by human faith alone. It is possible through the accomplishment of God's righteousness in Christ that was, according to Paul, promised in the scripture from the very beginning for both Jews and Gentiles. Paul considers Abraham's faith in a larger context of God's impartiality and accessibility for all the nations. See chapter 5.

Although the verse does not mention Christ here, Christ's faithfulness as God's revelation of his covenantal saving righteousness is implied. Paul unfolds the idea of God's saving righteousness/faithfulness revealed in Christ for all who believe, those who embrace and live out the consequences of what has been achieved by Christ (from faith to faith).

The dilemma with faith still remains. Paul is still to unfold the faith concept further (3:21—4:25; 9:31-33). The overall context is clear, though: Paul develops the theme of God's righteousness, his covenant faithfulness that is revealed and manifested through Christ's act, his obedience to the will of the Father. Hays rightly emphasizes that it would be peculiar to imagine that "the human's (Christian) disposition of faith towards God should be itself the source out of which God's eschatological righteousness is now revealed in a new way."[59] Even D. Moo, who prefers the objective interpretation of faith, realizes that "it is hard to see how God's faithfulness would be contingent on our faith."[60] It better refers to Christ's faithfulness. As L. Martyn notes, "Paul writes in the time after the apocalypse of the faith of Christ, the time therefore of rectification by that faith."[61] In this light Hays' proposition of a messianic interpretation of Rom 1:17 that the righteous one, ὁ δὲ δίκαιος, is a direct reference to Jesus makes sense.[62] We may pursue this point a little further.

3.3 Rom 1:17 in the Light of Christ's Faithfulness

Paul's discussion in 1:17 has clear connection with 1:2-4. Campbell argues that "a messianic reading of Habakkuk 2:4 directly fulfills the expectations that Paul set in motion in Romans 1:2-4."[63] In Rom 1:2-4 Paul writes that God's gospel is promised beforehand through the prophets in the scripture. It concerns his Son who is the promised Messiah of Davidic descendant and in whom all the nations are called into the obedience of faith. Now in 1:17 it is not an accident that Paul quotes from one of the prophets affirming and reinforcing the prophetic summary concerning God's Son, "The righteous one shall live by faith."[64]

59. Ibid., 208.
60. D. Moo, *Romans*, 46.
61. Martyn, "Apocalyptic Antinomies in Galatians," 418.
62. Hays, "The Righteous One," 209; and *The Faith*, 135-36.
63. Campbell, *The Deliverance*, 615.
64. In some Jewish texts "the Righteous One" is used to designate the deliverer of

Second, the verb ζήσεται (shall live) could refer to the one who lives in trust to God, as has been traditionally understood, but also it could point to Christ in Paul. The righteousness/faithfulness of God is revealed by God sending his Son to be the obedient Son (in contrast to Adam/Israel as in 5:18–19). He is vindicated by being raised from the dead because of his obedience. He dies but he is raised again to life. Christ is also the one who embodies all of God's big purposes in himself. He becomes an atoning sacrifice (3:25). He then becomes the corporate figure—the "in-Christ" language by which Paul refers to all who live in him, and whose righteousness is in him and in response to him. The quotation "ὁ δὲ δίκαιος ἐκ πίστεως ζήσεται" undoubtedly illustrates this whole picture[65] of life through faithfulness or participation in faithfulness with Christ. In other words, it includes the implication that the righteous one, namely Christ, lives because he is faithful to God. His faithfulness resulted in the righteousness of life (as in Hab 2:4) for all (5:18). Many shall be constituted righteous through Jesus' obedience and will live in him.

"From faith to faith" describes the fulfillment of faith: God's righteousness is revealed through Christ's faithful obedience (ἐκ πίστεως) to our faithful (εἰς πίστιν) participation in his faithful obedience that Paul referred to when he said "the righteousness of God is revealed from faith [Christ's] to faith [of Christ in us]" (1:17). This statement is very close to Paul's further development of the theme of God's righteousness revealed through faith where he identifies this faith in relation to Christ in 3:21–26.[66] Although Paul does not speak explicitly of Christ when he refers to God's righteousness revealed from faith to faith, his gospel of God concerning Christ and "faith" for Paul is entirely bound with God's

---

the End Time (*1 En.* 38:2; 53:6). It is uncertain though, whether the writing is pre-Christian because this part of *Enoch* was not found in Qumran. On the other hand, messianic reading would fit the story of the suffering "righteous one" in Wis 2:12–20. Although the righteous one in Wis is not a messianic figure, he is a suffering hero who received an eschatological vindication. See Suggs, "Wisdom 2:10–15," 26–53; and Campbell, *The Deliverance*, 614–15. Luke's account in Acts shows the references of the Christian Jews to Jesus as "the righteous one" (Acts 3:14; 7:52; 22:14; Luk 23:47). It appears in 1 John 2:1; 1 Pet 3:18. Heb 10:38, when quoting Hab 2:3–4, contextually suggests more the reference to Jesus himself and then the righteous one in Christ. See Fitzmyer, *To Advance the Gospel*, 243; and Hays, *The Faith*, 135–36.

65. Campbell, following Hays, rightly argues that Paul refers here to the story of Christ's passion metonymically so that one element may evoke the entire narrative. Campbell, "The Faithfulness," 62.

66. Also noticed and compared by Watson, *Paul*, 71–77.

saving action in Christ (1:1–5; 3:21–26; 5:12–21). The Christological explanation of Rom 1:17 derives from Paul's whole narrative.[67]

Furthermore, Habakkuk's interpretation by Paul can also be placed within his interpretation of Isaiah's prophecies of restoration and of the "Messiah," a person anointed or given power by God.

In the OT Isaiah speaks of the Messiah's kingdom, where justice and righteousness will reign. In Deutero-Isaiah this Messianic King is God's instrument to deliver Israel from Babylon (Isa 41:2), a light to the nations (Isa 42:6), and the righteous servant who will justify many (Isa 53:11). Isaiah reads, "Out of his anguish he shall see light; he shall find satisfaction through his knowledge. The righteous one, my servant, shall make many righteous, and he shall bear their iniquities." (Isa 53:11). Although, Habakkuk does not refer to the messianic figure, he gives assurance about God's revelation at the appointed time, about the end of wickedness (Hab 2:1–3). God's answer through Habakkuk for his people is to rely and hope in God's faithfulness that will be revealed.

The OT material is frequently conflated in Romans as, for example, in co-occurrences of Isaiah and Deuteronomy (in 10:19–21: Isa 65:1–2; Deut 32:21; in 11:8: Isa 29:10; Deut 29:3).[68] Paul echoes Isaiah throughout the letter (3:21–25; 4:24–25; 5:15–19; 10:16; 15:21) leaving his readers to "complete the trope" of these echoes in the light of Christ.[69] Although Paul cites directly from Habakkuk here, his awareness and sometimes use of the prophetic background helps him to obtain "some of the interpretive leverage he needs to recontextualize and reinterpret the prophet's oracles as a witness to his gospel and mission."[70]

Within Paul's interpretation of Rom 1:1–3 Isaiah's Messiah-language is certainly standing in the background. If we keep the Isaiah motif in the background while reading Paul's discussion on the righteousness of God revealed through Christ, the Habakkuk quotation becomes implicitly messianic. If "the righteous one" for Paul is now Christ who is faithful, who is raised from the dead and now lives because of his obedience, then the righteous people (Jews and Gentiles) who are in Christ may live with him. Christ had brought the gift of life to all people (5:18). In Christ they

---

67. Campbell also notices that Paul frequently quotes scripture in christocentric terms that adds up to a case for the Christological construal of Habakkuk in Romans (Campbell, *The Deliverance*, 615).

68. See Wagner, "Moses and Isaiah in Concert."

69. Hays, *Echoes*, 63.

70. Wagner, "Isaiah in Romans and Galatians," 118.

participate in his faithfulness and live in him by the power of the Spirit (cf. 2:29; ch. 8).

If Paul reinterprets Habakkuk as a realized prophecy[71] he is certainly not the only one. Hab 2:4 was reinterpreted in the first-century Judaism in 1QpHab VII, 17 (as has been shown in the first section) and Paul might presuppose it. The Qumran interpretation is surprisingly close to, but certainly different from Paul's concept of deliverance from judgment through faith. Paul reinterprets Habakkuk as the interpreter of Qumran does, as a prophecy that has more sense for the following generations (cf. 4:22–23; 15:4; 1 Cor 10:11). While the fulfillment of this prophesy has not yet taken place for the Qumran community, for Paul it has been fulfilled. For Paul, as for the Qumran community and Isaiah, the identity of "the righteous one" is bound up with the remnant.

For Paul, however, first, the remnant is both Jew and Gentile believers in Christ, the heir of Abraham (ch. 4) and of God himself (8:17). Second, the faith for Paul is faithfulness to God who counts it as righteousness (4:3) and raised Jesus from the dead for our justification (4:17). God's faithfulness is apart from the observance of the law (3:21) but based on Christ's faithfulness and obedience. Third, if for the Qumran community the Teacher of Righteousness is the interpreter of the law, for Paul Christ, God's Son, is the fulfillment of the law (10:4). Christ did what the law could not do. Being obedient he condemns sin so that the righteous requirements of the law might be fully met in people (8:3–4); so that they might submit to God's law through Christ and in Christ (8:9–11) and live in righteousness. In this regard, Brownlee says that "the implicit contradiction" between the gift of the divine righteousness and salvation through obedient faith "was never resolved except by Paul who identified God's righteousness with Jesus the Christ."[72] Thus, Paul's resolution is that God reveals his righteousness and redemption through Christ's faithful obedience up to death on the cross. The prophetic fulfillment is inaugurated by Jesus Christ's death and resurrection. It is through Christ's righteousness (his obedience and sacrificial death) that believers are brought into a right relationship with God and through which their disobedience has been removed by his obedience. This reconciliation with God is entirely the free gift of God's grace through the obedience of the Son for those who are in Christ (3:21–26). But Paul never implies that Christ's obedience removes the call for those

---

71. In the light of 1QHab as referring to the act of presaging a vision and its realization in history. See Brownlee, *The Midrash*, 26.

72. Ibid., 128–29.

who are in Christ to live lives of grace-enabled obedience. Paul explicitly claims that God dealt with sin by sending his Son in the likeness of sinful flesh so that the just requirement of the law might be fulfilled in those in Christ who walk according to the Spirit (8:3–4; see also 6:1–11). Paul sees the fulfillment of Habakkuk's vision christologically and this interpretation fits Paul's narrative.

In Romans 6:5 Paul states that we will be united with him in his resurrection. The faithful obedience of Christians continues the story of Jesus. In this sense Habakkuk serves Paul as "rubric and clincher of his argument."[73] In other words, Christ himself is the righteous one, who is faithful until death on the cross and is raised from death to life. The righteous ones among all the nations also die to sin and live a new life in Christ, in his faithfulness. The righteous one shall live by the faith of Christ. They will be united with him in resurrection and will live forever (6:2–5).

From the beginning of his epistle Paul intends to inform his readers about the very core of the gospel. This is the righteousness of God, God's promised redemption for both Jews and Gentiles that is finally revealed in Christ's faithfulness for all who believe. Faith, for Paul, is centered on Christ and issues in the in-Christ relationship. Both the faithfulness of Christ and participation in Christ build an inseparable concept. Paul's reference to Habakkuk serves as a key text for the disclosure of the divine righteousness that is by faithfulness. This faithfulness is of the righteous one, Christ himself, and by implication also of all who are in Christ and share the faith of Christ. They shall live as children of God sharing Christ's suffering and glory (8:14–17). Paul's interest in referring to Habakkuk is then not simply to connect faith and righteousness although they are positively correlated[74] but to confirm the revelation of God's righteousness in Christ's faithfulness for all nations, first to the Jews then also to the Gentiles. Only in Christ and through Christ many will become righteous (5:19) and grace reigns, bringing eternal life (5:21). Christ's faithfulness is the primary and central idea in Paul's view on God's redemption that has already taken place and is still to reveal its full glory (8:18–21). It has an eschatological dimension: both Jews and Gentiles that share the faith of Christ shall live. This interpretation, though, needs to be seen in Paul's further development of his argument (3:21–26; 5:12–21).

---

73. Hays, "The Righteous One," 211.
74. Watson, *Paul*, 56.

4. Christ's Faithfulness in Rom 3:21-26

4.1 3:21-26 within Paul's Narrative

In his comment on Rom 3:21-26 Richard Hays writes, "God has solved the problem of human unrighteousness and Israel's faithfulness by putting forward as a sacrifice the one perfectly faithful human being, Jesus. Though others rebelled and refused to give glory to God, he remained faithful. His death is an act of *pistis* [faith]: human . . . and divine."[75] The human faith of Christ Hays describes as an act of perfect obedience through which many will become righteous. The divine faith of Christ affirms God's love and faith-keeping.[76]

Hays' words sound very persuasive especially within Paul's narrative as he unfolds the theme of God's faithfulness/righteousness and the significance of Christ in God's redemption. The context of Rom 2:17—3:20 is highly important to see Paul's conclusion in 3:21-25 concerning God's righteousness through Christ's faithfulness. In Rom 2:17—3:20 Paul demonstrates that Israel's corporate life was marked out as faithlessness. They all were under the power of sin (3:9) along with the Gentiles (1:18-32). Although Israel was chosen by God and elevated into the status of his son so that God's people would be a light to the other nations and that God's name would be proclaimed in the whole world, they failed to obey God (2:21-24). The result of Israel's disobedience and dishonoring God is that the name of God is blasphemed among the Gentiles (2:24). Paul supports his arguments from the scripture, referring to Isa 52:5 and Ezek 36:22.[77] In both OT passages exile has come because of Israel's disobedience. God's people are mocked by Gentiles and God's name is constantly blasphemed. Although the words from Isaiah and Ezekiel sound like a sharp rebuke in Rom 2:24, both prophetic passages deliver a message of hope that underlines two major ideas. The first is that God will act through Israel. The second is that God will act for the glory of his own name in spite of Israel's disposition.

Paul's conclusion in 3:20 that he also reads from the scripture (in Rom 3:9-20 Paul alludes to Ps 14:1-3; 53:1-3; Eccl 7:20; Isa 59:7-8) is that no one (no Gentile and no Jew; with or without the law) can be

---

75. Hays, "*PISTIS CHRISTOU*," 45.

76. Hays, *Faith*, 170-74.

77. See further discussion on that in Hays, *Echoes*, 46; Wagner, *Heralds of the Good News*, 174-80.

justified before God. The future, approached in such terms, is bleak. In the light of the scripture though, the expectation is that God himself will act and he will still act through Israel. That is why at the beginning of his letter Paul introduces this stunning news (1:1–3, 16–17): God has acted in his Son who is the promised Jewish Messiah and the obedient Son.[78] God has acted through him as he would have acted through the obedient Israel calling other nations into the obedience of faith. Christ is like the embodiment of Israel. God exalted him as Lord at the resurrection after he demonstrated total obedience to God the Father. In him God's purposes are fulfilled for Israel and for the whole world so that God's name is glorified.

In 3:21–25 Paul offers God's solution to human sin as it has been intended from the very beginning and the Jewish scripture testifies about it. Paul offers almost a summary statement of what God has done in Christ. The righteousness of God has been disclosed through the faithfulness of Jesus Christ for all who believe with no distinction (3:21–22). They (all who believe with no distinction) are justified through the redemption that is in Christ Jesus. God put him forward as an atoning sacrifice (ἱλαστήριον) through faith in his blood (3:24–25a). The following context also becomes clear, if we continue the interpretation in the same Christological key. God did it [sent his Son to deal with sin] to show his righteousness. Although God's forbearing withheld well-deserved punishment for sins, now through Christ's faithfulness he deals with sin (3:25). Paul shows that the law that was for so long a means to seek God's righteousness did not work; rather it brought wrath and realization of sinfulness (cf. 4:15; 8:3) but was finally fulfilled in Christ (10:4). God's righteousness and faithfulness come only through the faithfulness of Christ. God demonstrates his righteousness through Christ, justifying those who are of the faith of Christ, meaning those who participate in Christ's faithfulness (3:26; cf. chs. 5–8).

In this interpretation faith as the faithfulness of Christ plays a major role. Of course, it is arguable that πίστις Χριστοῦ in 3:22 is an equivalent reference to faith in Christ, however, the further phrase "for all who believe" (εἰς πάντας τοὺς πιστεύοντας) would be particularly redundant in this reading. The subjective interpretation, on the contrary, is perfectly coherent with the εἰς πάντας τοὺς πιστεύοντας recognizing the necessity of Christians to have faith in Christ and to participate in his faithfulness.

---

78. See chapter 3 above.

The subjective interpretation illuminates the ultimate significance of Christ's faithful obedience for God's purposes, the unity between God and Christ, and finally the divine initiative and completion in the work for human redemption.[79]

In 3:26 the phrase ἐκ πίστεως Ἰησοῦ (from the faith of Christ) by itself is even less clear than in 3:22. James Dunn sees here a close parallel to Abraham's pure faith and trust in the Lord in 4:16, which makes him argue that this faith in 3:26 and elsewhere is the reference to human faith.[80] Alongside Dunn, Moo interprets faith as a human response on the ground that Paul nowhere clearly speaks of Christ believing or being faithful.[81] However, both scholars recognize that Paul's theology presupposes a story about Jesus. Both of them admit that Paul includes the larger story of God and his purpose for his people and his creation. In this larger story of God's redemption Christ's faithfulness makes better sense. God's covenantal righteousness/faithfulness to Israel and eventually to the whole world is manifested in Christ's faithfulness to God as the obedient Son undoing the disobedience of Adam and Israel. The subjective reading of faith best corresponds with the narrative logic of the letter. For R. Hays again, the faith that is in view is the faith of Christ and his faithfulness up to atoning death.[82] B. Matlock also questions, "How could the divine power of justification—how the very revelation of the righteousness of God!—lie in doffing the mental cap in the appropriate direction, in cultivating the proper spiritual disposition?"[83] Rather, it is Christ's faithfulness to God up to death on the cross that affirms God's unbreakable faithfulness. Paul indeed unpacks the meaning of "the faithfulness of Christ" not only here but also in other texts when he refers to the crucifixion of Christ (Gal 2:16, 19, 21; Phil 2:5–11, 3:9).[84]

Paul develops the idea of God's righteousness expressed in Christ's faithful obedience from the very beginning (1:1–7; 1:16–17). Christ's

---

79. See other fundamental affirmation in favour to the faith of Christ in Gorman, *Cruciformity*, 116.

80. Dunn, "ΕΚ ΠΙΣΤΕΩΣ."

81. D. Moo, *Romans*, 83.

82. Hays, *The Faith*, 284.

83. Matlock, "Detheologizing the ΠΙΣΤΙΣ ΧΡΙΣΤΟΥ Debate," 22.

84. Some scholars (Bill Salier, Peter Bolt, Bruce Lowe, David deSilva) argue that the concept of Jesus' obedience and faithfulness is expressed in the narratives of the biblical authors outside of Paul's writings as well. See Bird and Sprinkle, eds., *The Faith of Jesus Christ*, 209–59.

faithfulness correlates with Paul's further description about Christ's obedience (5:12–21). In Romans 5:8 God demonstrates his love by means of what Christ did showing the unity of purpose and activity of God the Father and God's Son. Through Christ's obedience all can come into relationship of One God and Father (8:9–15). So, human faith turns out to be a participation in the faithful obedience of Jesus (8:17, 29–30). As long as the notion of God's action on the basis of his own righteousness and the unity of action between God the Father and Jesus the Son is maintained in Paul's letter, Christ's faithfulness in 3:22, 26 becomes clear. In 3:26 then Paul implies that "God's saving righteousness extends to those who share in and derive their identity from Jesus' faithfulness."[85]

Now, the language in 3:21–26 is very heavily loaded with Old Testament imagery: redemption, atoning sacrifice, faith in his blood, and sins committed beforehand unpunished. The language is highly sacrificial and recalls the idea of the atoning sacrifice from sin in the OT. The question is: how does the sacrificial theme serve to unfold the theme of Christ's faithfulness, if at all?

4.2 Christ's Faithfulness as Atoning Sacrifice

For Paul God's redemption is in Christ, in what he has accomplished through his faithfulness. God's righteousness is revealed and his justice is demonstrated not because some people have an extraordinary faith that deals with sin and provokes God's revelation and not because the Jews tried hard to obey the law and could not succeed in that. Paul still emphasizes that all have sinned and fallen short of God's glory (3:23). Rather, God himself has acted through his Son, through his faithfulness. Πίστις Χριστοῦ most likely in this context is Christ's own faithfulness and not people's. Paul sees this act of Christ's faithfulness in the light of the things predicted and explained in the OT.

Paul explains Christ's faithfulness in terms of atoning sacrifice for sin (the idea is present also in 8:3) through his blood. The language Paul uses concerning Christ's atonement was most certainly known to the first century Christianity (1 Cor 15:3).[86] This might be an explanation why Paul delivers surprisingly little on this subject. Even if Paul is citing an

---

85. Jipp, "Rereading the Story," 232.
86. See also D. Moo's review on that in *Romans*, 233.

existing liturgical formula here,[87] still all the major terms (redemption, atoning sacrifice and his blood) are descriptive of Jesus and deserve special attention.

Paul depicts the act of Christ as ἱλαστήριον according to the OT, which apparently shows not a break with the Jewish tradition but the recognition of its deeper meaning.

The idea of atoning sacrifice is closely related with Israel's sacrificial structure as atoning from sin (Lev 4–5). In the LXX, the word ἱλαστήριον, the Hebrew כַּפֹּרֶת or the "mercy seat," is from the same root as the verb "make atonement for" (כפר). The blood of the sin offering was sprinkled on it annually on the Day of Atonement (Lev 16).[88] On that day Aaron and later the priest who was anointed and succeeded him as a high priest would make an atonement with the blood of the atoning sin offering for the generations to come (Exod 30:10). On the one hand, the ritual dramatizes the fact that sin separates people from God. On the other, through this redemptive ceremonial act God could stay among people and the place of his worship would be cleansed from the sin of his people.[89] The cleansing would be temporary only. The sacrificial ritual has to be repeated (Lev 16:29–34).

---

87. If Paul quotes an early Christian tradition at this point, it still suites his argument and creates another point of contact with the new for him audience in Rome, see D. Moo, *Romans*, 220–21.

88. The term ἱλαστήριον is also used for the cover of the ark in Exod 25:16–22, however, the combination of ἱλαστήριον with ἀπολυτρώσεως, ἐν τῷ αὐτοῦ αἵματι; thematic parallels between 3:21–22 with other passages in the NT (Heb 9–10), where the Day of Atonement is implied suggest that Lev 16 is the background for the Roman text. See further debate on the meaning and usage in Fitzmyer, *Romans*, 349–50; D. Moo, *Romans*, 230–39; N. T. Wright, "The Letter to the Romans," 474. The parallel is even more developed in Heb 10 with the idea of insufficiency of the blood of animals to remove the defilement of sins (Lane, *Hebrews 9–13*, 262).

89. Some OT passages note that the sin offering is for the purpose of atoning for unintentional sin (Lev 4:2, 13, 22, 27; 5:15, 18; Num 30:27). If anyone sins defiantly, blasphemes the Lord, that person must be cut off; his guilt remains on him (Num 15:30–31; 35:31–32). Although the penalty of the defiant sin is cutting off from the divine theocracy, this does not eliminate the possibility of atonement and forgiveness. Achan, before he is stoned to death for taking loot from those whom God has placed under the ban (Josh 7) is given a chance to confess, repent, and bring glory to the Lord. Atonement does not erase the temporal penalties and consequences of sin, but it is a matter of peace and reconciliation with God. The idea of forgiveness available apart from the sacrificial structure to those who truly repent is also not foreign to the OT (2 Sam 12:13; Ps 51). However, even on the Day of Atonement people have to deny themselves (Lev 23:32). "The external points to the internal," Swanson, "Offering for Sin in Leviticus," 14. Forgiveness grounds a new life in the prophetic language (Isa

Christ's Faithfulness as Fulfillment of the Father's Faithfulness 109

Paul explains that something different happens in relationship between God and people. People are justified by Christ whom God presents as ἱλαστήριον, which recalls atoning sacrifices at the Day of Atonement (3:25). Paul shows the efficiency of Christ's ἱλαστήριον. The ritual of animal sacrifice is not so much substituted by Christ as fulfilled in him. The atonement is complete and does not need to be repeated. God's righteousness has been revealed through Christ's obedience. Here Paul views Christ's faithfulness as beneficially working for Israel where God's covenantal faithfulness is renewed. God has put him as a sacrifice of atonement to bring himself into right relationship with his people. This way Paul underlines God's truthfulness in the history of Israel and Christ as a new means of access to God that reaches beyond the sins of Israel.[90] Paul sees Christ's obedient death on the cross as an atoning sacrifice that deals with Israel's sin and in this sense abolishes the OT sacrificial system by that. New life in obedience to God is in Christ.

When Paul describes Jesus as a ἱλαστήριον he might also recall the self-giving sacrifice of the Jewish martyrs who died vicariously as ἱλαστήριον on behalf of the law for the sake of Israel (cf. *4 Macc.* 17:20–22).[91] However, Paul does not imply any redemptive purposes connected

---

43:25; 53:10–12; Jer 31:31–34). Sacrifice alone is not effective as the prophets declare. True repentance and obedience is inward; it is circumcision of the heart (Deut 10:16; 30:6). Israel's sin is so great that there are not enough sacrificial offerings to cover it (Mic 6:7). From the OT it is evident that disobedience and sin that separate God and his people leads to the broken covenant and relationship with the Father. The prophets prophesized that Israel is to re-inhabit the land only with all iniquity removed (Zech 3:1–10). Jeremiah says that when the kingdom is restored people will look all over Israel and Judah for iniquity and sin, but they will not find any (Jer 50:20). The only way to turn away from the sins is to turn back to God. The prophets continuously call Israel to repentance before God, to obedience to God and emphasize Israel's failure to do so. The hope and redemption is still expected from God's side (Ezek 36:22). Isaiah proclaims the ways of God's own servant who makes an offering (Isa 53:10); who takes our infirmities (Isa 53:4); by whose wounds there is a reconciliation to God (Isa 53:5).

90. Jewett, *Romans*, 286.

91. The death of Jewish martyrs is described as some sort of vicarious atonement for the Jewish people (2 Macc 7; 14:37–46; *4 Macc.* 6:27–29; 17:20–22). The martyrs died on behalf of the law so that God might be satisfied by their punishment for the sake of Israel (*4 Macc.* 6:27–29). They died as a ransom (ἀντίψυχον) for the sin of the nation. Διὰ τοῦ αἵματος τῶν εὐσεβῶν ἐκείνων and τοῦ ἱλαστηρίου τοῦ θανάτου αὐτῶν divine providence preserved Israel (*4 Macc.* 17:20–22). See van Henten, *The Maccabean Martyrs*, 140–56. Campbell also sees the martyrological tradition behind the terminology here in 3:25. See Campbell, *The Deliverance*, 655. Perhaps, in the Jewish thinking of 2TP the idea of the suffering of the righteous Jew might have some atoning overtones for Israel, as a sacrifice does. This idea has some connection with

with the righteous Jews. If Paul has the imagery of the martyrs in mind, he uses it to explain the act of Christ. For Paul Jesus Christ is the most pious Jew, the righteous one and the perfect martyr. He is the Son of God who faithfully obeys the Father up to death on the cross. Christ's ἱλαστήριον obviously supersedes any other ἱλαστήριον. His faithfulness is supreme for God's redemption, particularly for Israel. God sent his own to redeem his own.

At the same time, Paul is universally optimistic: Christ's atonement is not just for Israel as sacrificial ἱλαστήριον was in the scripture, but for the Gentiles as well. On the one hand, Paul demonstrates the whole depth of sin and disobedience of people before God including the Gentiles' disobedience (1:18—3:20). On the other hand, for Paul it is important to show that God has dealt with sin and disobedience including the Gentiles' through Christ. Christ's atoning sacrifice covers all people not just Israel's sin. Jesus suffers on behalf of his people as the true Messiah, Son of David (1:1–5) and Adam's antitype (5:12-21) whom God has sent to redeem humanity. Hays is right that for Paul Christ's faithfulness up to death is "an act of *pistis* [faith]: human . . . and divine."[92] It is not a mere substitutionary act, but, in Gorman's words, "the quintessential covenantal act in which the love of God and of neighbor are joined and embodied in the one act of a faithful, loving death."[93] It is God's fulfillment of his bigger purposes. Christ's faithfulness (πίστις) is not only a counteract to Israel's unfaithfulness (ἀπίστια), it is an act of perfect obedience through which many will be made righteous (5:19). Christ as a true Israel's representative became a light to the nations. God's faithfulness in Christ has an effect on Gentiles as well. All who participate in his sacrifice, in his obedience, in his righteousness are part of God's family led by his Spirit (cf. 5:21; 8:14–17). Longenecker is helpful in explaining that, "Rather than gentiles blaspheming the name of the covenant God of Israel due to Israel's own disobedient faithlessness, gentiles can now enter into the salvation offered by God by means of their faith, due to the obedient faithfulness of Jesus Christ."[94]

Abraham's offering Isaac (we will return to this theme in chapter 5) who has become a model of obedience and an example for the Jewish martyrdom (4 *Macc*. 16:20; 18:12). See further N. T. Wright, *Jesus and the Victory of God*, 576–84.

92. Hays, "PISTIS CHRISTOU," 45.

93. Gorman, *Inhabiting the Cruciform God*, 62.

94. B. Longenecker, *The Triumph of Abraham's God*, 100.

Paul's point is similar when he refers to Abraham (ch. 4) saying that he was justified by faith as an uncircumcised Gentile. Accordingly, he is the father of Jews and Gentiles. Both Jews and Gentiles have an access into a covenant relationship with God on the basis of faith that was prefigured in Abraham and not according to the Mosaic law. Paul's point is that our faith should be directed toward the same God of Abraham who now raised Jesus from the dead (4:24).[95] For Paul justification is indeed possible by faith but not by human faith alone as such (although it is a condition to participate in the faith of Christ) and not by person's own faithfulness. It is possible through the accomplishment of God's righteousness in Christ, which was, according to Paul, promised in the scripture for both Jews and Gentiles (9:30—10:4). D. Garlington suggests that justification for Paul "is to be submitted under the more inclusive category of the righteousness of God."[96] Now God's righteousness is revealed in Christ universally to all the nations with no distinction.

Paul's arguments on Christ's death for many become lucid in the light of Isaiah 53. Although Paul's sacrificial language in 3:21-26 differs from Isa 53:10-11,[97] Isaiah's theme of the suffering servant sounds in the background.[98] Paul echoes Isaiah in 5:15, 19; 10:16; 15:21. In 4:25 Paul's language "who was handed over (παρεδόθη) to death for our trespasses (τὰ παραπτώματα ἡμῶν)" echoes Isa 53:6, " the Lord has laid (παρέδωκεν) on him the iniquity of us all (ταῖς ἁμαρτίαις ἡμῶν)" and Isa 53:12, "and made intercession (παρεδόθη) for the transgressors (τὰς ἁμαρτίας)."

In 8:3 Christ is a sin offering (περὶ ἁμαρτίας) as the suffering servant is a sin offering (περὶ ἁμαρτίας) in Isa 53:10. God condemned sin in the flesh (8:3), i.e., in the flesh of Christ. Christ is, for Paul, the suffering servant whose death deals with the sins of many. "Many" in Paul's view, are certainly Jews and Gentiles in Christ. In Christ then, Isaiah's prophesy that, for Paul, includes all the nations comes true. Christ is the suffering servant; through his ἱλαστήριον many will become righteous (5:19).

Christ's blood also covers for all who believe in Christ or who are in Christ (Paul's language in chs. 5–6). His blood is more precious than that of animals[99] and of Jewish martyrs if Paul has them in mind. Christ's

---

95. More on that in chapter 5.
96. Garlington, A "New Perspective" Reading of Central Texts in Romans 1–4, 7.
97. N. T. Wright, "The Letter to the Romans," 475
98. Hays, Echoes, 63.
99. The blood itself is an important reminder of life and the costliness of sin (Lev

death deals with sin. God's superior act in Christ deals with Israel's past in relation to sacrifices. Paul envisages the sacrificial system of Israel in some manner ineffective when he says that in his divine forbearance God had passed over the sins previously committed (3:25). Instead Paul places Christ's faithfulness as fulfillment of atonement for the sins of Israel and for all the Gentiles.

The blood of the Son of God that was shed on the cross not only deals with sin but also brings a new life and leads to a new life: all who died with him, died to sin and will be united with him in resurrection (6:4). Christ's righteousness through his obedience and sacrificial death is a share of all believers (cf. 5:2–21). They all will become righteous through his obedience (5:19). They are eventually to conform to him (8:29).

Paul underlines both corporate and dynamic consequences of Christ's faithfulness. Paul's concern throughout Romans is not so much then how a person is justified in the sight of God as how both Jews and Gentiles, the righteous ones because of Christ's act, can belong to God's renewed family as his true children and heirs. Through Christ's obedience this access is granted to all now, as they die to sin with Christ (6:4) and conform to his image (8:29), and in the future, when the whole creation will be renewed (8:17ff). So, Paul thinks of people's life in Christ as a process of ongoing offering to God (12:1–2), as a response to his grace in Christ, and as a process of orientation to Christ and mind set on the Spirit of Christ (8:4–17).

For Paul God acts, not in contradiction to the law that was a way of life and behavior for the Jews for a long time and that could not deal with sin (8:3), but in accordance with the law (3:21). Paul implies that the scripture anticipated that God would act in a special way dealing with sin. Neither any rituals nor the law *per se* could deal with it. For Paul Christ as the fulfillment of the law in himself (10:4) accomplished the anticipated redemption. In a nutshell, Paul's answer to the problem of human unrighteousness and Israel's unfaithfulness (1:18—3:20) is that God's faithfulness to Israel and eventually to his whole created world is revealed through his Son's faithfulness up to death on the cross. With his coming, the law has fulfilled its "divinely intended, though limited, function."[100] Some continue to pursue the law with zeal, but their zeal is misplaced (10:2). Paul himself testifies about his zeal misunderstood in

---

17:11). Blood is given to make atonement for one's life; it is not to be consumed (Lev 17:1–12).

100. Westerholm, *Understanding Paul*, 142.

the past (Gal 1:11–16), which did not reflect God's intended purpose. However, even in the case of Jewish rejection there will be benefit of others, reconciliation of the world because God's Son made his obedient offering complete.

For Paul, righteousness always comes by faith in God and his promises (4:13; 9:31). God takes initiative through Christ to restore relationship with all the people. The atoning sacrifice of Christ is supreme since through his faithfulness God's righteousness is finally revealed. The law did not do it. Some Jews must have insisted that all the Gentiles who were brought into this new faith must be circumcised, perform the Jewish ceremonies, and follow all the Mosaic laws. This is the theme that is more explicitly raised by Paul in Galatians (Gal 2:11–21). For Paul in Galatians and here, however, both Gentiles and Jews could be justified before God not by following the details of the observance of the law but through the act of God's Son Jesus Christ (9:30–32; cf. Acts 15). Paul could not have stated it any more clearly. He underlines that no one can be declared righteous at once and forever by keeping the law and offering sacrifices. The only way sinners can be declared righteous before God is by God himself (cf. Ps 32:1–2 in Rom 4:6) and their response to God who has acted through Christ's faithfulness (4:24). Jesus Christ came with the purpose to save sinners (5:8). He does it by establishing the only righteousness that demands the eternal life and salvation of all those for whom Christ established it at the cross.[101] In this light, both Jews and Gentiles, for Paul, restore their relationship with God only through Christ, the only acceptable ἱλαστήριον.

Furthermore, Paul points out that all are justified by God's grace through Christ's faith (3:24). "God's grace" explains Paul's overall principle of his understanding of how God acts in the life of people. God acts on basis of his righteousness by his grace. This understanding Paul derives from the OT. Deuteronomy, in particular, is a vivid example of Israel's special belonging to God and God's work of redeeming Israel out of Egypt not on the basis of Israel's righteousness but on the basis of God's righteousness (Deut 9; 32). For Paul God's purposes and their fulfillment are not limited by human unfaithfulness and inability to keep the promises (ch. 3). If the Jews fail to keep their part of the covenant (2:17–29), God's faithfulness in making promises and keeping them is not invalidated (3:4). It is to say that God remains true to his obligations

---

101. C. Wright, *The Mission of God*, 528.

and promises that, according to Paul, include both Jews and Gentiles. Now, all are justified by God's grace through Christ's faithfulness. No human effort is sufficient for that. God's grace as divine gift or favor is tied with Christ, God's only Son. God's grace works through Christ's obedience. Through Christ's faithful obedience there is access into grace by our faith as a dynamic participation in Christ's faithfulness (5:2–3).

Christ's faithfulness until death corresponds with sacrificial death known in the scriptures but Christ's death has redemptive consequences not only for Israel but for all (3:22). In this light Christ is the fulfillment of all sacrifices; and God's story of redemption sounds anew: both Jews and Gentiles have been embraced by God and restored in their relationship with God through the same channel—God's Son Christ Jesus, the obedient Son and the ἱλαστήριον for all.

5. Conclusions

The main focus of this chapter was the extent to which Paul reflects the idea of God's faithfulness/righteousness that cannot be separated from Christ's faithfulness. Paul discloses Christ's faithfulness as the faithfulness of God's own Son and the righteous One of Israel who faithfully obeys the Father up to death on the cross, revealing God's truthfulness in Israel's history and fulfilling God's bigger purposes that the scripture has testified.

By Christ's faithfulness the function of being a light to other nations is fulfilled, the one that Israel failed to accomplish in order that the Gentiles may rejoice with Israel. Therefore, through Christ's faithfulness it is possible to call all the nations to the obedience of faith that is into renewed covenantal relationship as God's children. Through Christ's faithful obedience many will be made righteous because Christ overcomes not only Israel's unfaithfulness but all human unrighteousness and sin. He dies as ἱλαστήριον, the Jewish martyr, and the suffering servant for all. Paul uses his Jewish heritage to draw a picture of how God's redemption came about through his Son's obedience as a new reality for all.

Christ's faithfulness calls forth participation language. All believers participate in Christ's obedience, i.e., faithfulness; in that they are faithful to God and reconciled to him. God raises Jesus Christ from death to life. So, all believers who die to sin with Christ and in him are obedient with him and in his obedience and will be raised by him to life.

Christ's Faithfulness as Fulfillment of the Father's Faithfulness

Having given a firm account on Christ's faithfulness as the fulfillment of God's truthfulness and righteousness in the history of Israel and humanity, Paul refers to Abraham, a great and respected figure, the ancestor of Jews. Paul considers this essential for the establishment of his argument. Does Abraham's story reveal God's covenantal faithfulness and his intention to redeem the world? Does Abraham fit Paul's account of Christ's faithfulness? Or, is Christ's obedience related to Abraham's faith according to Paul?

CHAPTER V

Christ's Obedience and Abraham's Faith

1. Introduction

The most prevalent view in traditional Protestant exegesis is that Abraham's justification for Paul is "explicitly predicated upon faith and not works."[1] In this approach Abraham is an illustration from the law of a sinner justified by faith not by works. It is also a proto-example for Christians' justification by faith not by works. The majority of contemporary scholars (Schreiner, Dunn, Wright, Campbell, Hays) interpret Abraham's example not so much as an example of one justified by faith, as in terms of God's salvation history, but as proof of the equality of Jews and Gentiles, with the result that the Gentiles join the Jews in the people of God as the children of Abraham.[2] Moreover, they recognize that Paul's argument on Abraham is multifaceted and cannot be reduced to one linear theme.[3] Within this perspective to study the nature of Abraham's faith and Paul's reason for discussing it at length is quite challenging.

James Dunn, for example, approaches Romans 4 as an example of Abraham's pure faith or trust in God's promises, not his faithfulness. Thus, what is in view throughout for Paul is "faith in the life-giving power of God (manifested in the conception of Isaac, and in the resurrection of Christ), not faithfulness (either of Abraham or Christ)."[4] Faith for

---

1. Jipp, "Rereading the Story," 217.
2. Schreiner, *Romans*, 209.
3. Jipp, "Rereading the Story," 218.
4. Dunn, "Once More, PISTIS CRISTOU," 265. See also Schreiner, *Paul Apostle of God's Glory in Christ*, 214–16.

Paul is faith or pure trust in Jesus Christ and not Christ's faithfulness.[5] Although Dunn is right and the sense of the believers' faith in Christ is certainly present in Paul's teaching (1:16; 3:22b), the case for a christocentric explanation of faith, as stated in the previous chapter, is cogent and comprehensive. The questions for this research are then: does Paul really set faith as trust and not as faithfulness or obedience when he refers to Abraham? Does faith in chapter 4 contradict Paul's overall emphasis on Christ's faithful obedience? Finally, what kind of faith plays a role in God's purposes of redemption?

2. Abraham's Example in Rom 4:1–25

2.1 Abraham's Example within Paul's Context

The fact that the theme of "faith versus works" runs throughout 3:27—4:25 pointing out that it is Abraham's faith, his complete assurance and trust in God and not his work, that matters for God, cannot be denied. But is this a sufficient explanation for Paul's extensive discussion of Abraham? In order to see the implications of Abraham's faith one must place Abraham's example in the flow of the letter.

Paul presents the gospel of God concerning his Son that brings salvation to the Jews and Gentiles on the basis of faith. As shown above, Paul clarifies this by saying that God's righteousness comes from faith to faith, implying that God's righteousness is revealed in Christ's faithfulness for all believers who participate in Christ's faithfulness (1:1–17). Paul's further explanation is that neither a Jew nor a Gentile is justified, in a right relationship, before God (1:18—3:20). With the statement that only God is true and everybody is a liar (3:4) Paul places both Jews and Gentiles on the same scale of sinfulness and unrighteousness before one true God, which is a fairly audacious claim. Paul explains that the advantages of the Jews are not particular laws or instructions but the possession of God's promises in general or the witness of the Jewish scripture. They concern all people and point to God's impartiality that eventually is fulfilled in Christ's obedience for all who believe (3:3–22). Hence, Paul's conclusion is that the only way of justification for all is by God himself on the basis of Christ's faithfulness and believers' participation in Christ's faithfulness (3:21–26).

---

5. Dunn, "ΕΚ ΠΙΣΤΕΩΣ," 351–66

In 3:27–31 Paul further substantiates the theme of faith and accessibility of God's righteousness to all. If there are some Jews who claim that God is the God of the Jews only (3:29) Paul reminds his readers that God is one and as the one God he must be the God of both Jews and Gentiles in the same way. If there is a claim among Paul's audience that the Gentile Christians must go under the law (3:27) Paul's answer to this is that the person is justified apart from the works of the law. Paul says that God will justify the circumcised and the uncircumcised on the same basis (3:30). Paul implies that neither works nor circumcision has value with regard to God's justifying activity.

There is more depth to the questions that Paul's imaginary interlocutors might have. If God is the God of both and justifies the Jews as well as the Gentiles on the same basis, what is then the significance of God's long history with the Jews, their election that starts with Abraham? Moreover, what about the law observance demanded in scripture and tradition? Should the new Gentile Christians not convert to Judaism? If Paul claims that God is the God of the Jews and Gentiles and that the Gentiles are also included in covenant relationship, then this raises serious questions about God's faithfulness in covenant with Israel and how the Gentiles enter into God's family. These issues especially trouble Paul's Jewish audience; however, they are of interest to the Gentiles as well since they are adopted by God who is the God and Father of Israel in the first place.

Paul's view on the Gentile inclusion apart from the law might have sounded radical, given that the focus in later Judaism is even more on the strict observance of the commandments, reinterpreting Biblical texts for that purpose.[6] During the Maccabaean revolt the Gentiles in the areas occupied by the Jews were forced to be circumcised and to observe the law as a token of their acceptance of Judaism (*Ant.* 13:318–19). The sons of the Jewish parents who abandoned the rite of circumcision were forcibly circumcised by Mattathias (1 Macc 2:45–46). Torah, circumcision, and food observance were clearly the identity marks of Judaism and the way for the Gentiles to join in Judaism, at least as some 2TP texts describe it.[7]

In contrast, Paul teaches that the Gentiles are welcomed by God apart from the law. Moreover, their justification works in the same way as for the Jews. Paul sounds even more radical when he says that not only the Gentiles are justified apart from the works of the law but the Jews

---

6. This is the case with the interpretation of Hab 2:4 in 1QpHab, as shown above. See also chapter 2 on that.

7. Reed, *Archaeology*, 26.

also are justified apart from them. Although the Jews are chosen and entrusted with the very words of God and the law, they cannot boast about their obedience to them (3:27). God's purpose for Israel and the desire to restore it has far reaching goals: his son Israel is to be obedient to God and to proclaim his name in all the earth (Deut 32:43 in 15:10). Obedience and law observance were important but they were the outcome of God's election and not the prerequisite of it. Now God has acted in Christ through his obedience. In Christ the law is fulfilled (10:4). For Paul the law or circumcision is not the way to attain righteousness, and not something superior in any way in relation to God that is now through Christ. The law, for Paul, now is the "law of love manifested in the obedience/faith/death of Christ,"[8] the fulfillment of God's promises.[9] In this sense, the law is upheld by faith (3:31).

So, Paul considers the Gentiles' inclusion as a part of the whole picture of God's redemption and fulfillment of his promises to the Jews. God's promises are based on his own faithfulness. This faithfulness is accomplished through Christ's faithfulness (3:22) for all who believe.

To illustrate the multiple statements made in 3:21–31 and the development of God's gospel concerning his Son for both Jews and Gentiles Paul refers to Abraham.[10] Abraham's faith becomes a key element in reckoning righteousness, in not boasting before God, in re-considering circumcision, in considering him a father of many nations, and even in a continuation Abraham's story for us (4:23). In its immediate context Paul's argument revolves around the point that Abraham's faith was reckoned to him as righteousness with reference to Gen 15:6. In 4:17 Paul also alludes to Gen 17. What are significant events in Gen 15, 17 that may shed light on Paul's usage of them in his teaching of Abraham?

---

8. Gorman, *Inhabiting the Cruciform God*, 84.

9. More on the law as the exclusive prerogative of the Jewish community and the law that transcends the Jewish community and its own written embodiment see Watson, *Paul, Judaism, and the Gentiles*, 212–16.

10. D. Moo, *Romans*, 259, assumes that Paul raises the question in 4:1 about Abraham. Hays also ascribes the question to Paul emphasizing that Paul is asking "whose father is Abraham and in what way his children are related to him" ("Have We Found Abraham?," 97). Jipp argues that in 4:1 Paul's interlocutors raise the question about Abraham in the light of the previous polemics (3:27–31) and Paul's radical statements. They refer to "the premier figure of Israel's Scripture," Abraham, "as a potentially damaging witness to Paul's gospel" compelling Paul to respond "to a recognizable Jewish discourse about their forefather" (Jipp, "Rereading the Story," 221). The most important thing, though, is that Paul does not avoid the discussion on Abraham but draws continuity between Abraham and the gospel of God revealed in Christ, as we shall see.

2.2 Abraham in Genesis 15, 17[11] and Jewish Tradition

In Gen 11:26—12:3 God chooses Abram among all the people of the world promising him land and blessings upon him, his descendants and all the nations through him. Thus, the destiny of Israel is described as bringing blessing to all the nations. Abram obeys God and leaves the country of his ancestors. In Gen 13:15-16, after Lot parted from Abram, God repeats his promise of the land and of innumerable offspring. In Gen 15 Abram is doubtful of God's promises since he still remains childless. God, however, confirms his promises that as many as the stars in heaven as many Abram's offspring shall be (Gen 15:5). Abram believes God, and God reckons it to him as righteousness (Gen 15:6).

For von Rad Abram's faith in God's promises sufficed to declare him righteous or acceptable to God. He describes it this way, "God has indicated his plan for history, namely, to make of Abraham a great people; Abraham 'has firmly assented' to that, i.e., he took it seriously and adjusted to it" adopting "the only correct relationship to God."[12] Abram believed God's promises of a numerous progeny, and this faith was credited to him as righteousness. Jewett asserts that von Rad's explanation of Gen 15:6 is "the clearest" one and suggests its consideration for understanding Romans.[13] Fitzmyer also defines faith as Abram's acceptance of God's word and "his willingness to trust and abide by it even when he had no perceptible evidence. It involved his personal confidence and included hope in a promise that no mere human could guarantee (4:18)."[14] Hartley recognizing the idea of acceptance also points to the verb "credit," "which implies some type of official action; that is, God declared Abram's belief to be the basis for his having full standing in God's presence."[15] It is as if God recognizes Abram's faith and counts on him to carry out his purposes for all the nations. Abram's response "marks the successful completion of the

---

11. Gen 22 describes a real stretch of Abraham's faith as obedience. Paul alludes to Gen 22 in 8:32. This particular event, its interpretation, and Paul's allusion to it are very important in Romans and will be considered separately in the second half of this chapter.

12. Rad, *Genesis*, 185.

13. Jewett, *Romans*, 312.

14. Fitzmyer, *Romans*, 373.

15. Hartley, *Genesis*, 156. Rad suggests a cultic background where the priest declares that a gift is properly offered (Lev 7:18). In response to Abraham's faith God as a priest (although outside of a worship setting) declares Abraham righteous, *Genesis*, 184–85.

divine act of promise-making."[16] Abram is recognized righteous by virtue of God's declaration in view of his faith in God's promises concerning Abraham's offspring.

In Genesis 16 Ishmael is born but he is not the promised son. In Genesis 17 two major changes take place. First, God reassures Abraham of his promise saying that he will establish his covenant as an everlasting covenant with Abraham and all his descendants that are to come. God even changes the name of Abram to Abraham anticipating his new identity as the father of many nations (Gen 17:2–8). Second, God "prescribes circumcision"; Isaac "will be the first heir of the covenant."[17] This is again an affirmation that the promise is of divine and not human initiative.[18]

Nehemiah 9:7–8 recalls Genesis 15, 17.[19] Nehemiah 9:7 writes that God called Abraham, brought him from Ur—which suggests the exodus motif (Gen 11; cf. Exod 20:2; 32:11–12)—and he changed his name (Gen 17). Nehemiah 9:8a says that God found Abraham's heart faithful to him and made a covenant with Abraham to give to his descendants the land. Finally, according to Nehemiah, God has kept the promise because God is righteous (Neh 9:8b). Nehemiah confirms the ideas present in Gen 11, 15, 17. God takes the initiative calling Abraham and making a covenant with him. God keeps his promises; the fulfillment of the promises demonstrates God's righteousness in relationship to Abraham "inspiring a confidence that God will not allow his promises to go by default."[20] God also sees the heart of Abraham. The whole phrase, that God found his heart faithful (9:8), is "balanced with the righteousness of the Lord at the end of the verse."[21] It shows that God makes the promise and fulfills it because he is righteous. Abraham accepts and participates in God's promise but it is God who fulfills it.

---

16. Watson, *Paul*, 179.

17. Hartley, *Genesis*, 169.

18. Ishmael is the son of human efforts or initiative. He represents "human falsification of the divine promise." Divine promise is fulfilled in Isaac. Sarah's demand for "Ishmael's expulsion together with the divine confirmation" serves "the theological point" of incompatibility of these two sons. Abraham has to learn that "flesh and promise are to be differentiated" (Watson, *Paul*, 205).

19. On differences and similarities, see Schliesser, *Abraham's Faith in Romans 4*, 160.

20. H. G. M. Williamson, *Ezra, Nehemiah*, 312.

21. Fensham, *The Book of Ezra and Nehemiah*, 229.

In 2TP Abraham's faith is understood more and more in terms of his faithfulness and as a fine example for his descendants.²² The author of the 1 Maccabees draws the teaching on the phrase from Gen 15:6 connecting it with Abraham's testing (most likely Gen 22). In First Maccabees 2:52 Mattathias says to his sons, "Was not Abraham found faithful (εὑρέθη πιστός) when tested, and it was reckoned to him as righteousness?" Mattathias refers to Abraham (and other figures from the scripture) to show the importance of zeal for the law (2:51). He instructs his sons to give their lives for the covenant of the ancestors (2:51) and to grow strong in the law, for by it they will gain honor (2:64). Abraham becomes a paradigm of faithfulness and an example to follow in this reading. In *Jubilees*, Gen 15:1–17 and Gen 17:5 are inserted without much change (*Jub.* 14:1–16; 15:7). However, in *Jubilees* 17:15–18 there is an interesting addition to the story of Abraham. Before the sacrifice of Isaac God was aware that Abraham was faithful in all of his afflictions (*Jub.* 17:17). His life is read as a series of events that demonstrate his faithfulness to every divine command (*Jub.* 17:17–18). Abraham himself claims in *Jub.* 21:1–3 that, "throughout all of the days of my life I have been remembering the LORD and sought with all my heart to do his will and walk uprightly in all his ways." He also instructs Isaac to keep God's commandments and ordinances (*Jub.* 21:5).

In Sirach Abraham is described as the father of nations (cf. Gen 17:4) and "no one has been found like him in glory. He kept the law of the Most High, he entered into covenant with him; he certified the covenant in his flesh, and when he was tested he proved faithful" (Sir 44:20). In the vision of *2 Baruch*, Abraham and his children were implanted with "the unwritten law" in them (*2 Bar.* 57:2). In 4QMMT the reference to Gen 15:6 is made in the framework of the deeds of righteousness that include following the rules of the community.²³ From the foregoing it is evident that further understanding of Abraham's faith as faithfulness is related to his deeds and to the exemplary model of following the law.

---

22. In the modern Jewish commentary on Gen 15:6 Abraham's faith has meritorious consequences. It is translated as, "And because he put his trust in the LORD, He reckoned it to his merit" (Plaut et al, *The Torah*, 109).

23. More on that in the next section.

2.3 Paul and the Genesis Motif

Paul refers back to Genesis 15 claiming that Abraham was placed in right relationship with God apart from his deeds so that he could not boast before God. The implication is that God is the main agent of Abraham's reckoning him righteous. At this point, Dunn is right saying that the faith that is in Paul's view about Abraham is faith in God's faithfulness.[24]

Then Abraham receives circumcision as a sign of righteousness attained by faith (4:11), which leads Paul to a significant twofold implication. Abraham is the father of all uncircumcised who believe; and God's righteousness might be reckoned to them (4:11). He is also the father of all circumcised who walk in the footsteps of the faith of Abraham before he was circumcised (4:12).

Abraham is set by Paul not as an example of faithfulness but as a model of how God himself justifies both the circumcised and uncircumcised on the basis of faith. Or, as Paul puts it in 4:16, God's promise is by grace and guaranteed to all Abraham's descendants, not only to those who are of the law but also to those who are of the faith of Abraham. Abraham believed the promise that he would become the father of many nations while he was still uncircumcised. This means that these nations may include uncircumcised people who share Abraham's faith in God and they would still be considered his descendants. For Paul, using Watson's language, promise and flesh are distinct matters just as God taught Abraham.[25] Not all Abraham's descendants are his children (9:7).

When Paul refers to Genesis 15:6 (4:3) he calls him "Abraham" already including the alterations that God made to Abraham's name later: Abraham is "a father of many nations" (Gen 17:4–5). The change of name secures God's election of Abraham and especially his call to a particular role within God's purposes through a child of God's promise. Paul refers to Genesis as a narrative where God's covenant with Abraham has far reaching goals.[26] The particular place when the name was changed is not significant from the narrative point of view as long as it is shown that whenever God calls Abraham, he makes promises based on his own purposes concerning the nations; and he eventually fulfills his promises in Abraham's life, in Jewish history and now as the Gentiles finally join the Jews in a new family of God. God's promise is by faith or acceptance

---

24. Dunn, "Once More, PISTIS CRISTOU," 265.
25. Watson, *Paul*, 205.
26. On the covenant idea in Genesis, see P. Williamson, *Sealed with an Oath*.

of the promise and by God's grace for all the nations (4:16). Abraham as a great hero and an obedient man cannot boast before God (4:2) because it is God who calls him and makes him the progenitor of many nations.

Paul still alludes to the change of Abraham's name (Gen 17:5) in Rom 4:17, however, he alludes to these words as already fulfilled prophesy. In Gen 17:5 Isaac is not born yet and God confirms his promises in anticipation. Paul claims in 4:17 that Abraham is our father (and the context determines that "our" includes all Abraham's descendants, Jews and Gentiles) in the sight of God whom he believed. Paul's point is still the same: God fulfills his promises that he has made long ago, promises that concern all the nations. Abraham is just a part of them (cf. Rom 9:6–22). In the same sense Paul uses allusion to Gen 15:5 in Rom 4:18. Abraham became a father of many nations as God promised him.

Then Paul specifies the nature of God who fulfills the promises: he gives life to the dead and calls into existence things that do not exist (4:17). These words are known in a 2TP Jewish liturgical formula that describes God as the powerful God and Creator (*Jos. As.* 20:7; *2 Bar.* 21:4; 48:8; 2 Macc 7:23, 28–29).[27] However, in Paul's context it refers to the Genesis motif, to God's miraculous power to open up the womb of barren Sarah to conceive Isaac (4:18–19). God makes Abraham the father of many nations as he promises performing a miracle in order to accomplish that. Fitzmyer suspects that these words in Paul's view also "connote the influence of God on the numerous Gentiles destined to be called into being as children of Abraham."[28] We may pursue this point a little further.

The words in 4:17 may be further enlightened by Paul in 4:24–25. Abraham is the father of many nations not only because God performed a miracle and Sarah bore a child; but also because God performed a miracle of raising Jesus from the dead and by opening the way for both Jews and Gentiles to join in God's family and as such, Abraham's family. Abraham is the father of nations retrospectively because God has fulfilled his promises to bless the nations through him in Christ. Paul could think of that even more literally: Abraham is the father of the nations through Christ, his seed, if we take Paul's view in Gal 3:16 into account. In any case, Abraham is the father of many nations because of God's act in Christ and because of God's power to give life to the dead that is fully revealed in Christ's resurrection. Some scholars understand "calls into existence the

---

27. Jewett, *Romans*, 334.
28. Fitzmyer, *Romans*, 386.

things that do not exist" (καλοῦντος τὰ μὴ ὄντα ὡς ὄντα) as a reference to God's creative power just as it is supported by Jewish tradition.[29] But Paul most likely links God's creative power with the establishing of the family, also known in the scripture.[30] For Paul God establishes Abraham's full family because he has already acted powerfully through the obedient Son (1:1–5; 3:21–25; 5:1–21; 8:14–17).

Paul's whole point that Abraham believes and God makes him the father of many nations finds its fulfillment at the present time in Christ. As Schreiner notes, Paul is "not so much interested in the past creative work of God as in faith in God's future work to produce a worldwide family for Abraham."[31] Paul wants to show that Abraham's hope based on faith in God's ability to fulfill what he promised has been fulfilled. This message concerns Paul's audience in a very significant way because OT expectations are fulfilled by God as he raised Christ from the dead. Christ is delivered for our sins and he is raised so that we may live with him (4:24). Together with the idea of the fulfillment of OT expectations there is a degree of the future fulfillment as well, as Paul indicates further (cf. Rom 8:18–27; 10:9–10). Paul believes that what has happened to Christ will also happen to the believers (6:8). In Christ a new era of God's redemption for all the nations has began.

Referring to Abraham Paul describes the fate of Israel and the inclusion of the Gentiles in relation to God's action. So, when Paul argues, "it was reckoned to him as righteousness," it is because Abraham was fully convinced that God is able to fulfill what he had promised (4:18–22). No act was necessary from Abraham's part. Abraham believed that it was all God who acts on behalf of his righteousness and fulfills his promises in a miraculous way. Precisely this relationship between God and Abraham becomes paradigmatic for all believers (4:24). In other words, our faith should be directed toward the same God of Abraham who makes and fulfills promises to his people, both Jews and Gentiles.

Now, God fulfills his promises by delivering Jesus over to death for our sins and raising him up to life for our justification (4:24–25). While Paul still refers to Abraham, using the words "faith" and "reckon" the

---

29. Cranfield, *Romans*, 1:244; Dunn, *Romans 1–8*, 218. See Isa 48:13; Wis 11:25; 2 Macc 7:28; *2 Bar.* 21:4.

30. As God establishes his people Israel (Isa 64:8; Mal 2:10; Deut 32:6–7). See chapter 2 above.

31. Schreiner, *Romans*, 237.

content of the believers' faith differs substantially.[32] The believers' faith is closely related to God's act in Christ. This conclusion almost verbatim repeats Paul's summary statement in 3:21–25. Abraham's example is then another of Paul's supportive argument for God's righteousness through Christ's faithfulness to all who believe, Jews and Gentiles. Without mentioning Christ in this chapter, Abraham would be understood as "a hero, and the stress falls on the persistence and quality of the human response, rather than on the divine promises."[33] For Paul justification is indeed possible by faith but not by human faith alone as such and not by individual human faithfulness. It is possible through the accomplishment of God's righteousness in Christ, which was, according to Paul, promised in the scripture for both Jews and Gentiles. Paul considers Abraham's faith in the larger context of God's impartiality and accessibility for all the nations. Abraham's faith is subordinated to the redemption motif that God brought about in Christ. Abraham's story is only foreshadowing Christ's.

Paul also draws a parallel between Abraham's faith and David's words in Psalm 32:1–2 that are repeated in Rom 4:6–8, "Blessed are those whose iniquities are forgiven, and whose sins are covered; blessed is the one against whom the Lord will not reckon sin." The psalm serves Paul as a supportive argument for Gen 15:6. Paul introduces the psalm with the words from Genesis of the blessedness of the person to whom God reckons righteousness apart from works (4:6) and then he returns to his argument concerning Abraham again. However, the psalm helps Paul to appeal to the other great witness in the Jewish scripture to confirm his argument: David, "the man after God's own heart" (1 Sam 13:14). Even though David believed God, he was a sinner and needed God's forgiveness. The message of the psalm is that God forgives David granting righteousness apart from works, in this case, apart from previous sinful deeds. God establishes a new relationship with David.

It is interesting that 4QMMT provides a reference both to the sin and forgiveness of David in terms of obedience to the law.[34] The laws commanded by MMT are most likely designed to mark out the scroll community against other groups within the wider Jewish world.[35] The

---

32. Stowers, *Rereading of Romans*, 247–48.

33. Cousar, *A Theology of the Cross*, 69.

34. Fr. 14–17 *col.* II (= 4Q 399 I-II; 4QMMT C 25–32), Martinez, *The Dead Sea Scrolls*, 2:803.

35. N. T. Wright, "Paul and Qumran," 18–54.

document, using the quotation of Gen 15:6, describes God as the One who assesses and judges deeds, who has

> [forgiv]en (their) sins. Remember David, who was a man of the pious ones, [and] he, too [was] freed from many afflictions and was forgiven. And also we have written to you some of the works of the Torah which we think are good for you and for your people, for we s[a]w that you have intellect and knowledge of the Law. Reflect on all these matters and seek from him that he may support your counsel and keep far from you the evil scheming{s} and the counsel of Belial, so that at the end of time, you may rejoice in finding that some of our words are true. And it shall be reckoned to you as justice when you do what is upright and good before him, for your good and that of Israel.

The manuscript underlines that David's deeds are somehow important for his forgiveness and counting him righteous. David's deeds are referred to in connection to the works of the Torah that the scroll community values, follows, and asks the recipients to accept. These works are decisive for the welfare of the people of Israel since doing them is doing righteous and good for God. This will be counted as righteousness with allusion to Gen 15:6. These precepts or community rules (although not fully described) offered in the text are like boundary markers of God's people Israel in the present time and in the future.[36]

When Paul quotes the words of the psalm, he insists that God reckons righteousness apart from any works of the law, which is apparently not how 4QMMT interprets it. Paul supports the Gen 15 language of God reckoning righteousness on the basis of faith apart from works with reference to Ps 32. In its context Ps 32 functions as a testimony to God's character as a gracious and forgiving God. The reality of divine forgiveness encompasses the reality of sin. The psalm goes on to speak of the forgiven as "the righteous" ones (32:11). To be righteous then is not a matter of being sinless or rigid in following the law, or being circumcised but a matter of being forgiven by God and being accepted by God. If for some audience the understanding of the righteousness that flows from the psalm were a matter of following God's instruction (especially in the light of Ps 1:2) then Paul shifts the meaning slightly. Paul transforms the message of the psalm into the reality of God's acceptance of a person "unconditionally into the relationship of righteousness."[37] This is the case

---

36. N. T. Wright, "4QMMT and Paul," 112.
37. Jewett, *Romans*, 317.

with Abraham and David whose past was forgotten, who were blessed by God and became a part of the covenantal history.

Paul emphasizes that these examples are not only for the Jews but also for the Gentiles (4:9). Thus, Paul applies Gen 15:6 and Ps 32:1–2 not only to Israel but to the Gentiles also. He implies that both the circumcised (like David) as well as the uncircumcised (as Abraham before his circumcision) can be forgiven, blessed with a new reassured relationship with God apart from circumcision and law observance. Paul uses the psalm within his overall theme that God is the God of Jews and Gentiles. It is a reminder from Paul that doing works of the law does not make anyone (within or without the law) righteous (cf. 3:27–31). Faith in God's faithfulness is counted in maintaining relationship with God but God initiates and restores broken relationship.

Paul refers to Christ as an atoning sacrifice and God's Son who deals with sin (3:25; 8:3). For Paul being accepted by God, being righteous, again, is through the faithfulness of Christ (3:22). Christ's death is beneficial not only for the Gentiles but for the Jews also. Psalm 32 fits well with Paul's emphasis on the divine mercy and grace in forgiving human sin and acceptance of people into God's family on a bigger scale: for all nations and apart from the works of the law through the faithfulness of Christ. If so, then Paul transforms the message of the psalm "against whom the Lord will not reckon sin" into the anticipatory message of God's redemptive act through Christ. In this sense Paul held a version of the same covenantal and eschatological scheme of thought as 4QMMT; but in his scheme the place that MMT gave to "works of Torah" was taken by "faith."[38] This is for Paul God's faithfulness fulfilled through Christ's and then the participatory faith of the believers.

For Paul God's grace is all-embracing and outside following the works of the law. He made his point quoting Ps 32:1–2a that the words of blessedness refer to the circumcised and to the uncircumcised (4:9ff.). Paul returns to this theme of the new identity in Christ later when he points to Christ's death for our sins and his resurrection for our justification (4:25; cf. 3:22–25; 8:3ff.; 10:5ff.). For Paul the complete restoration of the relationship with God and removal of the sin came about in Christ, in his obedience.

In sum, Gen 15:6, 17:5 (and Ps 32) serve Paul as a supportive argument for God's bigger redemptive purposes apart from the works of the

---

38. N. T. Wright, "4QMMT," 112.

law. If Abraham's faith was interpreted in the 2TP more as his own faith/ faithfulness in a sense of merit or virtue, or obedience in following the Torah, and in this sense as archetypal for later generations, Paul shifts the meaning of it. Faith is always dependent on God and his big purposes. Faith is always faith in God's faithfulness that includes response to or acceptance of God's promises and purposes in the life of his people. For Paul God always acts on behalf of his righteousness/faithfulness and takes the initiative in restoring relationship with people, both Jews and Gentiles. Paul's reference to the scripture has deeper meaning in the narrative of Christ's faithfulness as the revelation of God's faithfulness for all (3:21–25). This anticipates his further explanation of the fulfillment of God's purposes in the light of Christ who upholds the law in himself (5:12–21; 8:1–27; 10:4).

2.4 Paul's Implications of Abraham's Example

Paul considers Abraham's faith in the larger context of God's impartiality and accessibility for all the nations. Abraham's faith is subordinated to the redemption motif that God brought about in Christ. There are several implications from Paul's illustration of Abraham for this study.

First, Paul sets up a "crucial test case" of Abraham[39] in contrast with some 2TP traditions. For Paul Abraham is not the father of the Jews only. The observance of the law does not lead to Abraham's justification before God. Paul refers to the fact that Abraham was justified before his circumcision and without the law of Moses. Abraham was justified by faith as an uncircumcised Gentile, which makes him the father of all uncircumcised who, as Abraham, may turn to God on the same basis of faith in God. Paul's significant conclusion is that Abraham's offspring is more inclusive than 2TP Judaism might present it. All Gentiles who believe are welcomed and righteousness might be credited to them (4:11–12). In Christ this became explicit (1:1–5; 3:21–25).

Second, Paul does not deny that Abraham is the father of all circumcised. Circumcision is the seal of righteousness that he has received by faith (4:11). Abraham's circumcised children still have to walk in the footsteps of his pre-circumcised faith that was considered as righteousness (4:11–12). They are to trust and believe God who alone may reckon people righteous. God alone can forgive the circumcised (Ps 32:1–2 in

---

39. Dunn, *Romans 1–8*, 196.

4:4–6). God alone forgives in Christ because God's Son deals with sin (3:21–25). True circumcision for Paul is not physical but inward, circumcision of heart (3:30; 2:28–29).

Dunn believes that Gen 15:6 has "to be understood prior to and independent of the latter accounts of Abraham's circumcision (4:9–15), and, by implication, of Abraham's offering of Isaac."[40] However, this is not how Paul sees it. Abraham's faith and God's declaration of righteousness (Gen 15:6) are prior but not independent from circumcision. Abraham receives circumcision as a seal of righteousness, as a seal of his covenantal relationship with God based on faith that already includes trust, confidence, fidelity and obedience.[41] Paul extends the understanding of circumcision even further.

Paul explains the notion of circumcision as the circumcision of the heart (2:28–29), which echoes the Deuteronomic idea that the true circumcision is the circumcision of the heart (Deut 10:16–20). Israel was circumcised in the flesh but it was never sufficient. In Deuteronomy the day of this fulfillment is anticipated, "The LORD your God will circumcise your heart and the heart of your descendants, so that you may love him with all your heart and with all your soul, and live" (Deut 30:6). This theme is present in the prophets. Israel was called to circumcise their heart which was reflected in loving and serving the Lord and others, even aliens (cf. Jer 4:4; 9:25–26; Ezek 44:9). Circumcision of the heart is Jeremiah's call in his new-covenant prophesy (Jer 31:31–34). Earlier when Paul considers the value of circumcision he dismisses it as a sign that saves somehow by virtue of being applied to the body (2:25–29). The circumcised Jews who violate God's law are not members of God's people. Paul already proved that that all are under sin (3:9). Not all who are descendants of Israel are Israel (9:7). The true Jew is so inwardly (2:29). The true Jews are circumcised in heart, not by the written code but by the Spirit.

It appears that for Paul Abraham's true descendants are not those who are circumcised or those who follow the observance of the Mosaic law (which is against some 2TP texts, as 1QpHab VII, 17; Jub. 1:23–26) but those who follow the Spirit (2:29). The possibility to follow in Spirit

---

40. Dunn, "Once More, PISTIS CRISTOU," 265.

41. Although circumcision is not a bad thing, it is only a pointer to the covenant relationship based on faith. Paul does not go far off from Gal 3 where he indicates the temporality the covenant of circumcision superseded by Messiah and universal availability of Abrahamic faith. N. T. Wright, "The Letter to the Romans," 494.

for Paul is given in Christ (ch. 8). The true circumcision is then the matter of following Christ. Paul is confident that the Spirit of Christ can guide the believers more effectively than the law. The Spirit of Christ signifies the inauguration of the redemptive history and adoption into the family of God of all nations not just Israel (cf. *Jub.* 1:24–26), as Paul discloses in ch. 8.[42] Thus, for Paul Abraham is the father of all uncircumcised as well as of all circumcised who believe in God's faithfulness revealed through Christ and who are guided by the Spirit of Christ.

Third, Paul reinforces the idea that the covenant relationship is based on God's acceptance of Abraham not on the ground of his special merit or personal qualities, not of his observance of the law (that he did not have yet), not of Abraham's works but on the ground of God's call and Abraham's response to God. Paul refers to Gen 15 to show that God recognizes Abraham's faith and counts him righteous for carrying out his purposes for all the nations. God's acts in the life of Abraham and consequently of Israel are based on God's and not on human righteousness (cf. Deut 9, 32). God always takes the initiative. Abraham's faith is considered within God's bigger purposes (Gen 12:1–3). Paul writes that Abraham was fully persuaded that God had power to do what he has promised (4:21). Faith and God's promise are closely interrelated (4:14).

This concept allows Paul to specify the real children of Abraham and of God himself who are not of natural descendants but according to the promise and by implication according to the faith of Abraham (4:16–17; see also 9:7–8). Although Paul still includes the Jews as chosen by God and the descendants of Abraham, they are no longer automatically to consider themselves the heirs of the promise, Abraham's true children or children of God (9:6–9). Paul demands that they reform and follow Christ. Such a demand could be considered the beginning of attempts at "disinheriting the Jews."[43] However, in Paul's view, it is not so much "disinheriting" as finding true inheritance through Christ by the Holy Spirit (8:14–17; 9:3–8). Paul claims that Abraham's true descendants are children of the promise (9:8). The children of promise are those whom God has called. This promise depends on faith so that it may rest on grace and be guaranteed to all Abraham's descendants (4:16). If God has called both Jews and Gentiles in Christ and they have responded in faith, then they are his true inheritance (8:14–17) and Abraham's descendants (4:16).

---

42. See chapter 3 above.
43. Siker, *Disinheriting the Jews*, 52ff.

Fourth, Paul raises the issue of works and boasting (3:27; 4:2–5). In 4:3 the quote from the LXX of Gen 15:6 is slightly altered by replacement of καί with δέ "thus giving rhetorical emphasis to the antithesis between the scripture and the human tendency to boast." Jewett addresses the issue of boasting in terms of the whole of humanity.[44] Since in Paul the idea of boasting is applied to both Jews and Gentiles (3:27; 4:4–5) it is sensible to say that "Paul praised works that flowed from faith but criticized works that were animated by human pride."[45] If any, Jews or Gentiles, were tempted to boast in their works Paul reminds them that no one's goodness merits God's righteousness (4:4–5).

It is unlikely that Paul introduces the theme of boasting in the works as indictment of the Jews only or as a claim that all Jews were legalists; rather his audience, that consists of both Jews and Gentiles, is reminded that no one's goodness deserves boasting before God. Legalism is neither the point for Israel nor for the Gentiles. The whole emphasis in Paul's view falls on God's faithfulness and his bigger purposes for all nations from the very beginning. No one, starting with Abraham, deserves boasting for themselves in God's project that God himself accomplishes (3:23).

Gathercole approaches the question of boasting in connection with "early Jewish soteriology" exploring Israel's confidence before God and its distinctiveness from the nations. Gathercole suggests that Jewish soteriology was based on both divine election and on final salvation by works.[46] Paul opposes this view. On the one hand, Paul stresses the continuity with the traditional faith of Judaism "at the conceptual level, in the one God." On the other hand, "the God on whom the boast depends has revealed himself decisively in Christ, and so any boast in God must also be "through our Lord Jesus Christ" (5:11)." Gathercole concludes that Paul replaces Torah-boasting with Christ-boasting. Eventually Jews and Gentiles in Christ boast in God through Christ.[47] Thus, Paul (and other believers) may boast in the power of God for the salvation of everyone who believes (1:16).[48] Paul clarifies it even further: they may boast in God through our Lord Jesus Christ, through whom we have received now rec-

---

44. Jewett, *Romans*, 311.

45. Schreiner, *Romans*, 218.

46. Gathercole, *Where is Boasting?*, 90.

47. Ibid., 261.

48. In 1:16 Paul says that he is not ashamed of the power of God revealed in Christ. The language is so strong that implies the opposite: Paul is proud (boasting) of God's power in Christ.

onciliation (5:11). In Romans the theme of boasting does not necessarily raise the contrast between pure faith or trust and good works but points to the significance of God's act in Christ.

Moreover, Abraham's faith and obedience to God is the key issue in relationship with God and deeply rooted in the history of Israel, as stated earlier. When Paul is arguing that Abraham's faith was reckoned to him as righteousness, how could he exclude the obedience notion? Paul does not say that the works are useless. In fact, earlier he affirms that God will give to each person according to what he has done. There will be trouble and distress for both Jews and Gentiles who do evil; and there will be glory, honor and peace for everyone who does good (2:6, 9–10).[49] Paul's emphasis on faith in Romans is on faith and faithfulness and it does not contradict good works. In fact, it flows out of Jewish inclusive concept of faith as trust, faithfulness, obedience honesty, fidelity, and integrity.[50] All the nuances complement and supplement each other. Paul recognizes it even in Abraham's life, "Yet he [Abraham] did not waver through unbelief regarding the promise of God, but was strengthened in his faith and gave glory to God" (4:20). Faith and obedience to the will of God are closely related for Paul. Moreover, they are related with what Christ has accomplished as a part of God's righteousness (cf. 1:5; 15:8; 16:26). Paul insists that God's people, on their part, need to express true obedience to God as circumcision of their hearts (2:28–29; 10:6–16), which is, according to Paul, in Christ, through Christ, and by the Spirit of Christ. Obedience is an outcome of the restored relationship with God through Christ.

When Paul appeals to Abraham's faith referring to Gen 15 he points to Abraham's trustful belief without disregarding other aspects of faith in Abraham's relationship with God. Paul just wants to demonstrate that God recognized Abraham's acceptance of God's promise to bless the nations through him as righteousness while he is still childless and is virtually a Gentile (4:10). On this basis the Gentiles can be justified as well. Although Abraham was considered by the Jews as their ancestor, the basis of his justification is the divine endorsement. Abraham's faith as participation in divine promises makes him the ancestor of both Jews and Gentiles. Abraham's faith/faithfulness continued to be the right response to his relationship with God (4:20–21). In this sense, Abraham's

---

49. The problem of a Jew in ch. 2 is an unrepentant heart. His obedience to Torah or circumcision does not make him a true Jew. See also Gathercole, *Where is Boasting?*, 197ff.

50. See discussion on Hab 2:4 in Rom 1:17.

faith is paradigmatic or archetypal for all Jewish and Gentile believers: faith as not a precondition of receiving God's blessings, but an appropriate response to God's given blessing.

Thus, when Paul turns to Abraham he considers Abraham's faith in the larger context of God's impartiality and accessibility for all the nations. Paul refers to Abraham to show that God's covenant with Abraham embraces the redemption of the whole world and that Abraham is the forefather of more than just his physical descendants (4:13, 16). Paul's point then is not to demonstrate the contradiction of obedience and pure faith. However, he implicitly disagrees with Abraham's meritorious idealization in later Judaism and the narrow perspective on the works of the law within God's covenant with Israel only or simply following the rules. His point is to show that Abraham's faith, including his faithfulness, obedience and righteousness, are understood only in terms of God's own action toward him and his descendants, who are not according to the flesh, law, or even circumcision, but who are children of God's promises (cf. 9:6ff.). For Paul the principle of faith, including all its aspects, is revealed within God's purposes of redemption for the whole world (4:13).

Finally, Abraham's faith in God's faithfulness does not contradict Paul's overall emphasis on Christ's faithful obedience, but allows for "Christ's orientation toward God."[51] Abraham's faith is anticipatory faith in God who calls, promises, and fulfills his promises for Abraham, his physical descendants and for all the nations by raising Jesus from the dead (4:23–25). The redeeming faithfulness comes with Christ who fulfills and reveals God's promises for all the nations. Abraham's story only foreshadows Christ's.

3. Christ's Redemptive Death and the Aqedah[52] Motif

3.1 Introduction: Paul and the Aqedah

Paul sees some resemblance between God giving his Son Jesus and Abraham's binding of Isaac. In 8:32 Paul writes that God gives over his Son to

---

51. Campbell, *The Quest*, 194.

52. Although the term "Aqedah," הדקע (also known as "Binding of Isaac"), taken from Hebrew verb דקע (Gen 22:9), does not appear until the second century AD, and some scholars reserve this term only for the later hermeneutic interpretation of the sacrifice of Isaac (see Davies, Chilton, "The Aqedah," 514–46), other scholars note the interest and the interpretation of Gen 22 throughout Jewish history and prefer to use

redemptive death using the aorist active of the verb, παρέδωκεν. The first part of the phrase, ὅς γε τοῦ ἰδίου υἱοῦ οὐκ ἐφείσατο, in 8:32 echoes the word of the angel to Abraham in Gen 22:12, 16, "you have not withheld your son, your only son."[53] In 4:25 Paul writes that Jesus was delivered over to death for our sins using the aorist passive form of the same verb, παραδίδωμι (παρεδόθη), which may also point to the Aqedah motif.[54]

Some scholars doubt whether the allusion to the Aqedah has any significant force for understanding Paul's letter, since Paul does not develop this theme.[55] Others emphasize the significance of the Aqedah in the OT, in later Judaism, and consequently in Paul.[56] Although much has been suggested in the past, the Aqedah in relation to Romans has not attracted thorough scholarly attention.[57]

Before we study Paul's interaction with Gen 22, it is important to examine the story itself in scripture and in 2TP interpretation.

---

the term generally for the story of Gen 22 in the HB and the following tradition. See R. Daly, "The Soteriological Significance," 45–75; Segal, "He Who Did Not Spare His Own Son," 173; Moberly, "The Earliest Commentary." This study refers to the Aqedah in accordance with the latter group of scholars.

53. The LXX translates וְלֹא חָשַׂכְתָּ אֶת־בִּנְךָ אֶת־יְחִידְךָ מִמֶּנִּי by καὶ οὐκ ἐφείσω τοῦ υἱοῦ σου τοῦ ἀγαπητοῦ δι' ἐμέ, which is also closely related to the theme of God's love to his Son picked up by Paul (8:31–39) and John 3:16. G. Wenham, *Genesis*, 2:117.

54. R. Daly, "Soteriological Significance," 72.

55. For the view that the Aqedah has not been not developed in Paul's time or that Paul repeats the traditional phrasing that contains such an allusion without making any use of it, see Davies and Chilton, "The Aqedah," 530–31; Käsemann, *Romans*, 247; Paulsen, *Überlieferung*, 167; Fitzmyer, *Romans*, 532.

56. The assumption that Romans alludes to the Aqedah is so old and widespread that it is impossible to summarize the history of its interpretation within this research. Most commentators on Romans recognize Paul's allusion to Gen 22 without further development (see, for example, Barrett, D. Moo, Jewett, Wright). Others see God's giving of Jesus as analogous to the Aqedah. See Schwartz, "Two Pauline Allusions," 259–68; Hayward, "The Sacrifice of Isaac," 292–306. Some argue that the Aqedah and its redemptive significance prefigures the redemption of Christ in Paul. See Vermes, *Scripture and Tradition*; Swetnam, *Jesus and Isaac*. Dahl believes that the handing over of Jesus is God's reward to Abraham and his descendants for Abraham's willingness to hand over his son. See Dahl, "The Atonement," 137–53. R. Daly thinks that Paul develops his Christological soteriology from the Aqedah. See his "Soteriological Significance," 66–67. More recently, Campbell also emphasizing the influence of this Jewish tradition upon early Christianity, Paul, and, perhaps, Jesus himself, offers a martyrological reading of Gen 22 in Paul. He suggests considering Jesus' atonement (3:25) as complexity of images, including Isaac's sacrifice on the mount (*The Deliverance*, 653–56, 1106n51). See also Moberly, *The Bible, Theology, and Faith*, 133–34.

57. Campbell, *The Deliverance*, 655.

3.2 The Aqedah in Scripture and Tradition

Von Rad describes Gen 22 as a story where "one must from the first renounce any attempt to discover one basic idea as *the* meaning of the whole. There are many levels of meaning, and whoever thinks he has discovered virgin soil must discover at once that there are many more layers below that."[58] This story begins with God's promise to Abraham (Gen 15:4) being fulfilled only with the birth of Isaac after a long delay (Gen 21:1–7). Isaac is the promised son through whom God is going to make Abraham a father of nations, not Ishmael (Gen 16:15), nor other children from Keturah (Gen 25:2). This does not mean that Ishmael and other children are excluded from the relationship with God. Genesis is very specific in showing how God takes care of them (Gen 21:8–21). It simply means that God's promises to bless Abraham's descendants, and eventually all the nations, are based on his grace and election. Only Isaac is God's heir of promise and election. But on God's command this one (the only son as Gen 22:12, 16 emphasizes) is to be sacrificed. Among an array of other possibilities, the implication of this command then is that the gift of promise is still a gift.[59] Moberly sees here the combination of both God's absolute rights over human life and hope, and his mercy.[60]

The text itself shows that this is God's test for Abraham (Gen 22:1), which, according to Wenham, "will strain Abraham's faith and obedience to the uttermost in order to reveal his deepest emotional attachment."[61] Jon Levenson emphasizes more the reverential obedience in which God's trial of the righteous demonstrates the inner logic and vindication of God's election.[62] Robert Hamerton-Kelly puts it this way, "The unnatural act of turning against one's son . . . becomes the model of faith, which trusts the invisible God to bless one, in his own mysterious way. It is a breaking of the familial ties of patriarchy, a rendering of the order of nature for the sake of opening oneself to the experience of grace."[63] Although Hamerton-Kelly is more interested in analyzing the dynamics of restoring the family relationship within a bigger picture of relationship with God, he is helpful in pointing toward "the initiative of grace and its

---

58. Rad, *Genesis*, 243.
59. Rad marks this implication, ibid., 244.
60. Moberly, "The Earliest Commentary," 305–6.
61. G. Wenham, *Genesis*, 2:113.
62. Levenson, *The Death and Resurrection of the Beloved Son*, 138–39.
63. Hamerton-Kelly, *God the Father*, 31.

transforming power."⁶⁴ It is a test of Abraham's obedience to God as well as a celebration of "the divine initiative of grace," mercy and "transforming power."⁶⁵ A parallel conclusion is drawn by Moberly, who analyzes the meaning of *nissah* (to test) in the context of Gen 22 and a similar occurrence in Deut 8:2 (in relation to Israel): although the emphasis falls upon the appropriate human response, God's involvement is clear. God is "engaged within the encounter in such a way that the outcome is a genuine divine concern."⁶⁶

In Gen 22:5, before the trial, Abraham assures his servants that he and Isaac will come back, which leads to a question: Does Abraham as a man of faith believe that God could raise the dead if that is necessary to fulfill his promise? Genesis does not explain it on those terms; however one NT writer clearly reinterprets this event as Abraham's assurance that God could raise the dead (Heb 11:17–19). In Genesis Abraham simply says, "God will provide" (Gen 22:8). Abraham's faith is faith in the God who is taking care and is trustworthy. In Gen 22 a ram is caught in the thicket and this is God's provision of sacrifice. Abraham names the place Moriah, which means "God will provide" or where "the Lord may be seen", commemorating God who intervenes; God who is faithful and trustworthy, and who "draws near those in deepest distress."⁶⁷

The idea of God's provision and seeing (Gen 22:8, 13, 14) through Abraham's sacrifice of the ram instead of Isaac (v. 13) makes "foreshadowing and subtle allusion" to the burnt offering in the Temple.⁶⁸ First, the name Moriah as the place of seeing (Gen 22:2, 14) is possibly identified as the Temple mount (2 Chr 3:1). Second, the phrase "mount of the LORD" (Gen 22:14b) alludes "to the Temple as the place where Yahweh always 'sees' and provides for his people."⁶⁹

64. Ibid., 34.
65. Moberly, *The Bible, Theology, and Faith*, 106.
66. Ibid., 107.
67. G. Wenham, *Genesis*, 2:115.
68. Moberly, "The Earliest Commentary," 320.
69. Ibid.; also Moberly, *The Bible, Theology, and Faith*, 108–12.This idea finds more expression in post-biblical Judaism. Rabbinic writings show that the "offering of sacrifices were intended as a memorial of Isaac's self-oblation" (Vermes, *Scripture and Tradition*, 209). The firstborn sons of Israel were saved at the time of the first Passover in the light of the blood of the Binding of Isaac. Jews call upon God in prayer to remember to their benefit that sacred act of Abraham and to look favorably and compassionately upon them as a result of it. *Exod. Rab.* 23, 5; *Levi Rab.* 29, 9; *Gen Rab.* 56, 10. See Vermes, *Scripture and Tradition*, 206–9.

The climax of the story is that Abraham obeyed God; and God recognizes this in Gen 22:12, "Now I know that you fear God, because you have not withheld from me your son, your only son." In Gen 22:16 God's recognition of Abraham's obedience has more powerful consequences. His faithful obedience is rewarded with God's blessing, "I will surely bless you and make your descendants as numerous as the stars in the sky and as the sand on the seashore . . . through your offspring all nations on earth will be blessed, because you have obeyed me" (Gen 22:17–18). It appears that Abraham's obedience toward God triggers God's reciprocal action by confirming and fulfilling his promises to Abraham. Von Dobbeler believes that this act of sacrifice corresponds with Abraham's faith and is endowed with the gift of salvation.[70]

However, God confirms his promises that he has made earlier (Gen 12:1–4, 15:5; 17:3–8), implying that they are rooted in the goodwill and purposes of God. Only here these blessings are explicitly pronounced as a reward for Abraham's action. Moberly, therefore, concludes, "A promise which previously was grounded solely in the will and purpose of Yahweh is transformed so that it is now grounded *both* in the will of Yahweh *and* in the obedience of Abraham. It is not that the divine promise has become contingent upon Abraham's obedience, but that Abraham's obedience has been incorporated into the divine promise. Henceforth Israel owes its existence not just to Yahweh but also to Abraham."[71]

He proposes that Gen 22:15–18 is a later addition to the text and, as such, they are a profound canonically recognized commentary within the Abraham cycle as a whole. Their theological implication then is "to draw out the significance of Abraham's obedience in such a way that Abraham can be seen to have a role within the salvation-history of Israel."[72] Whether it is a later addition or not, Gen 22:16 displays the importance of Abraham's obedience of faith that affirms and extends God's previous promises; and finds further theological development in Judaism.

In the 2TP Abraham "emerges as the paragon of uprightness"[73] and as an observer of the law. In *Jubilees* the story of Isaac's sacrifice has a different narrative nuance, as Prince Mastema tempts Abraham to offer Isaac. As in *Jubilees*' reading of Job 1–2 Mastema tries to "cross God's

---

70. Dobbeler, *Glaube als Teilhabe*, 119.

71. Moberly, "The Earliest Commentary, 321. He affirms his conclusions more recently in Moberly, *The Bible, Theology, and Faith*, 119–20.

72. Moberly, "The Earliest Commentary, 321.

73. Fitzmyer, *Romans*, 370.

plan and to make ineffective God's promise to Abraham of a progeny numerous as the stars" (*Jub*.17:15—18:13, cf. 4Q225).[74] But God knows that Abraham is faithful even before the trial because he tested him many times (*Jub*. 17:17–18). When Abraham is asked to offer his beloved son, he again obeys God. Mastema is ashamed and God pronounces his blessing as in Gen 22:12, 16 (*Jub*. 18:11, 15-16). However, *Jubilees* adds an interesting phrase to God's blessing, "And I have made known to all that you are faithful to me in everything which I say to you" (*Jub*. 18:16b). It appears that God sets up Abraham as an example of faithfulness making him known to all. Then Abraham observed "the feast of the LORD" for seven days and it was ordained for Israel to observe this feast (*Jub*. 18:18–19). Abraham lived a long life also because he "was perfect in all his actions with the Lord and was pleasing through righteousness all of the days of his life" (*Jub*. 23:10).

In First Maccabees 2:52 Abraham was found faithful, when tested, alluding to both Gen 15 and 22. In Sirach Abraham is described as the father of nations (cf. Gen 17:4) and "no one has been found like him in glory. He kept the law of the Most High, he entered into covenant with him; he certified the covenant in his flesh, and when he was tested he proved faithful" (Sir 44:20). It appears that Abraham's obedience certainly has significant beneficial consequence for his descendants.[75]

The second important point in the development of the Aqedah is the role of Isaac. The Genesis account is silent about Isaac's attitude to the offering while the Aqedah tradition attributes to him willingness to offer himself in obedience to God. In Judith 8:26 Isaac is also tested by God, "Remember what he [God] did with Abraham, and how he tested Isaac." While Gen 22:17 pronounces a solemn blessing of Abraham, 4Q225 concludes with the blessing of Isaac, "And God YHWH blessed Isa[ac all the days of his life . . .]" (4Q225 2 II, 10).[76]

In later Jewish texts, such as in *4 Maccabees*, Isaac is the proto-martyr. He was offered as a burnt offering (*4 Macc.*18:12). He is listed among

---

74. Martinez, "The Sacrifice of Isaac in 4Q 225," 49–51; Oh, "Holiness of Abraham," 185–89. Jealous angels prompted God to demand the sacrifice of Isaac in Pseudo-Philo (*Bib. Ant.* 32:2, 4).

75. A modern Jewish prayer to God asks to remember us (Jews) on the basis of Abraham's sacrifice evoking "the binding with which our father Abraham bound his son Isaac on the altar appear before Thee" (Machzor for Rosh Hashanah, in Plaut et al., *The Torah*, 153).

76. See further on that Martinez, "The Sacrifice of Isaac in 4Q 225," 56.

those who surrendered their bodies to suffering for piety's sake and were not only admired by humankind but were also deemed worthy of a divine portion (*4 Macc.* 18:3; cf. *4 Macc* 14:20ff.; *Bib. Ant.* 40:2–3). In 16:20, Isaac, seeing his father's hand with a knife in it, did not flinch. This text also exhorts to endure hardship for God's sake (*4 Macc.* 16:19–20), implying that the righteous one does endure all for God's sake (*4 Macc.* 16:21). The author lists Abraham, Isaac and Daniel among those people. In *4 Macc.* 13:12 Isaac "gave himself to be sacrificed for piety's sake." In the rabbinic tradition the development of this idea went further. In the words of Rabbi Akiva, as reported by R. Meir, "Isaac bound himself upon the altar" (*Sif. Deut* 32;[77] cf. Pseudo-Philo *Bib. Ant.* 18:5; 32:2–4; 40:2;[78] Josephus *Ant.* 1:225–36).[79]

In *Biblical Antiquities* 18:5 Isaac's offering is acceptable before God on account of his blood. It is related to God's blessings of Abraham's seed. Isaac plays a significant role in the offering as he answers Abraham, "Yet have I not been born into the world to be offered as a sacrifice to him who made me? Now my blessedness will be above that of all men, because there will be nothing like this; and about me future generations will be instructed and through me the peoples will understand that the LORD has made the soul of a man worthy to be a sacrifice" (*Bib. Ant.* 32:3).

Isaac encourages Abraham to consider his offering positively and beneficially. Moreover, in the light of animal sacrifices (*Bib. Ant.* 18:3) this is "a claim of expiatory efficacy for Isaac's sacrifice."[80] This section concludes with God's words to Abraham, "Now your memory will be before me always, and your name and his will remain from one generation to another (*Bib. Ant.* 32:4). But since the importance of Isaac's "full, active and consenting status" in the story is already established, "Isaac's submissive cooperation" becomes "essential to the divine plan" and together with Abraham's obedience "a warrant of God's blessings upon Israel."[81] While the latter referred texts are at least as late as 70 CE and post-Pauline, they

---

77. See Fitzmyer, "The Sacrifice of Isaac," 228.

78. On Pseudo-Philo, see Fisk, "Offering Isaac," 481–507.

79. Martinez, "The Sacrifice of Isaac in 4Q 225," 53; Fitzmyer, "The Sacrifice of Isaac," 219, 229.

80. Fisk, "Offering Isaac," 495.

81. Ibid. Vermes who studied Rabbinic texts, concludes that "Isaac's merit was due Israel's salvation and the preservation of his descendants from death and divine disfavour" (*Scripture and Tradition*, 207).

do not diminish, but rather support earlier references about Isaac's involvement in the drama and his importance for the future of Israel.

In sum, the theme of human obedience in Genesis 22 became more prominent in 2TP. Later Judaism paints Abraham as an observer of the law. It ascribes Abraham a reward for his fidelity to God's commandments when he was tested. Moreover, not only Abraham, but also Isaac became a model of obedience and an example for Jewish martyrdom. As a consequence, Abraham, Isaac and his descendants were rewarded by God. In this approach the faithfulness of God and his pro-active agency is no longer the primary focus. The Aqedah with its emphasis on human obedience became a significant part within God's redemptive plan for Israel.

3.3 The Aqedah and Obedience in Paul

Paul makes no direct reference to the Aqedah when he describes Abraham. Given the importance of Abraham's obedience in the 2TP literature, it is likely that Paul was aware of the Aqedah and therefore alluded to it.[82] It is unconvincing that in 8:32 Paul uses a known liturgical formula that refers to the Aqedah, but he himself does not refer to it.[83] The evidence advanced above supports Daly's view that the Aqedah was already known in the first century.[84] But his reason that the Aqedah was too Jewish or that readers would recognize even the slightest allusion to it does not explain Paul's treatment of the subject.

This study proposes that the Aqedah has some influence on Paul's theological argument in the letter. If Abraham's obedience and Isaac's sufficient sacrifice became significant factors in God's redemptive plan for Israel in 2TP, then Paul shifts the focus to God. He rethinks the Aqedah against his Jewish background and develops it theologically in the light of God's act through Christ's obedience that concerns Israel and all the nations.

For Paul, God fulfills his purposes for humankind based on his own faithfulness and righteousness that has been revealed through Christ's faithful obedience (3:22; 5:12–21). When he describes Abraham in chapter four, he does not give just an example of someone who is justified

---

82. Against Fitzmyer, *Romans*, 532.

83. Against Käsemann, *Romans*, 247. Even if it is a liturgical formula, Paul uses it for his own purposes in the letter.

84. R. Daly, "Soteriological Significance," 72.

by faith.[85] Paul refers to the Genesis narrative to emphasize God's initiative and faithfulness toward his promises to all the nations. He considers Abraham as the father of the nations in the sight of God who gives life to the dead (4:16–17) and who raised Jesus from the dead. God's righteousness, redemption, and purposes for humanity have been revealed in Christ because of his obedience (1:1–5; 3:22; 5:12–21). Abraham's not sparing his son and Isaac's almost sacrifice did not have redemptive consequence. Redemption depended upon the act of God in Christ, God's own Son (3:21–26). Abraham became the father of the nations in anticipation through God's faithfulness fulfilled in Christ's obedience.

Paul acclaims this result through some careful moves. When he alludes to Gen 22 in 8:32, he builds up a parallel between Abraham and God. For Paul, the language of God being the Father who redeems through his Son is crucial. Thus, the parallel between God and Abraham undoubtedly emphasizes the fatherhood of God. Abraham loved his son, the only son of the promise, yet was ready to sacrifice him in obedience to God. In the same way, God is a loving Father who offers his only Son.

This is true in 8:31–39 where Paul sums up the love of God manifested in Christ after he had shown that in Christ there is redemption from death, sin, self and even the law. Paul praises the divine love of God who gave the best he possibly could, his own Son. L. Hurtado sees in this act "God's great generosity and the length he went to in order to secure redemption of the elect."[86] The elect ones in Paul's context are Jews and Gentiles in Christ. Abraham expresses trust and obedience to God, believing that God fulfills his promises for him and his descendants. When God gives up his Son, he expresses his love toward humanity (ὑπὲρ ἡμῶν πάντων). God's intention is to redeem it even if he has to hand over his own Son in order to accomplish it. So, if Paul draws a parallel between Abraham in Gen 22 and God, this parallel is only a limited analogy that he reinterprets it in the light of God's faithfulness through Christ's obedience for all who believe (3:21–25; 5:12–21).

While the majority of scholars notice the partial parallel between Abraham and God's not sparing his Son, only a few see the parallel between the Aqedah and God who did not spare his son Israel in Rom 11.[87] Hays explains that Abraham did not spare his son and received him

---

85. N. T. Wright, *Justification*, 190.
86. Hurtado, "Jesus' Divine Sonship," 232.
87. Hays, *Echoes*, 62.

through God's intervention. God did not spare his Son, but vindicated him through resurrection. This also applies to Israel, God's son.[88] God did not spare (ἐφείσατο) his son Israel but broke it off as branches for the sake of the Gentiles (11:21). Paul uses the same verb in Greek for not sparing Israel as for his Son in 8:32, which echoes LXX Gen 22:12, 16.

If Hays is right and Paul really has this threefold parallel in his mind, there might be room for further theological reflection. Paul draws parallels not only between Abraham and God who gives up his Son but also between Jesus and Israel alluding to Gen. 22 language. God is faithful to Abraham and Israel not only for the sake of Israel but for the sake of all people so that God's universal purposes would be fulfilled (10:11–13). God did not spare Israel for the sake of the Gentiles. This thought is expressed in 11:11. In Hays' words, Israel "undergoes rejection for the sake of the world, bearing suffering vicariously."[89] However, Paul's main emphasis is on Christ's obedience. While Israel is disobedient, Christ is the obedient Son. God's salvation comes despite Israel's transgression through the faithfulness of God's Son to all who believe (3:22; 5:12–21). Christ confirms the promises given to the patriarchs and in order that the Gentiles might glorify God (15:8–9). Even Israel's failure is of great benefit for the Gentiles (11:11–12), which is already the blessing of the nations in action. Israel's transgression (11:11–12) and disobedience (11:30) is "the necessary context for the Messiah's death, and as such [it] has become part of the saving plan."[90] If Paul alludes to the Aqedah in this discussion, he again re-thinks it in the light of God's action through Christ's obedience where Israel plays an important sacrificial role and points to a greater sacrifice of God's own Son.

Paul takes a slightly different tack in 4:23. Here he draws a parallel between Abraham's faith and the faith of Christians. Their common faith is directed toward God who makes and fulfills his promises. Again, Paul's idea of Abraham's faith (4:1–25) is not to show how his faith or obedience plays an important role in God's justification. Rather, he refers to Abraham's faith to prove God's universal purposes. In this context Moberly notes, "Abraham is not a model of blessing to which others aspire, but a channel of blessing to which others, through faith, attain."[91] Hays

---

88. Ibid.
89. Ibid., 61.
90. N. T. Wright, "The Letter to the Romans," 680.
91. Moberly, *The Bible, Theology, and Faith*, 121.

sharpens the description of their common faith even further, "Abraham typologically prefigures Christian believers, whose faith—note carefully—is said to be directed not toward Jesus but toward the God who raised Jesus."[92] The emphasis in both cases falls on God who begins and brings to completion the promises of blessing the nations.

When Paul draws the parallel between Abraham's faith and Christians', he may be alluding to Gen 22. If so, he may also imply that Abraham believed in God who could raise Isaac from the dead. Paul is not as explicit as Hebrews is on this (Heb. 11:17–19); however he states that Abraham believed in God as the one who gives life to the dead (4:17) and who had power to do what he has promised. In other words, Paul may describe not only the way of God's opening of Sarah's womb, which was dead and providing an heir, but also Abraham's growing faith in God who fulfills his promises even by raising from the dead. If so, then Paul means Abraham's faith, including his hope, trust and faithfulness in God of resurrection and life, are typological for the believers (4:24).

Moreover, Paul does not easily distinguish between believing in God and being loyal to God (cf. 10:9–10 where he combines verbal confession with belief in the heart).[93] Abraham's faith includes trust, belief, fidelity and faithful obedience. Abraham grows strong in his faith (4:20–21). Abraham's faith/faithfulness continues to be the right response to his relationship with God. In this sense, Abraham's faith is paradigmatic or archetypal for all Jewish and Gentile believers: faith as not a precondition of receiving God's blessings, but an appropriate response to God's given blessing.

Although there is a parallel between the faith of Abraham and Christians as faith in God, the content of the faith differs: Paul particularly stresses the fact of Jesus' death and resurrection as a part of Christian faith in God (4:25). Their faith is in God who already gave Jesus over to death for their sins and raises him for their justification. For Paul, Christian faith is specified by Christ's obedient act that he has fully developed in his letter. For Paul, God acts on behalf of his own righteousness that is revealed in Christ's faithful obedience (1:17; 3:22; 5:12–21). Through his obedience and in him people may be made righteous (5:19) and live a new life (6:4). Abraham's faith is anticipatory faith in God, who fulfills promises. Christian faith is in God who has already acted in Christ and in whom the new era of redemption has begun. In Christ, on the basis

---

92. Hays, *The Faith*, 286.
93. N. T. Wright, "The Letter to the Romans," 468.

of faith both Jews and Gentiles join God's family (8:14–17) and live in obedience to God, conforming to the likeness of his Son (8:29) as living sacrifices, holy and acceptable to God (12:1).

Now, does Paul draw any parallel between the Aqedah and Jesus' faithful obedience? James Dunn does not think so. In fact, when Paul refers to Abraham in chapter 4, his intention is to show Abraham as the model of trustful faith, and the Aqedah would contradict the development of Paul's argument. Thus, Paul does not picture Abraham's faithfulness as a prototype of Jesus' faithfulness and consequently as a model of Jewish-Christian faithfulness. Rather, Abraham's faith in God is an objective faith, which is a prototype of objective trustful faith in Christ of all believers.[94]

First, Dunn is right that Paul draws a picture of Abraham's faith in God and God's faithfulness. God chooses Abraham not on the basis of his performance but on the basis of God's own righteousness and love in order to bless people through Abraham. Abraham is justified apart from his works. The problem with focusing on the Aqedah lies in the tendency to attend only to the "trial" itself, leaving aside the context and the history of the long God-Abraham relationship where God takes the initiative. By Gen. 22 Abraham not only believed God, he has developed a strong confidence in God's goodwill and competence.[95] Abraham continues to believe, trust and obey God who makes and affirms his promises in Gen. 12, 15, 17 and 22. Abraham puts his faith in God's faithfulness, thus God reckoned him righteous. This is the idea behind Paul's interpretation of Abraham in chapter 4.

Second, although Paul recognizes that Abraham grew in faith as his response to God, and gave glory to God (4:20), his obedient faith by itself was not redemptive for humankind, not even for Israel (2:1—3:20). Paul argues that sin has been in the world from the time of Adam over all Abraham's descendants (5:12–21). Christ's obedience is redemptive and brings righteousness to many; he liberates from sin (3:21–26; 5:1–21; 6:1–23). M. Hooker writes that, "in spite of his faith, Abraham was 'ungodly'—part of fallen mankind. It was necessary for Christ to come in the likeness of sinful man—to share our humanity—in order to receive the sin of Adam, and enable men and women to share his righteousness."[96]

---

94. Dunn, "Once More, ΠΙΣΤΙΣ ΧΡΙΣΤΟΥ," 265–66.
95. See discussion on that in Lee, "Abraham in a Different Voice," 377–400.
96. Hooker, *From Adam to Christ*, 170.

God finally reveals his righteousness to Jews and Gentiles through the complete faithfulness of his Son (3:22), which is unparallel to Abraham or Israel for that matter.

The question still remains whether there are any redemptive implications of the Aqedah in relation to Isaac that may impact Paul's view of Christ's redemptive death?

3.4 The Aqedah and Atonement in Paul

Since the Aqedah plays a significant part within God's redemptive purposes for Israel in later Judaism and is considered as a reward by God, Nils Dahl believes that the handing over of Jesus is God's reward to Abraham and his descendants for Abraham's willingness to hand over his son.[97] Vermes goes even further arguing that Isaac's self-offering served a key to the doctrine of redemption and was used by Paul to interpret the death of Jesus as atonement.[98]

Paul might have referred to Abraham's willingness to obey God when he speaks about God handing over his Son (8:32 or Israel in 11:11–32), emphasizing the idea of God the Father who redeems through his Son (4:25). However, Paul lacks any allusion to Isaac. One reason could well be that any parallel breaks down over the resurrection. Although Isaac is returned to Abraham, he dies again. Jesus dies but is resurrected by God. Isaac's almost death is certainly not a key to interpret Jesus' death and resurrection.

Behind the Aqedah for Paul is divine intervention just as behind the death of God's Son is divine action: God reconciles us to himself (5:10; 8:3). Moreover, God's divine action is inseparable from Christ's atonement (3:21–26). The atoning sacrifice becomes effective through Christ's faithful obedience (3:22, 26) that has redemptive consequences for all (cf. 5:12–21). Campbell describes it succinctly when he refers to Christ's ἱλαστήριον "as something singular in relation to the broader process of atonement and reconciliation."[99] For Paul, because Jesus was obedient to death, he was vindicated by God through resurrection (6:4). In the same way, all Christians who have been united with Christ in his death will be

---

97. Dahl, "The Atonement," 137–51.

98. Vermes, *Scripture and Tradition in Judaism*, 218. Earlier Shoeps, "The Sacrifice of Isaac," 385–92.

99. Campbell, *The Deliverance*, 654.

united with him in his resurrection (6:5). Isaac's almost sacrifice could not and did not accomplish that.

Christ's obedience to the death takes on deeper poignancy when it is viewed as the death of God's Son himself. Thus, the parallel between Isaac and Jesus is not adequate to show the depth of Christ's faithful obedience and redemptive consequences for all the people. Indeed, Jesus' sacrificial death rather corresponds with the death of the ram.[100] It is possible that Paul sees Jesus as a sacrificial ram when he describes Jesus' atoning sacrifice (3:25; 8:3) that completes and abolishes Israel's sacrificial system (3:21–26).

Campbell looks at Christ's death as both a recapitulation of the "Yom Kippur cultus" and in relation to the death of the Jewish martyrs in 4 Macc.[101] If Abraham's sacrifice of the ram anticipates the burnt offerings in the temple and Mount Moriah is associated with the Temple mount, then Jesus is truly the fulfillment of the sacrifices and the fulfillment of God's promises to Abraham and all the nations. However, if the temple sacrifices were associated with the merit of Isaac, or if Isaac's obedience was redemptive in any sense, as the later Jewish development of the story demonstrates, then Paul shifts the focus away from Isaac's obedience to Abraham and to the divine initiative and faithfulness accomplished in the obedience of God's own Son. Paul's emphasis is on the gospel of God concerning his Son, through whom all the Gentiles are called into obedience of faith (1:1–5).

Christ's obedience to death is qualitatively different from either the deaths of any martyrs or the almost sacrifice of Isaac. Jesus' death is better understood in terms of the suffering servant of Isaiah 53.[102] Like Abraham, the servant makes an offering and he will see his offspring (Isa. 53:10). Like Isaac he was "like a lamb that is led to the slaughter" (Isa. 53:7). Like the Isaac of the Aqedah tradition, he offered himself, rather than anyone else. But unlike Abraham and Isaac, the servant actually died (Isa. 53:8–9), bearing the sin of many (Isa. 53:12). Paul alludes several times to the

---

100. The analogy between the lamb being sacrificed and the appellation of Jesus as "the Lamb of God" is explicit in the NT (John 1:29; 1 Pet 1:19–20). Already Melito, Bishop of Sardis (AD 150–180), draws a parallel between Jesus and the ram, arguing that just as the ram redeemed Isaac, so does the Lord redeem the world. Melito of Sardis, *From the Catena on Genesis*.

101. Campbell, *The Deliverance*, 655.

102. The possibilities of the suffering servant motif are also discussed by Hengel, *Atonement*, 36; Segal, "'He Who Did Not Spare His Own Son,'" 178; Jipp, "Rereading the Story," 229–30.

suffering servant motif of Isaiah throughout Romans (4:24-25; 5:15-19; 10:16; 15:21). Although Paul does not draw this imagery into an explicit basis for his interpretation of Jesus, in Hays' words, Paul's "transumptive silence cries out for the reader to complete the trope."[103]

The only remaining parallel to Genesis here is that Abraham's blessing might come upon the Gentiles. In Gal. 3:13-14 Paul paraphrases Gen. 22:18 that "in your seed all the nations of the earth shall be blessed." But he argues strongly that all these blessings are fulfilled in Christ, the crucified and resurrected Messiah and the Son of God because of his faithful obedience (1:1-5; 5:12-21). In him Abraham's descendants according to the flesh and all the nations of the earth are called into obedience of faith and into God's family (1:5; 8:14). In this sense Jesus is the new kind of Isaac: in him Abraham's promises were fulfilled, and his obedience has redemptive consequences for Israel and all the nations. But Paul never explicitly draws out this connection.

4. Conclusions

Paul refers to Abraham to show that God's covenant with Abraham embraces the redemption of the whole world, and that Abraham is the forefather of more than just his physical descendants. Paul considers Abraham's faith within a larger context of God's impartiality and accessibility for all the nations. Paul's point is to show that Abraham's faith and obedience are understood only in response to God's primary action toward him and all the nations.

When Paul alludes to the Aqedah, he shifts the emphasis to God's act in the story. It is not Abraham's obedience that is redemptive, but the righteousness/faithfulness, mercy and love of God for the whole of humanity. God the Father, like Abraham, did not spare his own Son as he did not spare Israel for the sake of the world. Paul reinterprets the Aqedah in the light of God's action through Christ's obedience. Christ is like the new type of Isaac, in whom Abraham's promises to bless the nations were fulfilled. But he actually dies and is resurrected by God. Through his faithful obedience many will become righteous. Thus, Paul has a radical re-reading of the Aqedah as God's story of redemption that has come about in Christ's obedience to the Father.

103. Hays, *Echoes*, 63.

CHAPTER VI

Christ's Obedience versus Adam's Disobedience

1. Introduction

THE PROBLEM WITH ROMANS 5-8 generally, as A. Schweitzer observed some time ago, is that, instead of moving on to a new area of discussion, Paul picks up the same topic as in 1-4—the universality of sin, the role of the law, the death of Christ and the redemptive consequences for the believers—albeit from an altered perspective. Schweitzer explains this perspective as the distinction between "righteousness by faith" and the "mysticism of being in-Christ."[1] The majority of modern scholars recognise this alternative perspective as well (Wright, Jewett, Longenecker, Fitzmyer, Dunn).[2] However, they see it in terms of God's righteousness revealed in Christ and the consequences of being in Christ. Even within this view some scholars like Fitzmyer and Dunn still insist that Paul moves into an explanation of the consequences of faith in Christ Jesus leaving aside Paul's focus on Christ's own faithfulness in God's purposes for the created order and Christian participation in Christ's faithfulness.[3] But if Paul unfolds in Romans the theme of God's faithfulness revealed in the faithfulness of Christ (1:1-7; 1:16-17; 3:21-26) through whom we receive reconciliation (5:1-11), Paul's discussion on obedience in 5:12-21 becomes an explicit explanation of Christ's own faithfulness as the fulfillment of God's purposes for the world. This explanation comes

---

1. Schweitzer, *The Mysticism of Paul the Apostle*, 225-26.
2. N. T. Wright, "The Letter to the Romans," 508-14; Jewett, *Romans*, 344-47; R. Longenecker, "The Focus of Romans," 61-69; Fitzmyer, *Romans*, 405; Dunn, *Romans 1—8*, 242-44.
3. Fitzmyer, *Romans*, 393; Dunn, "Once More, ΠΙΣΤΙΣ ΧΡΙΣΤΟΥ," 265-56.

for Paul through the contrast between Adam and Christ, which requires some unpacking of the problem of Adam (5:12-14) before we can see what God has accomplished in Christ (5:15-21).

2. The Impact of Adam

In his commentary on Romans Fitzmyer writes,

> I distinguish "Adam" in Genesis 2-3 as a symbolic figure from "Adam" in 5:12-21 as a historical individual, or as a historicized individual, as he had already become in contemporary Jewish literature. Paul, however, knew nothing about the Adam of history. What he knows about Adam, he has derived from Genesis and the Jewish tradition that developed from Genesis. "Adam" for Paul is *Adam in the Book of Genesis;* he is a literary individual, like Hamlet, but not symbolic, like Everyman. Adam is for Paul what Jonah was for the evangelist Matthew (12:40) and Melchizedek for the author of the Epistle to the Hebrews (7:3). All three have been used as foils for Christ. But they are literary figures who have or have not been historicized, as the case may be.[4]

This statement raises a number of questions. How does Genesis depict Adam and what is the impact of Adam in Jewish thought that could be known to Paul? How does Paul reinterpret the tradition of Adam and to what extent does Adam serve as a foil for Christ? While most of these questions must remain unanswered in this study, some account must be given of how the contrast between Adam and Christ enables Paul to illuminate the theme of God's redemption made possible through Christ's obedience.

2.1 Adam's Disobedience in Scripture and Tradition

The etiology of Adam's disobedience derived from Gen 2-3 depicts Adam and Eve as having brought sin into life through yielding to the temptation of the serpent. The story states that sin originated not with God but with human beings who covet to become like God (3:5). The consequences of human disobedience are a distorted relationship with God, dysfunctional human relationships, ecological degradation and death. Genesis introduces the notion of Adam's broken condition in human life generation after generation (3:16-24).

---

4. Fitzmyer, *Romans*, 410.

Adam's name reappears briefly in the opening genealogy in 1 Chr 1:1. In Ezekiel 28:11-19 there is a description of the ruler of Tyre. This description has been drawn from the theme and imagery of Gen 2-3.[5] Ezekiel describes the ruler being in the garden of God, full of wisdom and blameless in his ways (Ezek 28:13, 15). The ruler's disobedience like Adam's came "through the abundance of trade" (Ezek 28:16). A human being was filled with violence and sinned (Ezek 28:16). The Lord turned him to ashes on the earth (Ezek 28:18). This allusion is pronounced in terms of judgment against Tyre and other nations. The day of God's wrath was soon to come, but not on Israel alone. Later, the author returns to the message of hope and redemption for the people of God, Israel (Ezek 33-48), bringing them back to life (Ezek 37) and to glory (Ezek 43).

In later Jewish tradition the theme of Adam becomes more prominent. It appears not only in terms of the creation of humanity (Tob 8:6; Sir 33:10) but also in terms of Adam's transgression and his influence upon following generations that brought death and cut off the years of those who were born from him (Sir 40:1). The whole multitude is going to corruption as a consequence (2 Bar. 48:42; cf. 17:3; 23:4; 54:15; 4 Ezra 3:7; 3:21; 7:118). Second Baruch 54:19 says that individuals are also responsible for their deaths, "Adam is, therefore, not the cause, except only for himself, but each of us has become our own Adam." *Fourth Ezra* holds that the evil heart from which Adam's sin proceeded had developed in all who were descended from him (4 Ezra 3:21-27; 4:30; 7:48, 118).

Other texts take a notoriously negative view of women; the origin of sin is traced to Eve and because of her we all must die (Sir 25:24; cf. 2 En. 30:17; Apoc. Adam 21:1; Apoc. Mos. 14; 32:1, 2; Sib. Or. 1: 50-54).[6] The transgressions and sin that are brought upon the generations are ascribed to "our parents" in Bib. Ant. 44:2 and 2 Bar. 48:42.

Some texts associate sin with the angels' involvement or the devil's envy. In Wisdom 2:23-24 God created man for incorruption and made him the image of his own eternity, but through the devil's envy death came into the world. In Wisdom 10:1-2 the allusion is made that wisdom herself delivered the first formed father of the world from his transgression, and gave him strength to rule over all things. The book of *Jubilees* establishes the angelic story of Gen 6:1-4 (Jub.3:17-31; 4:15, 22; 5:1-12; 7:21-25)

---

5. Ezekiel alludes to the story of the first human. See Darr, "The Book of Ezekiel, 1391-95; Block, *The Book of Ezekiel*, 110.

6. See Collins, *Jewish Wisdom in the Hellenistic Age*, 80-81.

where the depravity of humanity is traced to the daughters of humankind being seduced by the angels (cf. *1 En.* 6:1–6; 7:1; 10:8–9).[7]

In 1QS evil is conceived of as being instituted by God as part of creation.[8] 1QS III, 15 states that God is the sole creator of all things and that before they came into existence, he had "made all their plans," while 1QS III, 16 asserts that once things come into being, they will execute all their works in compliance with his instructions without altering anything. Another scroll states that people themselves walk in the ways of truth or injustice, respectively (1QS IV, 24). These passages emphasize a strong belief in predestination with the implication that the "sons of light" did not choose their way of life, but had been appointed by God at their creation. The righteous ones are righteous only because they have been chosen by God. Thus, in 1 QS IV, 23, when God destroys the spirit of deceit and all things associated with him, some will be purified and allowed to enter into "all the glory of Adam."[9]

Some other texts also emphasize the glory of Adam. In Sir 49:16 Adam is highly honored among other famous ancestors, but Adam's glory is above every living being. Adam is bestowed by God with blessings and he is regarded as one of the patriarchs (*Jub.* 19:25). In CD III, 20 the elect ones are promised the "glory of Adam."

In sum, the perception of Adam's disobedience recorded in Genesis is rather diverse in Jewish tradition. Some texts recognize Adam's disobedience (or the disobedience of both parents) and the influence of his consequences on his descendants. Some blame only Eve. Yet, some blame individuals for their own transgressions. Others depict the shift of the blame of sin towards angelic (based on Gen 6) or the devil's involvement and ascribe glory to Adam, which also will be given to the elect ones of Israel.

---

7. The author of *1 En.* does not even mention the Genesis 3 story giving full play to the angelic involvement in an epidemic of evil over generations possibly, according to Vanderkam, perceiving a deficiency in the text of Genesis. See Vanderkam, "The Interpretation of Genesis in 1 Enoch," 139.

8. Charlesworth, "A Critical Comparison of the Dualism, 80. It is possible that this concept of evil derives from Zoroastrian dualism, though it has been modified for a Jewish context, see Collins, *Seers, Sibyls and Sages*, 287.

9. See further Collins, *Apocalypticism in the Dead Sea Scrolls*, 48.

2.2 Paul's View of Adam's Disobedience

Apparently, Paul returns to the origin of the problem with Adam in 5:12–14. He begins in 5:12, "Therefore, just as sin came into the world through one man." Paul avoids any speculative formulations about the angels' or the devil's involvement that were present in the 2TP.[10] Likewise, he does not say anything about the single fault of Eve in the story of disobedience.[11] He does not even name Adam yet, although Adam is meant here as he unfolds the theme. Sin for Paul came into the world through one man. The focus is rather on sin related to human beings not God.

Historically, scholars tried to find the answer to the question of the origin of sin in Pauline writing.[12] However Paul does not develop a clear answer on that. Paul unfolds the universal consequences of sin rather than its origin. He simply says that sin entered the world through one man and death through sin (5:12). In verses 16, 18 Paul depicts the consequence of Adam's sin in terms of condemnation. If death is the consequence of sin, then condemnation is the divine sentence that is pronounced upon sin. In both cases the consequence is universal: for all people.[13]

Like Ezekiel, Paul pronounces judgment for all the nations, including Israel (cf. Ezek 28). Paul says that death came to all people. This agrees with Genesis and some 2TP texts (Sir 40:1; *2 Bar.* 48:42; cf. 17:3; 23:4; 54:15; *4 Ezra* 3:7; 3:21; 7:118). Paul, however, emphasizes more the concomitant cause of death in terms that "all have sinned."

---

10. The angelic language in general is not foreign to Paul. In 8:38–39 he says that no ἄγγελοι will be able to separate us from the love of God in Christ. Elsewhere Paul refers to ἄγγελοι as the otherworldly messengers either sent by God (Gal 1:8; 4:14; 1 Cor 4:9) or as fallen and posing a threat to humans (1 Cor 6:3; 11:10; 2 Cor 12:7). If Paul is familiar with the Jewish angelic tradition of the involvement in human transgression, he certainly does not connect it with the fall but admits that nobody, including ἄγγελοι, can contend with God who reveals his love and redemption in Christ (8:38).

11. In 2 Cor 11:3, Paul says that since the serpent deceived Eve the thoughts of humankind are led astray, also implying that it is through human beings sin came into the world. This time he refers to Eve, in Watson's words, "to ensure the balance of the analogy" (*Paul, Judaism, and Gentiles*, 274). In 1 Tim. 2:14–15 the author is more direct in blaming Eve, however, the relationship that is in view there is that of husband and wife, and not of man and woman.

12. Cranfield, *Romans*, 1:269–95; Tobin, *Paul's Rhetoric*, 161.

13. Paul does not use Jews/Gentiles language here anymore, that has dominated the letter up to this point. He rather embraces all people under the dominion of Adam.

Paul unfolds this all-embracing idea from the very beginning: all people sinned and are without excuse (1:20).[14] Generally speaking, in 1:18—3:20 Paul has delivered the message of both Jews and Gentiles being guilty before God and in the power of sin. Moreover, when 5:12-21 is read in the light of 1:18—3:20, v. 12 shows that Adam's sin and the presence of sin in the world are somehow connected. Paul says in 12b, "death came through sin, and so death spread to all because (ἐφ' ᾧ) all have sinned (ἥμαρτον)." The question is whether the verb ἥμαρτον refers to the actual sins of all people or to the primal act of Adam. It depends on how ἐφ' ᾧ is translated. If ᾧ is a masculine pronoun, it may refer to an implied law, death or Adam who passed hereditary depravity to his descendants. The meaning would be "in him all have sinned." However, in this case ἐν would be more appropriate than ἐπι. A neuter ᾧ gains the conjunctive sense of "because," "so that," which can be interpreted as a reference to the involuntary participation of humans in Adam's sin or to independent human actions following the example of Adam. This interpretation fits Paul's argument as we shall see.[15]

N. T. Wright is concerned that the aorist tense of the verb is better taken as a reference to Adam. However, he realizes that within Paul's narrative emphasis on "all have sinned," the former sounds plausible. Wright's conclusion is that, "Paul's meaning must in any case be both that an entail of sinfulness has spread throughout the human race from its first beginnings and that each individual has contributed their own share to it."[16] Paul presses home "a paradoxical combination" of Adam's influence over the world (cf. 5:19) and the idea that people were responsible for the spreading of sin throughout the world. This latter is especially consistent with Ezekiel's prophesy against the nations, including Israel (cf. Ezek 28). Paul does not explain exactly how Adam's sin interrelated with human sins but one thing is clear: for Paul all people, Jews and Gentiles, were alienated from God; they all were in solidarity with Adam's sin. It is as if sin "gained entry into the world" through Adam, the human, but now "all of the humanity since Adam has entered into the human condition in a

---

14. When Paul discusses the foolishness of people and their refusal to glorify God (1:20-23) the language is similar to Ezek 26 where the author also draws a prophetic image alluding to Gen 2–3. Hooker traces the language of Gen 2–3 in Rom 1 in her monograph, *From Adam to Christ*, 73–84.

15. See further debate in Jewett, *Romans*, 375; Fitzmyer, *Romans*, 413–17.

16. N. T. Wright, "The Letter to the Romans," 526–27.

context in which sin is already 'in' the world."[17] This corporate solidarity explains the notion of all in-Adam.

In 5:13–14 Paul continues to explain the consequence of sin, now in relation to the Torah. Sin was in the world before the law. Only before the law sin was not accounted (ἐλλογεῖται). This is also what Paul probably means in 4:15 when he says where there is no law, there is no transgression. Death reigned from the time of Adam to the time of Moses even over those who did not sin by breaking the command, as Adam did. Paul shows the priority of sin before the law implying that "no law can be granted universally applicable validity."[18] Moreover, sin is much more than just violation of the Jewish law. It was in the world before the Torah, thus it affects even those who have the Torah. Although the law is holy and just and good (cf. 7:14) it is not redemptive in the sense that it could not do what God did by sending his Son (8:3; cf. 3:28). In fact, it increases the realization of sin (5:20; cf. 4:15).[19] In Wright's commentary, the problem of Adam's sin was magnified by the Torah.[20] Sin for Paul is like a power that reduces humanity to a kind of slavery and death. Israel was in the same need of God's redemption as the Gentiles. All human beings came under sin's dominion (1:18—3:9). L. Keck addresses it this way, "However important are the election of Israel, the promise to Abraham, the gift of the law, the Davidic ancestry of God's Son, in no way do these exempt 'the Jews' from solidarity with the Gentiles in the human condition. It is the *human* problem that the gospel addresses."[21] The point that Paul is making is that the Jews or Israel belong within the Adamic humanity (ch. 2; 3:9–20; 5:13–14, 20; 6:14–15; 7:7–25).[22]

Paul is also far from tracing the idea of glory to Adam (cf. *Jub.* 19:25; CD III, 20). On the contrary, Adam became the type of disobedience for all people according to Paul (5:18–19). It is interesting that Paul depicts the same absence of glory in the Gentiles and the Jews (1:23; 3:23), which

---

17. Brower, *Living as God's Holy People*, 15–16.

18. Jewett, *Romans*, 377.

19. The implication is that without the law or God's command people had a hard time distinguishing between right and wrong. What about natural law, as Paul refers to in ch.1? Perhaps this is not the point for Paul at the moment. The point is that sin was before the law and the law helped sin be recognized and trespass increased. See further Tobin, *Paul's Rhetoric*, 181.

20. N. T. Wright, "The Letter to the Romans," 530.

21. Keck, "What Makes Romans Tick," 24.

22. Hooker, *From Adam to Christ*, 170.

is a further example of Adam's sin present in the world. On the other hand, glory for Paul belongs to God (1:23; 4:20; 5:2; 6:4) and to Christ in whom all believers can share his glory (6:4; 8:17).

So far, one may assume that Paul refers to Adam as a type of disobedience to show not so much the origin of sin, although Paul emphasizes human not divine involvement with this, but the universal presence of sin in the world since Adam's sin. Even the law for Paul does not release the Jews from solidarity with the Gentiles in this human condition. Adam for Paul is important in showing the human condition before Christ. Paul makes luminous what Christ had to restore and what God has accomplished in Christ (5:1–11; 5:15–21). The question, however, arises: if Adam is the type of disobedience for Paul, in what sense, then, is Adam a type (τύπος) of the one who was to come (5:14)?

3. Jesus' Obedience as Contrast to Adam's Disobedience

In 5:15–19 the theme of the obedience of Jesus Christ and those who are in him is contrasted with the sin of Adam's disobedience (cf. 1 Cor 15:20–22, 42–49). But Paul surprisingly says that Adam is τύπος of the one who was to come (5:14). Does τύπος stipulate any kind of similarity between the one of disobedience and the one of obedience?

The reason for similarity may be described in terms of the great impact upon many people who are connected to them, as we shall see later (5:18–19). However, as Paul develops further how Christ's life defines the future of the believers just as Adam's life defines the future of his descendants (5:15–21), it becomes clear that Adam is in fact "the antitypos" of Christ. The resemblance between type and antitype is antithetical.[23]

On the other hand, one cannot miss the similarity between Adam and Christ. God sends his Son in the likeness of sinful flesh, in the likeness of Adam (8:3) and thereby condemned sin in the flesh (8:4). Jesus for Paul is a fully human being just like Adam, but he did not commit sin. He condemned sin so that others can be conformed to his likeness (8:29; cf. 1 Cor 15:42–49) rather than Adam's.

In 5:15 Paul explicitly compares Adam and Christ. Adam's trespass is contrasted with Christ's gift. Paul says, "But the free gift is not like the trespass. For if the many died through the one man's trespass, much more surely have the grace of God and the free gift in the grace of the

---

23. Fitzmyer, *Romans*, 418; Jewett, *Romans*, 379.

one man, Jesus Christ, abounded for the many." Given Paul's previous argument on Christ's lavish act of reconciliation (5:1–11), the effect of God's gift through Christ's obedience here must greatly exceed the effect of Adam's trespass. The contrast between the two is in quantity. Paul thinks in terms of the greater degree of Christ's gift (5:15, 17): μᾶλλον (more), ἐπερίσσευσεν (abounded), περισσείαν (abundance), which means that in Christ there is much more gain than loss in Adam. Just as many died and were in sin through Adam's trespass (τὸ παράπτωμα), so also the grace of God and the free gift (ἡ χάρις τοῦ θεοῦ καὶ ἡ δωρεα) come "through Christ's redemptive work with the power to overcome the Adamic legacy."[24] Christ will not only ultimately undo all the consequences that Adam's sin affected, but he will accomplish "much more" by God's grace. The emphasis is placed on the greater achievements of grace (5:20–21). Paul's previous discussion on Adam finally reveals its purpose: Adam is a foil for Paul's view of Christ. If the disobedience of one man resulted in death for the entire human race, then the obedience of one man should accomplish much more. Paul indicates two particular results of this grace.

First, in 5:16 he says that the judgment followed one sin and brought condemnation, but the gift followed many trespasses and brought justification. In the case of Adam there is expansion outwards, from one to many; in the case of Christ, there is contraction inwards: many sins are all embraced in a single sentence of justification. N. T. Wright is right when he says that Christ picks up not where Adam began, but where he ended.[25] Paul's universal language emphasizes the lavishness of Christ's gift that exceeds human trespasses and results in redemption with God (5:11). In a sense Paul answers here his own question of 3:3 once again, whether human unfaithfulness, sin, or trespass can nullify God's faithfulness; whether God has to come up with another plan because of the Gentiles' and Israel's disobedience. Paul answers that God's action in Christ deals with many sins and many sinners. God's redemption in Christ for all people is one and the same purpose from the very beginning. God is true to his promises from the very beginning. They all are fulfilled through Christ.

Second, Paul contrasts the reign of death through Adam with the reign of life through Christ's gift of righteousness (5:17–21). Paul picks

---

24. Jewett, *Romans*, 379.
25. N. T. Wright, "The Letter to the Romans," 528.

up his language of 1:17 and 3:21–26.[26] There he has already pointed out that God's faithfulness is being revealed in the faithfulness of Christ on the cross. The One who has been faithful to the Father until death was raised by the Father from death to life (6:4). All believers participate in Christ's obedience, i.e., faithfulness in that they are faithful to God himself. Paul explains the participation in Christ's obedience in terms of dying with him and of living in unity with Christ "on the resurrection ground" (6:5ff.).[27] Paul speaks of living in the sphere of Christ's rule freed from sin when the old self (as the one in Adam) dies (cf. 6:6). Wright argues in this regard that Paul's argument "is not simply that one has died to sin and hence must not live in it anymore, but that one is already 'alive to God in Christ'" and he/she "must live accordingly" in this newness of life.[28] Although Christians still live in the world of the two realms of sin and grace (5:21), Paul is very clear about where Christians are supposed to be: in the realm of Christ controlled by the Spirit of Christ, belong to him and in him to God in covenantal relationship as God's children (8:14–17).

They can be raised by God to life as Christ is raised to life because of his obedience. Now he explicitly confirms the same concept in the "from lesser to the greater" manner.[29] God's righteousness through Christ's obedient faithfulness supersedes all human unfaithfulness and death. Christ opens the gift of life and the possibility to abide with God and to be his children (8:14–17). That which Adam lost is received in Christ.[30] Glory that is lost (3:23) is obtainable in Christ by conforming to him (8:17, 29).

Paul reaches the culmination by his final comparison between Adam's disobedience and Christ's obedience through which many will be made righteous (5:19). While some Jews expect the glory of Adam will be given to the elect ones of Israel (CD III, 20; 1 QS IV, 23; 1 QH XIV, 11–15), for Paul all have sinned, and like Adam fall short of God's glory (cf. 3:23). Paul ascribes glory only to God (1:23; 4:20; 5:2; 6:4) and to Christ because of his obedience to the Father. It is Christ's glory that will be given to the renewed Israel, all Jews and Gentiles who participate

---

26. See discussion in chapter 3 above.
27. N. T. Wright, "The Letter to the Romans," 538.
28. Ibid.
29. Barth, *Christ and Adam*, 15–24; Witherington III and Hyatt, *Paul's Letter*, 142.
30. Karl Barth assumes further that "man's essential and original nature is to be found, therefore, not in Adam but in Christ. In Adam we can only be prefigured. Adam can therefore be interpreted only in the light of Christ and not the other way round" (*Christ and Adam*, 41–45).

in Christ's obedience. Paul like Ezekiel pronounces the message of hope and redemption for the people of God, Israel (Ezek 33–48) bringing them back to life (Ezek 37) and to glory (Ezek 43). However, Paul expands the idea of the physical Israel. The message of hope for Paul is applicable to the many, all the Jews and the Gentiles, who conform to Christ.

In the previous passage Paul affirms that Abraham was not like Adam because Abraham gave glory to God (4:20). Abraham's faith in God who is able to fulfill his promise was reckoned to him as righteousness. Abraham's faith, though, could not be reckoned to everyone, only God could do it. Where Abraham's "reckoning" is present, disobedience is overcome (4:11–13). Apart from that, sin remained. Abraham's faith is an example and reminder to all Abraham's descendants to give glory to God who handed over Jesus for our trespasses and raised him for our justification (4:24–25). Abraham for Paul is only an anticipation of what has happened in Christ. Abraham was within the universal scope of condemnation (5:18a). Only Christ's act of righteousness leads to righteousness and life for all (5:18b–19). For Paul God has acted in Christ for everyone. Through Christ's faithfulness we all can stand in God's grace and boast in the hope of sharing God's glory (5:1). It is significant that after the discussion on Abraham (4:1–25) Paul emphasizes once again the redemptive role of the obedient Son (5:1–12) who is the Jewish Messiah, and then contrasts Jesus Christ with Adam (5:12–21). It is as if Paul continues his explanation of why God promised Abraham he would inherit the world (4:13; cf. Gen 12:1–3). Through the work of the Messiah the whole world has been reconciled to God. Jesus Christ has reversed the fall of Adam and has accomplished the redemptive work of Israel to which God called his people in the first place.[31]

There is, of course, an eschatological aspect in this. Although all people are still in their physical bodies like Adam and will experience physical death, in Christ there is hope and assurance of living forever with God (cf. 8:18ff.). However, what has been accomplished by Christ on the cross is already effective and will be beneficial and effective at the final judgment (5:9–10; cf. 3:21–26; 6:1–11).

In sum, Paul contrasts Adam with Christ to show the superiority of the latter. Although Christ like Adam, was born into sinful flesh, he acts like an obedient Son. In doing so he condemns sin and death allowing many people to reconcile with God and to have life now and forever.

---

31. N. T. Wright, "The Letter to the Romans," 512.

Paul draws the contrast between Adam and Christ in terms of sin, trespass, disobedience, condemnation, and death on the one side, and gift, grace, obedience, righteousness, and life on the other. It serves Paul to illuminate the theme of God's redemption that supersedes not only Israel's but human sin, trespass, and disobedience—all made possible through Christ's obedience.

4. Christ's Obedience and Redemption

"Christ's obedience was vicarious . . . in the full discharge of the demands of righteousness. His obedience becomes the ground of the remission of sin and actual justification."[32] Murray's statement is applicable to Paul in the sense that Paul considers Christ's obedience as a cornerstone of God's redemption. Unlike Adam, Jesus Christ was the obedient One. He heard and obeyed God fully until death on the cross. Christ's obedience for Paul deals with human sin.

However, Paul's view on Christ's obedience in terms of redemption is bigger than just "remission of sin." The "actual justification" is more embracing than just for Israel. Christ's obedience for Paul reveals God's bigger picture and purposes that concern not only Israel but the whole world. Through his obedience people can come into a relationship with the one God and Father (8:14–17). In contrast with Adam Paul presses home the idea that Jesus Christ, the Messiah of Israel is Lord of all (1:4: 10:12). Watson writes that in spite of a "particularistic Christology" (9:5; 15:8), Paul emphasizes Christ as the Messiah for all people.[33]

That being the case, the theme of obedience results in demonstration of the faithfulness of God to Israel. Christ confirms the promises made to the patriarchs so that the Gentiles may praise God together with the Jews (15:8–13). God's intention to redeem the world was from the very beginning and Israel was part of it. Paul affirms that God remains faithful to his people Israel despite their unbelief and that he will in the end affect their eschatological redemption as he had always promised (1:2; 3:21; 9–11).[34] Even the law as a reminder of God's rule did not and could not make human beings trust and obey God as they ought to (4:15; 5:13–14; 8:3). Indeed, the law has intensified the reign of sin (5:20). Paul's

---

32. Murray, *Redemption Accomplished*, 22.
33. Watson, *Paul, Judaism, and Gentiles*, 275.
34. Hays, *Echoes*, 75.

point is that those who are under the law are a part of fallen humanity (5:13–14).[35] But God has done what the law could not do (8:3–4). His grace has abounded where sin increased (5:20) "that is, in Israel itself."[36] God's abundance of grace in Israel "is presumably a further reference to the messianic work, and the messianic death, in which Jesus offered to Israel's God the faithful obedience that Israel could not."[37] With Christ's coming, the law has been fulfilled (cf. 9:31; 10:4). In other words, Christ's obedience has dealt with his people's sins; and his obedience that acquires righteousness is reckoned to all those in Christ.[38]

Christ takes over all the burden of the alienation of humanity. This means that the OT prophecies of the great tribulation, God's deliverance of Israel from oppressors, God's rule over the Gentiles and the establishment of his kingdom have been set in motion by Christ's life, death, resurrection, which are for Paul the same salvific event.[39] All that God has begun to do through Israel (despite its disobedience) he has brought to fulfillment in Christ. Christ has not only reversed the fall of Adam, he has also accomplished the redemptive work of Israel. In Christ God is proved to be true (cf. 3:3).

Christ's obedience within God's redemption has a corporate dimension. Paul is not thinking primarily in individual terms, but rather in collective terms as the contrast between being "in Adam" and "in Christ." These two eons are described as two spheres of power where there is no other option.[40] In Romans 6:17 Paul speaks about the end of sin's reign. Those who have been buried with Christ in a death like his are dead to sin (6:12). Further, Paul exhorts his readers not to allow the exercise of the authority of sin in their bodies (6:13) and to stop being "slaves" of sin. This way of living leads to death. Instead, Paul calls them to live as slaves of righteousness that results in sanctification, the way of living and being in relationship to Christ (6:16, 19), in his new dominion of the Spirit (8:4), which ultimately leads to eternal life. The same corporate and participation language must have been in view from the very beginning

---

35. Watson, *Paul, Judaism, and Gentiles*, 275.
36. N. T. Wright, "The Letter to the Romans," 530.
37. Ibid.
38. Ibid., 529.
39. Brower, *Living as God's Holy People*, 23.
40. Ibid., 17.

when Paul interprets Habakkuk in 1:17 in the light of Christ.[41] The implication is that throughout the letter Paul affirms that Christ himself is faithful to the Father until death on the cross; and he is raised from the dead to life by the glory of the Father so that those in him may also live a new life (6:4–5).

Christ's obedience for Paul is closely connected with his resurrection. N.T. Wright is concerned that this aspect was undermined in the past.[42] Christ's resurrection for Paul marks the beginning of a new life here and now (5:17–18; cf. 4: 23–25; 10:6–11; cf. 1 Cor 15: 3–6, 20–22). Living in the resurrection of Christ is living in obedience with him and with the mind set on God, on Christ, and on the Spirit (8:4–14). In this context Paul also speaks of the renewal of the mind (12:1). In Christ's obedience the old way of being in Adam has been brought to an end for those in Christ. Modern scholars (Hooker, Wright, Campbell, Brower) describe this process of reconciliation through Christ in terms of transfer (cf. 2 Cor 5:17).[43] Those who are in Adam are within the reign of sin and death. Those who are in Christ are in the reign of God through Christ. Those who are in Christ have been transferred from the realm of sin's dominion to the realm of God. In the light of Christ's obedient death and resurrection, Paul tells his readers, you also must consider yourselves dead to sin and alive to God in Christ Jesus (6:11). Reconciliation with God as a new relationship with God is the beginning of a different life that includes both a death and resurrection experience.[44]

For Paul, reconciliation was wrought by God through Christ for human beings and in human beings. It is while we were enemies that we were reconciled to God by the death of his Son (5:10). If God's people are obedient to him and accept Christ's offer God will redeem them fully, giving life from the dead. God's grace has the last word. Paul like Ezekiel repeats the judgment against nations, including Israel. Like Ezekiel he returns to the message of hope and redemption for the people of God, Israel (Ezek 33–48). However, the people of Israel are for Paul the Jews and the Gentiles, the children of God in Christ. The message of hope for Paul includes all the nations. God's righteousness is revealed for all. Paul

---

41. See discussion on Rom 1:17 in chapter 3 above.

42. N. T. Wright, *Justification*, 219.

43. See discussion in Brower, *Living as God's Holy People*, 33–37; N. T. Wright, "The Letter to the Romans," 528, 538–41; Hooker, *From Adam to Christ*, 26–41; Campbell, *The Deliverance*, 710, 825–27.

44. Gorman, *Inhabiting the Cruciform God*, 70.

emphasizes the supreme value of Christ's obedience unto death; this one who stood closest to God the Father is the means of reconciling people to God and the means of the life eternal in God's presence as his children.

5. Conclusions

God's redemption for Paul is made possible through Christ's faithful obedience that overcomes all human sin and death that has been in the world since Adam. It is significant that after the discussion on Abraham and his role in God's purposes, Paul returns to Adam. He considers all who are after Adam and before Moses under Adam's dominion of sin. Thus, Abraham's and Israel's story are part of God's universal story.

By contrasting Jesus with Adam Paul illuminates the superiority of Christ who being like Adam did not sin but obeyed God until death and condemned sin, reconciling humanity to God. This way Paul implicitly broadens the idea of God's fatherhood through the obedience of the Son as a reality for the whole of humanity.

Christ's obedience affirms God's universal purposes that include God's faithfulness to Israel. For Paul Christ confirms the promises made to the patriarchs so that the Gentiles may praise God just like the Jews. God's intention to redeem the world is from the very beginning and Israel is a part of it in spite of its disobedience. Christ has not only reversed the fall of Adam, but also accomplished the redemptive work of Israel.

Christ's obedience opens a new way of participation with him now and until the redemption is complete. People from among all nations are called now to be not in Adam but in Christ, i.e., to die to sin, to the old self and to live a new life in Christ's faithfulness, in the realm of Christ controlled by the Spirit of Christ. Those in Christ form a single family of the children of God and will be united with him in the life eternal.

Chapter VII

Conclusions

1. Summary and Conclusion

THIS STUDY SHOWS THAT the narrative substructure of Romans is based on the story of God's redemption as the act of God the Father accomplished in the Son. It develops the view that the foundation of Paul's picture of the Father who redeems comes from the Jewish scriptures. Chapter 2 examines OT and 2TP texts. It concludes that the notion of God the Father emerges together with the idea of God's redemption of Israel: first in the deliverance from Egypt and then in reference to God's persistent redeeming activity throughout the story of Israel. God enters into a covenant family relationship with Israel, giving it the status of his son and expecting Israel to obey. While God remains a faithful Father to his people, Israel as God's son is not obedient to the will of God, and does not live in righteousness before God. As such, it does not serve as a light to the other nations, and does not proclaim God's name in all the earth as is expected from God's son. Both OT and 2TP literature contain expectations that God as the Father and Redeemer will introduce a new era in a relationship with Israel whether it is with the whole of Israel or with a righteous remnant only. God may even name other people as his own; however, how the nations will be brought together to worship and to obey God remains a mystery. In later Judaism there are indications that God may act through a messianic figure to accomplish his promises.

This background helps to see Paul's development of redemption as the act of God the Father accomplished in Christ. Chapter 3 focuses on God's fatherhood and by implication on the family of God in Romans. Both Paul's language of God being the Father of Christ and of Christ being the Son enables him to unfold God's redemptive plan for Israel and through Israel for all the nations. God the Father acts through his obedient Son. Christ confirms God's righteousness/faithfulness to Israel. He is the expected Jewish Messiah who came to restore the relationship with Israel. As the obedient Son he is the light to other nations, the function that Israel failed to accomplish. It is possible to call all people to the obedience of faith because of his obedience. In Christ God's faithfulness to both Jews and Gentiles has been revealed. In this light Paul re-reads his scripture and reinterprets the idea of God the Father universally in relation to both Jews and Gentiles. In Christ Paul redefines the family of God that now consists of all in Christ led by the Spirit of God/Christ. Both Jews and Gentiles in Christ are incorporated into God's family conforming to the character of his Son. The implication is that all who participate in Christ's obedience belong to God as children.

Chapter 4 shows how God fulfills his redemption for both Jews and Gentiles in Christ, namely through Christ's faithfulness. Paul discloses Christ's faithfulness as the obedience of God's own Son and the righteous One of Israel. He obeys the Father up to death on the cross revealing how God is trustworthy in Israel's history and how he fulfills his bigger purposes to which the scripture has testified. Christ's faithfulness is a demonstration of God's righteousness to both Jews and Gentiles and God's faithfulness to his promises. Paul uses Jewish imagery to describe the universal consequences of Christ's faithfulness. He dies as ἱλαστήριον, as the perfect martyr and the suffering servant for all. Through Christ's obedience many will be made righteous because Christ overcomes not only Israel's unfaithfulness but all human unrighteousness and sin. This opens up a possibility for believers to participate in Christ's faithfulness. The participation language is variously explained throughout Romans. This includes: unity with Christ; living in the sphere of Christ's rule freed from sin when the old self in Adam dies; living as co-heirs with Christ and children of God in the newness of the resurrected life with the mind set on Christ and the Spirit; and living as holders of the eschatological hope of the final revelation when the whole creation will be liberated.

A critical question in this research is how Abraham's story and his faith contribute to Paul's sub-narrative of God's redemption that came about in Christ's faithfulness. This is addressed in chapter 5. Paul considers the story of Abraham within the larger context of God's impartiality and accessibility for all the nations. Paul refers to Abraham to show that God's covenant with Abraham embraces the redemption of the whole world and that Abraham is the forefather of Jews and Gentiles. Abraham's faith, including his trust, faithfulness and obedience is anticipatory faith in the God of Israel who calls, promises, and fulfills his promises for Abraham, his physical descendants and for all the nations by raising Jesus from the dead. The redeeming faithfulness comes with Christ who fulfills and reveals God's promises for all the nations. When Paul draws a parallel between God and Abraham he alludes to the Aqedah: God like Abraham did not spare his own Son Jesus Christ just as he did not spare his people Israel for the sake of the world. Nevertheless, the Aqedah is at most an implicit image on which Paul draws as if he rewrites it against his Jewish heritage in the light of Christ.

The final section brings forth Paul's emphasis on Christ's superior obedience as contrasted with the picture of Adam's disobedience. God's redemption for Paul is made possible through Christ's faithful obedience that overcomes all human sin and death that has been in the world since Adam. Even those who are under the law are part of Adamic fallen humanity. Paul contrasts Jesus Christ to Adam to show that Christ being like Adam did not sin but obeyed God till death. By his obedience until death Christ condemned sin. This is the context in which the created order awaits the eager expectation when the children of God will be revealed. Creation will join the freedom of the glory of the children of God through Christ.

In conclusion, there are two key elements that derive from Paul's re-reading of scripture and more generally from within his Second Temple literary context: God is the Father who redeems and Christ's death is his faithful obedience to the redeeming Father. Christ's faithfulness is a continuation of God's dealing with Israel and through Israel with all the nations.

2. Contribution to Research

This research contributes to the discussion of how Paul reads and interprets the scripture and how he re-evaluates his Jewish heritage. Four major contributions can be identified.

First, Paul reads the scriptural language of Father retrospectively through a Christological lens. In this reading the Jewish concept of God's persistent redeeming activity is defined in terms of the Father who seeks to establish a relationship with his people. This is foregrounded by Paul and recast in the light of Christ. Jesus is both the promised Jewish Messiah and the obedient Son of God. Furthermore, God is the Father who redeems not only Jews but also Gentiles through Christ because of his obedience. In Christ God's redemptive story is both for Israel and beyond Israel for the whole of humanity. According to Paul, however, this is not new: it is intended from the very beginning. In Christ Paul redefines the family of God. It now consists of all who participate in Christ's obedience.

Second, in this context, another look at the idea of the Aqedah in Paul is warranted. Although the idea itself is not new, in relation to Romans and in relation to the question of God's redemption accomplished in Christ's faithful obedience, it has not heretofore received sufficient attention. The emphasis in late Second Temple Judaism in particular is on the obedience of Isaac and Abraham. But for Paul the emphasis in the Aqedah is upon God's intervention rather than human obedience. The Aqedah is expressed in Paul's description of God the Father who like Abraham did not spare his Son Jesus, as he did not spare his people Israel to fulfill his bigger purposes in love for humanity. However, the Aqedah with its development of Isaac's role is not the most helpful imagery in Paul's view on Christ's obedience and his redemptive death. Paul re-thinks his Jewish heritage and develops the Aqedah theologically against his Jewish background in the light of Christ's obedience. For Paul Christ is a new kind of Isaac, he is God's own and faithful Son who fulfills God's redemptive purposes. He actually dies and is resurrected by God. Through his faithful obedience many will become righteous.

Third, the thesis makes a further contribution to the theological implications of a subjective reading of πίστις Χριστοῦ. For Paul God's bigger story is the story of the divine initiative and redemptive purposes accomplished through Christ's faithful obedience. Christ's redemptive faithfulness penetrates the whole story of God's redemption and his covenantal faithfulness. Paul draws a genuine unity between the Father and the Son and emphasizes that the act of the Son reveals God's purposes for Israel and humanity.

Fourth, this research poses a challenge to those who claim that God's reconciliation with the Gentiles through Christ serves his larger goal of the ultimate restoration of ethnic Israel exclusive of Christ. This thesis argues that for Paul the centrality of Jesus' work as an integral part of God's own activity and his obedience to God the Father is the means for unfolding God's purposes not only for Israel but for the whole world from the very beginning. Christ is the means of adopting of both Jews and Gentiles into God's renewed family.

Bibliography

Abegg, Martin G., Jr. "4QMMT, Paul, and 'Works of the Law.'" In *The Bible at Qumran: Text, Shape, and Interpretation*, edited by Peter W. Flint and Tae-Hun Kim, 203-16. Grand Rapids: Eerdmans, 2001.
Adams, Edward. "Abraham's Faith and Gentile Disobedience: Textual Links between Romans 1 and 4." *JSNT* 65 (1997) 47-66.
Aland, Kurt, Barbara Aland, and Erwin Nestle, editors. *Novum Testamentum Graece*. Instituto Studiorum Textus Novi Testamenti Monasteriensi Westphaliae. 27th ed. Stuttgart: Deutsche Bibelgesellschaft, 1993.
Alexander, Philip S. "The Qumran *Songs of the Sabbath Sacrifice* and the *Celestial Hierarchy* of Dionysius the Areopagite: A Comparative Approach." *RevQ* 22 (2006) 349-72.
———. "Orality in Pharisaic-Rabbinic Judaism at the Turn of the Eras." In *Jesus and the Oral Gospel Traditions*, edited by Dom Henry Wansbrough, 159-84. JSNTSup 64. London: T. & T. Clark, 2004. 1st ed. Sheffield: Sheffield Academic, 1991.
Andersen, Francis A. *Habakkuk: A New Translation with Introduction and Commentary*. AB. New York: Doubleday, 2001.
Anderson A. A. *2 Samuel*. WBC 11. Dallas: Word, 1989.
———. A. *The Book of Psalms*. NCB. London: Marshall, Morgan & Scott, 1972.
Babylonian Talmud. 30 vols. Translated and edited by Rabbi Isidore Epstein. London: Soncino, 1938.
Barr, James. "Abba isn't 'Daddy.'" *JTS* 39 (1988) 28-47.
Barrett, C. K. *Paul: An Introduction to His Thought*. London: Geoffrey Chapman, 1994.
Barth, Karl. *Christ and Adam: Man and Humanity in Romans 5*. Translated by T. A. Smail. Edinburgh: Oliver & Boyd, 1956.
Barton, John, and John Muddiman, editors. *OBC*. Oxford: University Press, 2001.
Bauckham, Richard. *God Crucified: Monotheism and Christology in the New Testament*. Didsbury Lectures 1996. Carlisle: Paternoster, 1998.
Beavis, Mary Ann. "The Resurrection of Jephthah's Daughter: Judges 11:34-40 and Mark 5:21-24, 35-43." *CBQ* 72 (2010) 46-62.
Bell, Richard H. *Provoked to Jealousy: The Origin and Purpose of the Jealousy Motif in Romans*. Tübingen: Mohr Siebeck, 1994.
Bird, Michael F., and Preston M. Sprinkle. *The Faith of Christ: Exegetical, Biblical, and Theological Studies*. Peabody, MA: Hendrickson, 2009.
Bird, Michael F., and Michael R. Whitenton. "The Faithfulness of Jesus Christ in Hippolytos's *De Christo et Antichristo*: Overlooked Patristic Evidence in the πίστις Χριστοῦ Debate." *NTS* 55 (2009) 552-62.

Bibliography

Block, Daniel I. *The Book of Ezekiel: Chapters 25–48.* NICOT. Grand Rapids: Eerdmans, 1998.

Bousset, Wilhelm. *Jesu Predigt in ihrem Gegensatz zum Judentum: Ein Religionsgeschichtlicher Vergleich.* Göttingen: Vanderhoeck und Ruprecht, 1892.

Brooke, George J. *Exegesis at Qumran: 4Q Florilegium in Its Jewish Context.* JSOTSup 29. Sheffield: JSOT Press, 1985.

———. "The Rewritten Law, Prophets and Psalms: Issues for Understanding the Text of the Bible." In *The Bible as Book: The Hebrew Bible and the Judaean Desert Discoveries,* edited by Edward D. Herbert and Emanuel Tov, 31–40. London: British Library, 2002.

Brower, Kent E. *Living as God's Holy People: Holiness and Community in Paul.* Didsbury Lectures 2008. Carlisle: Paternoster, 2010.

Brown, Joanne Carlson, and Carole R. Bohn, editors. *Christianity, Patriarchy, and Abuse: A Feminist Critique.* New York: Pilgrim, 1989.

Brownlee, William H. *The Midrash Pesher of Habakkuk.* SBLMS 24. Missoula: Scholars, 1979.

Bruce, F. F. *Paul: Apostle of the Heart Set Free.* Grand Rapids: Eerdmans, 1977.

———. *Romans.* 1963. Reprint, Downers Grove, IL: InterVarsity, 2008.

Brueggemann, Walter. "The Book of Exodus: Introduction, Commentary and Reflections." In *NIB* 1:677–981. Nashville: Abingdon, 1994.

Bultmann, Rudolf. "The Significance of the Old Testament for the Christian Faith." In *The Old Testament and Christian Faith,* edited by Bernard Anderson, 8–35. London: SCM, 1964.

Burchard, C. "Joseph and Aseneth." In *The Old Testament Pseudepigrapha: Expansions of the "Old Testament" and Legends, Wisdom and Philosophical Literature, Prayers, Psalms and Odes, Fragments of Lost Judeo-Hellenistic Work,* edited by James H. Charlesworth, 2:177–247. London: Darton, Longman & Todd, 1985.

Burke, Trevor J. *Adopted into God's Family: Exploring a Pauline Metaphor.* Downers Grove, IL: InterVarsity, 2006.

Campbell, Douglas A. *The Deliverance of God: An Apocalyptic Rereading of Justification in Paul.* Grand Rapids: Eerdmans, 2009.

———. "The Faithfulness of Christ in Romans 3:22." In *The Faith of Christ: Exegetical, Biblical, and Theological Studies.* Edited by Michael F. Bird and Preston M. Sprinkle, 57–71. Peabody, MA: Hendrickson, 2009.

———. *The Quest for Paul's Gospel: A Suggested Strategy.* New York: T. & T. Clark, 2005.

Caragounis, Chrys C. "בְּ" In *NIDOTTE* 1:671–77.

Caroll, Robert P. *Jeremiah.* OTL. London: SCM, 1986.

Cerfaux, L. *Christ in the Theology of St. Paul.* New York: Herder & Herder, 1959.

Charles, R. H., editor. *The Apocripha and Pseudepigrapha of the Old Testament in English.* 2 vols. 1913. Reprint, Oxford: Clarendon, 1976–1977.

Charlesworth, James H. "A Critical Comparison of the Dualism in 1QS 3:13—4:26 and the 'Dualism' Contained in the Gospel of John." In *John and the Dead Sea Scrolls,* edited by James H. Charlesworth, 76–106. New York: Crossroad, 1991.

Charlesworth, James H., editor. *The Old Testament Pseudepigrapha: Apocalyptic Literature and Testaments.* Vol. 1. London: Darton, Longman & Todd, 1983.

———. *The Old Testament Pseudepigrapha: Expansions of the "Old Testament" and Legends, Wisdom and Philosophical Literature, Prayers, Psalms and Odes,*

Fragments of Lost Judeo-Hellenistic Works. Vol. 2. London: Darton, Longman & Todd, 1985.

Chester, Andrew. "The Christ of Paul." In *Redemption and Resistance: The Messianic Hopes of Jews and Christians in Antiquity,* edited by Markus Bockmuehl and James Carleton Paget, 109–21. London: T. & T. Clark, 2007.

Childs, Brevard S. *Biblical Theology of the Old and New Testaments: Theological Reflection on the Christian Bible.* Minneapolis: Fortress, 1993.

———. *Exodus.* OTL. London: SCM, 1974.

———. *Old Testament Theology in a Canonical Context.* London: SCM, 1985.

Ciampa, Roy E. "Deuteronomy in Galatians and Romans." In *Deuteronomy in the New Testament: The New Testament and the Scriptures of Israel,* edited by Steve Moyise and Maarten Menken, 99–117. LNTS 358. London: T. & T. Clark, 2007.

———. "The History of Redemption." In *Central Themes in Biblical Theology,* edited by Scott J. Hafemann and Paul R. House, 254–308. Grand Rapids: Baker Academic, 2007.

Clements, Ronald E. "The Book of Deuteronomy: Introduction, Commentary and Reflections." In *NIB* 2:269–538. Nashville: Abingdon, 1998.

Cobb, John B., David J. Lull. *Romans.* St. Louis: Chalice, 2005.

Collins, John J. *Apocalypticism in the Dead Sea Scrolls.* London: Routledge, 1997.

———. "Ecclesiasticus, or The Wisdom of Jesus Son of Sirach." In *OBC* 667–98. Oxford: Oxford University Press, 2001.

———. *Jewish Wisdom in the Hellenistic Age.* Louisville: Westminster John Knox, 1997.

———. *The Scepter and the Star: The Messiahs of the Dead Sea Scrolls and Other Ancient Literature.* New York: Doubleday, 1995.

———. *Seers, Sibyls and Sages in Hellenistic-Roman Judaism.* New York: Brill, 1997.

Coppedge, Allan. *Portraits of God: A Biblical Theology of Holiness.* Downers Grove, IL: InterVarsity, 2001.

Corley, Kathleen E. "Women's Inheritance Rights in Antiquity and Paul's Metaphor of Adoption." In *A Feminist Companion to Paul,* edited by Amy-Jill Levine and Marianne Blickenstaff, 98–121. London: T. & T.Clark, 2004.

Cousar, Charles B. "Continuity and Discontinuity: Reflection on Romans 5–8." In *Pauline Theology, Volume III: Romans,* edited by David M. Hay and E. Elizabeth Johnson, 196–210. Minneapolis: Fortress, 1995.

———. *The Letters of Paul.* Nashville: Abingdon, 1996.

———. *A Theology of the Cross: The Death of Jesus in the Pauline Letters.* Minneapolis: Fortress, 1990.

Crafton, Jeffrey A. "Paul's Rhetorical Vision and the Purpose of Romans: Toward a New Understanding." *NT* 32 (1990) 317–39.

Craigie, Peter C. *The Book of Deuteronomy.* NICOT. Grand Rapids: Eerdmans, 1971.

Cranfield, C. E. B. *The Epistle to the Romans.* 2 vols. ICC. Edinburgh: T. & T. Clark, 1975.

Crawford, Sidnie White. *Rewriting Scripture in Second Temple Times.* Grand Rapids: Eerdmans, 2008.

D'Angelo, Mary Rose. "Abba and 'Father': Imperial Theology and the Jesus Traditions." *JBL* 3 (1992) 611–30.

Dahl, Nils A. "The Atonement: An Adequate Reward for the Aqedah?" In *Jesus the Christ: The Historical Origins of Christological Doctrine,* edited by Donald H. Juel, 137–53. Minneapolis: Fortress, 1991.

Daly, Mary. *Beyond God the Father: Toward a Philosophy of Women's Liberation.* Boston: Beacon, 1973.
Daly, Robert J. "Sacrifice Unveiled or Sacrifice Revisited: Trinitarian and Liturgical Perspectives." *TS* 64 (2003) 24–42.
———. "The Soteriological Significance of the Sacrifice of Isaac." *CBQ* 39 (1977) 45–75.
Darr, Katheryn Pfisterer. "The Book of Ezekiel: Introduction, Commentary, and Reflections." In *NIB* 4:1073–1607. Nashville: Abingdon, 2001.
Davies, G. N. *Faith and Obedience in Romans: A Study in Romans 1–4.* JSNTSup 39. Sheffield: JSOT Press, 1990.
Davies, P. R., and B. D. Chilton. "The Aqedah: A Revised Tradition History." *CBQ* 40 (1978) 514–46.
Davis, Ellen F., and Richard B. Hays, editors. *The Art of Reading Scripture.* Grand Rapids: Eerdmans, 2003.
Deissmann, Gustav Adolf. *The Religion of Jesus and the Faith of Paul: The Selly Oak Lectures, 1923 on the Communion of Jesus with God.* Translated by W. Wilson. London: Hodder & Stoughton, 1923.
Delaney, Carol. *Abraham on Trial: The Social Legacy of Biblical Myth.* Princeton: Princeton University Press, 1998.
Dobbeler, Alex von. *Glaube als Teilnahme.* Tübingen: Mohr/Siebeck, 1987.
Donaldson, Terence L. *Paul and the Gentiles: Remapping the Apostle's Convictional World.* Minneapolis: Fortress, 1997.
Dunn, James D. G. *Christology in the Making.* 2nd ed. London: SCM, 1989.
———. "EK PISTEWΣ: A Key to the Meaning of PISTIS CRISTOU." In *The Word Leaps the Gap: Essays on Scripture and Theology in Honor of Richard Hays*, edited by J. Ross Wagner et al., 351–66. Grand Rapids: Eerdmans, 2008.
———. *The New Perspective on Paul.* Rev. ed. Grand Rapids: Eerdmans, 2008.
———. "Once More, PISTIS CRISTOU." In *The Faith of Jesus Christ: The Narrative Substructure of Galatians 3:1—4:11*, edited by Richard B. Hays, 249–71. Grand Rapids: Eerdmans, 2002.
———. *Romans 1–8.* WBC 38a. Dallas: Word, 1988.
———. *Romans 9–16.* WBC 38b. Dallas: Word, 1988.
———. *The Theology of Paul the Apostle.* Grand Rapids: Eerdmans, 1988.
———. *Unity and Diversity in the New Testament: An Inquiry into the Character of Earliest Christianity.* London: Trinity, 1997.
Durham, John I. *Exodus.* WBC 3. Dallas: Word, 1987.
Ehrensperger, Kathy. *That We May Be Mutually Encouraged: Feminism and the New Perspective in Pauline Studies.* New York: T. & T. Clark, 2004.
Eichrodt, Walter. *Theology of the Old Testament.* Translated by John Baker. 2 vols. London: SCM, 1961.
Elliger, K., and W. Rudolf, editors. *Biblia Hebraica Stuttgartensia.* Stuttgart: Deutsche Bibelgesellschaft, 1967/1977.
Ellis E. Earle, *Paul's Use of the Old Testament.* Edinburgh: Oliver and Boyd, 1957.
Elwell, Walter A., editor. *Evangelical Commentary on the Bible.* Grand Rapids: Baker, 1989.
Erickson, Millard J. *God the Father Almighty: A Contemporary Exploration of the Divine Attributes.* Grand Rapids: Baker, 1998.
Esler, Philip F. *Conflict and Identity in Romans: The Social Setting of Paul's Letter.* Minneapolis: Fortress, 2003.

Evans, Craig A. "Abraham in the Dead Sea Scrolls: A Man of Faith and Failure." In *The Bible at Qumran; Text, Shape, and Interpretation,* edited by Peter W. Flint and Tae-Hun Kim, 149–58. Grand Rapids: Eerdmans, 2001.
Fee Gordon D. *God's Empowering Presence: The Holy Spirit in the Letters of Paul.* Peabody, MA: Hendrickson, 1994.
Fensham, Charles F. *The Book of Ezra and Nehemiah.* NICOT. Grand Rapids: Eerdmans, 1982.
Fisk, Bruce N. "Offering Isaac Again and Again: Pseudo-Philo's Use of the Aqedah as Intertext." *CBQ* 62 (2000) 481–507.
Fitzmyer, Joseph A. "4Q246: The "Son of God" Document from Qumran." *Biblica* 74 (1993) 153–74.
———. *According to Paul: Studies in the Theology of the Apostle.* Mahwah, NJ: Paulist, 1993.
———. *Romans: A New Translation with Introduction and Commentary.* AB. New York: Doubleday, 1993.
———. "The Sacrifice of Isaac in Qumran Literature." *Biblica* 83 (2002) 211–29.
———. *To Advance the Gospel: New Testament Studies.* New York: Crossroad, 1981.
Garlington, Don B. "'New Perspective' Reading of Central Texts in Romans 1–4." The Paul Page. Online: http://www.thepaulpage.com/Rom1-4.pdf.
———. *The Obedience of Faith: A Pauline Phrase in Historical Context.* Tübingen: Mohr/Siebeck, 1991.
Garnsey, Peter, and Richard Saller. *The Roman Empire: Economy, Society and Culture.* Berkeley: University of California Press, 1987.
Gathercole, Simon J. *Where Is Boasting: Early Jewish Soteriology and Paul's Response in Romans 1–5.* Grand Rapids: Eerdmans, 2002.
Gerstenberger, Erhard S. *Psalms, Part I: With an Introduction to Cultic Poetry (The Forms of the Old Testament Literature, Volume 14).* Grand Rapids: Eerdmans: 1988.
Goldingay, John. *Psalms.* Vols. 1–3. Edited by Tremper Longman III. Baker Commentary on the Old Testament Wisdom and Psalms. Grand Rapids: Baker Academic, 2006–2008.
Gorman, Michael J. *Apostle of the Crucified Lord: A Theological Introduction to Paul and His Letters.* Grand Rapids: Eerdmans, 2004.
———. *Cruciformity: Paul's Narrative Spirituality of the Cross.* Grand Rapids: Eerdmans, 2001.
———. *Inhabiting the Cruciform God: Kenosis, Justification, and Theosis in Paul's Narrative Soteriology.* Grand Rapids: Eerdmans, 2009.
Graystone, Kenneth. *The Epistle to the Romans.* London: Epworth, 1997.
Greathouse, William M. *Romans 1–8: A Commentary in the Wesleyan Tradition.* Kansas City: Beacon Hill, 2008.
———. *Romans 9–16: A Commentary in the Wesleyan Tradition.* Kansas City: Beacon Hill, 2008.
Green, Joel B. *Salvation.* St. Louis: Chalice, 2003.
Grieb, A. Katherine. *The Story of Romans: A Narrative Defense of God's Righteousness.* Louisville: Westminster John Knox, 2002.
Grisanti, Michael A. "גאל." In *NIDOTTE* 1:882–84.
Hamerton-Kelly, Robert. *God the Father: Theology and Patriarchy in the Teaching of Jesus.* Philadelphia: Fortress, 1979.
Hampson, Daphne. *Theology and Feminism.* Oxford: Blackwell, 1990.

Hartley, John E. *Genesis*. NIBC. Carlisle: Paternoster, 2000.

Hay, David M., and E. Elizabeth Johnson, editors. *Pauline Theology, Volume III: Romans*. Minneapolis: Fortress, 1995.

Hays, Richard B. *The Conversion of the Imagination: Paul as Interpreter of Israel's Scripture*. Grand Rapids: Eerdmans, 2005.

———. *Echoes of Scripture in the Letters of Paul*. New Haven: Yale University Press, 1989.

———. *The Faith of Jesus Christ: The Narrative Substructure of Galatians 3:1—4:11*. Grand Rapids: Eerdmans, 2002.

———. "Have We Found Abraham to Be Our Forefather According to the Flesh? A Reconsideration of Rom 4:1." *NT* 27 (1985) 76–98.

———. "Is Paul's Gospel Narratable?" *JSNT* 27 (2004) 219–39.

———. "*PISTIS CHRISTOU* and Pauline Theology: What Is at Stake?" In *Pauline Theology, Volume IV: Looking Back, Pressing On*, edited by E. Elizabeth Johnson and David B. Hay, 35–60. Atlanta: Scholars, 1997.

———. "Psalm 143 and the Logic of Romans 3." *JBL* 99 (1980) 107–15.

———. "'The Righteous One' as Eschatological Deliverer: A Case Study in Paul's Apocalyptic Hermeneutics." In *The New Testament and Apocalyptic*, edited by Joel Marcus and Marion L. Soards, 191–215. JSNTSup 24. Sheffield: JSOT Press, 1989.

Hayward, C. T. R. "The Sacrifice of Isaac and Jewish Polemic Against Christianity." *CBQ* 52 (1990) 292–306.

Hengel, Martin. *Atonement: The Origins of the Doctrine in the New Testament*. Translated by John Bowden. Philadelphia: Fortress, 1981.

Henten, Jan Willem Van. *The Maccabean Martyrs as Saviours of the Jewish People: A Study of 2 and 4 Maccabees*. Leiden: Brill, 1997.

———. *The Son of God*. Translated by John Bowden. London: SCM, 1976.

Hodge, Caroline Johnson. *If Sons, then Heirs: A Study of Kinship and Ethnicity in the Letters of Paul*. Oxford: Oxford University Press, 2007.

Hooker, Morna D. *From Adam to Christ: Essays on Paul*. Eugene, OR: Wipf & Stock, 1990.

———. *Not Ashamed of the Gospel: New Testament Interpretation of the Death of Christ*. Didsbury Lectures 1988. Carlisle: Paternoster, 1994.

———. "Pistis Christou." *NTS* 35 (1989) 321–42.

Horsley, Richard A., editor. *Paul and the Roman Imperial Order*. London: Trinity, 2004.

Houtman, Cornelis. *Exodus*. HCOT. Vol. 1. Kampen, Netherlands: Kok, 1993.

Hughes, R. Kent. *Preaching the Word: Ephesians: The Mystery of the Body of Christ*. Wheaton, IL: Crossway, 1992.

Hultgren, Arland J. "The Pistis Christou Formulation in Paul." *NovT* 22 (1980) 248–63.

Hurtado, Larry W. "Jesus' Divine Sonship in Paul's Epistle to the Romans." In *Romans and the People of God*, edited by Sven K. Soderlund and N.T. Wright, 217–33. Grand Rapids: Eerdmans, 1999.

———. *Lord Jesus Christ: Devotion to Jesus in Earliest Christianity*. Grand Rapids: Eerdmans, 2003.

Jeremias, Joachim. *New Testament Theology: The Proclamation of Jesus*. Translated by John Bowden. New York: Scribner's Sons, 1971.

———. *Prayers of Jesus*. Translated by John Bowden. Philadelphia: Fortress, 1967.

Jewett, Robert. *Romans: Hermeneia: A Critical and Historical Commentary on the Bible*. Minneapolis: Fortress, 2007.

Jipp, Joshua W. "Rereading the Story of Abraham, Isaac, and 'Us' in Romans 4." *JSNT* 32 (2009) 217–42.
Johnson, E. Elizabeth. "Romans 9–11: The Faithfulness and Impartiality of God." In *Pauline Theology, Volume III: Romans*, edited by David M. Hay and E. Elizabeth Johnson, 211–39. Minneapolis: Fortress, 1995.
Johnson, Elizabeth A. *She Who Is: The Mystery of God in Feminist Theological Discourse*. New York: Crossroad, 1992.
Johnson, Luke T. *Reading Romans: A Literary and Theological Commentary*. New York: Crossroad, 1997.
———. *Religious Experience in Earliest Christianity: A Missing Dimension in New Testament Study*. Minneapolis: Fortress, 1998.
———. "Romans 3:21–26 and the Faith of Jesus." *CBQ* 44 (1982) 77–90.
———. *The Writings of the New Testament: An Interpretation*. Philadelphia: Fortress, 1986.
Jonge, Marinus de. "Christian Influence in the Testament of the Twelve Patriarchs." In *Studies on the Testaments of the Twelve Patriarchs: Text and Interpretation*, edited by Marinus de Jonge, 193–246. Leiden: Brill, 1975.
Kaiser, Walter C., et al. *Three Views on the New Testament Use of the Old Testament*. Edited by Stanley N. Gundry et al. Grand Rapids: Zondervan, 2008.
Käsemann, Ernst. *Commentary on Romans*. Translated and edited by G. W. Bromiley. London: SCM, 1980.
———. "'The Righteousness of God' in Paul." In *New Testament Questions of Today*, translated by W. J. Montague, 168–82. London: SCM, 1969.
Keck, Leander E. "'Jesus' in Romans." *JBL* 8 (1989) 443–60.
———. *Paul and His Letters: Proclamation Commentaries*. Philadelphia: Fortress, 1973.
———. "What Makes Romans Tick?" In *Pauline Theology, Volume III: Romans*, edited by David M. Hay and E. Elizabeth Johnson, 3–29. Minneapolis: Fortress, 1995.
Keener, Craig S. *The IVP Bible Background Commentary: New Testament*. Downers Grove, IL: InterVarsity, 1993.
Keesmaat, Sylvia. *Paul and His Story: (Re)Interpreting the Exodus Tradition*. JSNTSup 181. Sheffield: Sheffield Academic, 1999.
Kinneavy, James L. *Greek Rhetorical Origins of the Christian Faith*. New York, Oxford: Oxford University Press, 1987.
Kittel, Gerhard. "ἀββᾶ." In *TDNT* 1:5–6.
Kittredge, Cynthia B. *Community and Authority: The Rhetoric of Obedience in the Pauline Tradition*. Harrisburg, PA: Trinity, 1988.
Koch, Dietrich-Alex. "Der Text von Hab 2:4b in der Septuaginta und im Neuen Testament." *ZNW* 76 (1985) 68–85.
———. *Die Schrift als Zeuge des Evangeliums. Untersuchungen zur Verwendung und zum Verständnis der Schrift by Paulus*. Tübingen: Mohr/Siebeck, 1986.
Kolarcik, Michael. "The Book of Wisdom: Introduction, Commentary, and Reflections." In *NIB* 5:435–600. Nashville: Abingdon, 1997.
Kugel, James. "4Q369 'Prayer of Enosh' and Ancient Biblical Interpretation." *DSD* 5 (1998) 119–48.
Kugler, Robert A. *The Testament of the Twelve Patriarchs*. Sheffield: Sheffield Academic, 2001.
Kunin, Seth Daniel. "The Death of Isaac: Structuralist Analysis of Genesis 22." *JSOT* 64 (1994) 57–81.

Ladd, George Eldon. *A Theology of the New Testament*. Grand Rapids: Eerdmans, 1911.
Lampe, P. *Die Stadtrömischen Christen in den Ersten Beiden Jahrhunderten: Untersuchungen zur Sozialgeschichte*. WUNT 2:18. 2nd ed. Tübingen: Mohr/Siebeck, 1989.
Lane, William L. *Hebrews 9–13*. WBC 47b. Dallas: Word, 1991.
Lee, Jung H. "Abraham in a Different Voice: Rereading "Fear and Trembling" with Care." *RS* 36 (2000) 377–400.
Levenson, Jon D. *The Death and Resurrection of the Beloved Son: The Transformation of Child Sacrifice in Judaism and Christianity*. New Haven: Yale University Press, 1993.
Lidgett, John Scott. *The Fatherhood of God in Christian Truth and Life*. London: Kelly, 1913.
Lim, Timothy H. "The Qumran Scrolls, Multilingualism, and Biblical Interpretation." In *Religion in the Dead Sea*, edited by John J. Collins and Robert A. Kugler, 57–73. Grand Rapids: Eerdmans, 2000.
Longenecker, Bruce W. "ΠΙΣΤΙΣ in Romans 3.25: The Neglected Evidence for the 'Faithfulness of Christ'?" *NTS* 39 (1993) 478–80.
———. *The Triumph of Abraham's God: The Transformation of Identity in Galatians*. Edinburgh: T. & T. Clark, 1998.
Longenecker, Bruce W., editor. *Narrative Dynamics in Paul: A Critical Assessment*. Louisville: Westminster John Knox, 2002.
Longenecker, Richard N. "The Focus of Romans: The Central Role of 5:1—8:39 in the Argument of the Letter." In *Romans and the People of God*, edited by Sven K. Soderlund and N. T. Wright, 49–69. Grand Rapids: Eerdmans, 1999.
———. *Paul: Apostle of Liberty*. New York: Harper & Row, 1964.
Longenecker, Richard N., editor. *Patterns of Discipleship in the New Testament*. Grand Rapids: Eerdmans, 1996.
MacCasland, Vernon S. "Abba, Father." *JBL* 72 (1953) 79–91.
Machen, J. Gresham. *The Origin of Paul's Religion*. James Sprunt Lectures 9. 1925. Reprint, Grand Rapids: Eerdmans, 2003.
Macintosh, A. A. *Hosea*. ICC. Edinburgh: T. & T. Clark, 1997.
Martinez, Florentino Garcia. *Qumran and Apocalyptic: Studies on the Aramaic Texts from Qumran*. STDJ 9. New York: Brill, 1992.
———. "The Sacrifice of Isaac in 4Q 225." In *The Sacrifice of Isaac: The Aqedah (Gen 22) and its Interpretations*, edited by Edward Noort and Eibert J. C. Tigchelaar, 44–57. Leiden: Brill, 2002.
Martinez, Florentino Garcia, and Eibert J. C. Tigchelaar. *The Dead Sea Scrolls: Study Edition*. 2 vols. Grand Rapids: Eerdmans, 1997–1998.
Martyn, Louis J. "Apocalyptic Antinomies in Galatians." *NTS* 31 (1985) 410–24.
———. *Theological Issues in the Letters of Paul*. London: T. & T. Clark, 1997.
Matlock, R. Barry. "The Arrow and the Web: Critical Reflections on a Narrative Approach to Paul." In *Narrative Dynamics in Paul: A Critical Assessment*, edited by Bruce W. Longenecker, 44–57. Louisville: Westminster John Knox, 2002.
———. "Detheologizing the ΠΙΣΤΙΣ ΧΡΙΣΤΟΥ Debate: Cautionary Remarks from a Lexical Semantic Perspective." *NT* 42 (2000) 1–23.
———. "The Rhetoric of pistis in Paul: Galatians 2.16; 3.22, Romans 3.22, Philippians 3.9." *JSNT* 30 (2007) 173–203.

———. "Saving Faith: The Rhetoric and Semantic of πίστις in Paul." In *The Faith of Christ: Exegetical, Biblical, and Theological Studies*, edited by Michael F. Bird and Preston M. Sprinkle, 73–90. Peabody, MA: Hendrickson, 2009.
McCann, Clinton, Jr. "The Book of Psalms: Introduction, Commentary, and Reflections." In *NIB* 4:641–1280. Nashville: Abingdon, 1996.
Melito of Sardis. *From the Catena on Genesis*. Translated by B. P. Pratten. In *ANF*, edited by Alexander Roberts and James Donaldson, 8:759–60. Online: http://www.ccel.org/ccel/schaff/anf08.x.v.xii.html.
Miller, James C. "Jewish Context of Paul's Gentile Mission." *TynBul* 58 (2007) 101–15.
———. *The Obedience of Faith, the Eschatological People of God, and the Purpose of Romans*. SBLDS 177. Atlanta: SBL, 2000.
Minear, Paul S. *The Obedience of Faith: The Purpose of Paul in the Epistle to the Romans*. Studies in Biblical Theology Second Series 19. London: SCM, 1971.
Moberly, R. W. L. "אמן." In *NIDOTTE* 1:427–33.
———. *The Bible, Theology, and Faith: A Study of Abraham and Jesus*. Cambridge: Cambridge University Press, 2000.
———. "The Earliest Commentary on the Aqedah." *VT* 3 (1988) 302–23.
———. *Old Testament Theology: The Theology of the Book of Genesis*. Cambridge: Cambridge University Press, 2009.
Moo, Douglas J. *Encountering the Book of Romans: A Theological Exposition*. Grand Rapids: Baker Academic, 2002.
———. *The Epistle to the Romans*. NICNT. Grand Rapids: Eerdmans, 1996.
Moo, Jonathan. "Romans 8.19–22 and Isaiah's Cosmic Covenant." *NTS* 54 (2008) 74–89.
Moore, George F. "Christian Writers in Judaism." *HTR* 14 (1921) 197–254.
Morris, Leon. *The Atonement: Its Meaning and Significance*. Downers Grove, IL: InterVarsity, 1983.
———. "Redemption." In *DPL* 784–86.
Moyise, Steve, and Maarten Menken, editors. *Deuteronomy in the New Testament: The New Testament and the Scriptures of Israel*. LNTS 358. London: T. & T. Clark, 2007.
Murphy-O'Connor, Jerome. *Paul and Qumran: Studies in New Testament Exegesis*. London: Chapman, 1968.
Murray, John. *Redemption Accomplished and Applied*. Grand Rapids: Eerdmans, 1955.
Nanos, Mark D. *The Mystery of Romans: The Jewish Context of Paul's Letter*. Minneapolis: Fortress, 1996.
Nunnally, Wave E., Jr. "The Fatherhood of God at Qumran." PhD diss., Hebrew Union College-Jewish Institute of Religion, 1992.
Oh, Won Keun. "Holiness of Abraham in Genesis and in the Rewritten Bible." PhD thesis, Nazarene Theological College, Manchester, 2007.
Oswalt, John N. *The Book of Isaiah: Chapters 40–66*. NICOT. Grand Rapids: Eerdmans, 1998.
Paulsen, Henning. *Überlieferung und Auslegung in Römer 8*. Wissenschaftliche Monographien zum Alten und Neuen Testament 43. Düsseldorf: Neukirchener, 1974.
Perdue, Leo G., et al. *Families in Ancient Israel*. Louisville: Westminster John Knox, 1997.
Plaut, W. Gunter, et al. *The Torah: A Modern Commentary*. New York: Union of American Hebrew Congregations, 1981.

Porter Stanley E., and Andrew W. Pitts. "Πίστις with a Preposition and Genitive Modifier: Lexical, Semantic, and Syntactic Considerations in the πίστις Χριστοῦ Discussion." In *The Faith of Christ: Exegetical, Biblical, and Theological Studies*, edited by Michael F. Bird and Preston M. Sprinkle, 33–56. Peabody, MA: Hendrickson, 2009.

Prior, David. *The Message of Joel, Micah and Habakkuk*. The Bible Speaks Today. Leicester: InterVarsity, 1988.

Quarles, Charles L. "From Faith to Faith: A Fresh Examination of the Prepositional Series in Romans 1:17." *NovT* 45 (2003) 1–21.

Rad, Gerhard von. *Deuteronomy*. OTL. Translated by Dorothea Barton. London: SCM, 1966.

———. *Genesis*. OTL. Translated by John H. Marks. London: SCM, 1972.

———. *God at Work in Israel*. Translated by John H. Marks. Nashville: Abingdon, 1974. 2nd ed. 1981.

Ralphs, Alfred. *Septuaginta*. 2 vols. Stuttgart: Wüttembergische Bibelanstalt, 1935.

Reasoner, Mark. *Romans in Full Circle: A History of Interpretation*. Louisville: Westminster John Knox, 2005.

Reed, Jonathan L. *Archaeology and the Galilean Jesus: A Re-Examination of the Evidence*. Harrisburg, PA: Continuum, 2002.

Roberts, J. J. *Nahum, Habakkuk, and Zephaniah*. OTL. Louisville: Westminster John Knox, 1991.

Sanders E. P. *Paul and Palestinian Judaism*. London: SCM, 1977.

Schlatter, Adolf. *The Theology of the Apostles: The Development of New Testament Theology*. Translated by Andreas J. Köstenberger. Grand Rapids: Baker, 1998.

Schliesser, Benjamin. *Abraham's Faith in Romans 4: Paul's Concept of Faith in Light of the History of Reception of Genesis 15:6*. Tübingen: Mohr/Siebeck, 2007.

Schneider, J., and C. Brown. "λύτρον." In *DNTT* 3:189–223.

Schoeps, H. J. "The Sacrifice of Isaac in Paul's Theology." *JBL* 65 (1946) 385–92.

Schreiner, Thomas R. *Paul, Apostle of God's Glory in Christ: A Pauline Theology*. Downers Grove, IL: InterVarsity, 2001.

———. *Romans*. BECNT. Grand Rapids: Baker Academic, 1998.

Schuller, Eileen M. "4Q372 1: A Text about Joseph." *RevQ* 14 (1990) 343–70.

———. "The Psalm of 4Q372 1 Within the Context of Second Temple Prayer." *CBQ* 54 (1992) 67–79.

Schwartz, Daniel R. "Two Pauline Allusions to the Redemptive Mechanism of the Crucifixion." *JBL* 102 (1983) 259–68.

Schweizer, Albert. *The Mysticism of Paul the Apostle*. Translated by David Smith. New York: Seabury, 1968.

Scott, J. M. "Adoption, Sonship." In *DPL* 15–18.

Segal, Alan. "'He Who Did Not Spare His Own Son . . .': Jesus, Paul and the Akedah." In *From Jesus to Paul: Studies in Honour of Francis Wright Beare*, edited by Peter Richardson and John C. Hurd, 169–84. Waterloo, ON: Wilfrid Laurier University Press, 1984.

Siker, Jeffrey S. *Disinheriting the Jews: Abraham in Early Christian Controversy*. Louisville: Westminster John Knox, 1991.

Smith, Barry D. "'Spirit of Holiness' as Eschatological Principle of Obedience." In *Christian Beginnings and the Dead Sea Scrolls*, edited by John J. Collins and Craig A. Evans, 75–99. Grand Rapids: Baker Academic, 2006.

Smith, Ralph L. *Micah-Malachi*. WBC 32. Waco: Word, 1984.
Sprinkle, Preston M. "Πίστις Χριστοῦ as an Eschatological Event." In *The Faith of Christ: Exegetical, Biblical, and Theological Studies*. Edited by Michael F. Bird and Preston M. Sprinkle, 165–84. Peabody, MA: Hendrickson, 2009.
Stanley, Christopher. *Paul and the Language of the Scripture: Citation Technique in the Pauline Epistles and Contemporary Literature*. SNTMS 69. Cambridge: Cambridge University Press, 1992.
Stendahl, Krister. *The School of St. Matthew and its Use of the Old Testament*. 2nd ed. Philadelphia: Fortress, 1968.
Stowers, Stanley K. *Rereading of Romans: Justice, Jews and Gentiles*. New Haven: Yale University Press, 1994.
Stuart, Douglas. *Hosea-Jonah*. WBC 31. Waco: Word, 1987.
Stubbs, David L. "The Shape of Soteriology and the Pistis Christou debate." *SJT* 61 (2008) 137–57.
Suggs, M. J. "Wisdom 2:10–15: A Homily Based on the Fourth Servant Song." *JBL* 76 (1957) 26–53.
Swanson, Dwight D. "Offering for Sin in Leviticus, and John Wesley's Definition." *European Explorations in Christian Holiness* 1 (1999) 9–22.
———. "'Original' Sin in the Primeval Narratives." In *European Explorations in the Christian Holiness* 2 (2001) 180–203.
Swetnam, James, S. J. *Jesus and Isaac: A Study of the Epistle to the Hebrews in the Light of the Aqedah*. Rome: Biblical Institute Press, 1981.
Tasker, David R. *Ancient Near Eastern Literature and the Hebrew Scriptures about the Fatherhood of God*. New York: Lang, 2004.
Taylor, John W. "From Faith to Faith: Romans 1.17 in the Light of Greek Idiom." *NTS* 50 (2004) 337–48.
Thielman, Frank. *The NIV Application Commentary: From Biblical Text to Contemporary Life*. Grand Rapids: Zondervan, 1995.
Thiessen, Matthew. "4Q372 1 and the Continuation of Joseph's Exile." *DSD* 15 (2008) 380–95.
Thompson, J. A. *The Book of Jeremiah*. NICOT. Grand Rapids: Eerdmans, 1980.
Thompson, Marianne Meye. "'Mercy upon All': God as Father in the Epistle to the Romans." In *Romans and the People of God*, edited by Sven K. Soderlund and N.T. Wright, 203–16. Grand Rapids: Eerdmans, 1999.
———. *The Promise of the Father: Jesus and God in the New Testament*. Louisville: Westminster John Knox, 2000.
Tobin, Thomas H. *Paul's Rhetoric in its Context: The Argument of Romans*. Peabody, MA: Hendrickson, 2004.
Van Wijk-Bos, Joanna W. H. *Reimagining God: The Case for Scriptural Diversity*. Louisville: Westminster John Knox, 1995.
VanderKam, James C. *The Dead Sea Scrolls Today*. Grand Rapids: Eerdmans, 1994.
———. "Recent Scholarship on the Book of Jubilees." *CBR* 6 (2008) 405–31.
Verhoef, Peter A. *The Book of Haggai and Malachi*. NICOT. Grand Rapids: Eerdmans, 1987.
Vermes, Geza. *The Complete Dead Sea Scrolls in English*. London: Penguin, 2004.
———. *Jesus the Jew: A Historian's Reading of the Gospels*. 1973. Reprint, London: SCM, 1983.

———. *Scripture and Tradition in Judaism: Haggadic Studies*. Rev. ed. Leiden: Brill, 1973.

Wagner, J. Ross. *Heralds of the Good News: Isaiah and Paul in Concert in the Letter to the Romans*. Leiden: Brill, 2003.

———. "Isaiah in Romans and Galatians." In *Isaiah in the New Testament*, edited by Steve Moyise and Maarten Menken, 117–32. London: T. & T. Clark, 2005.

———. "Moses and Isaiah in Concert: Paul's Reading of Isaiah and Deuteronomy in Romans." In *As Those Who are Taught: The Reception of Isaiah from the LXX to the SBL*, edited by Claire Matthews McGinnis and Patricia K. Tull, 87–106. SBLSS. Atlanta: SBL, 2006.

Wallace, Daniel B. *Greek Grammar Beyond the Basics*. Grand Rapids: Zondervan, 1996.

Watson, Francis. "By Faith (of Christ): An Exegetical Dilemma and its Scriptural Solution." In *The Faith of Christ: Exegetical, Biblical, and Theological Studies*, edited by Michael F. Bird and Preston M. Sprinkle, 147–63. Peabody, MA: Hendrickson, 2009.

———. *Paul and the Hermeneutics of Faith*. London: T. & T. Clark, 2004.

———. *Paul, Judaism, and Gentiles: Beyond the New Perspective*. Grand Rapids: Eerdmans, 2007.

Watts, John W. *Isaiah 34–66*. WBC 25. Dallas: Word, 1987.

Wedderburn, Alexander J. M. *The Reasons for Romans*. Edinburgh: T. & T. Clark, 1991.

Wenham, David. *Follower of Jesus or Founder of Christianity?* Grand Rapids: Eerdmans, 1995.

———. *Paul and Jesus: The True Story*. Grand Rapids: Eerdmans, 2002.

Wenham, Gordon J. "The Akedah: A Paradigm of Sacrifice." In *Pomegranates and Golden Bells: Studies in Biblical, Jewish, and Near Eastern Ritual, Law, and Literature in Honor of Jacob Milgrom*, edited by David P. Wright, et al., 93–102. Winona Lake, IN: Eisenbauns, 1995.

———. *Genesis 1–15*. WBC 1. Waco: Word, 1987.

———. *Genesis 16–50*. WBC 2. Dallas: Word, 1994.

Westerholm, Stephen. *Understanding Paul: The Early Christian Worldview of the Letter to the Romans*. 2nd ed. Grand Rapids: Baker Academic, 2004.

Westermann, Claus. *Isaiah 40–66*. Translated by David Stalker. OTL. London: SCM, 1969.

Wicks, Henry J., and R. H. Charles. *The Doctrine of God in the Jewish Apocryphal and Apocalyptic Literature*. New York: KTAV, 1971.

Widdicombe, Peter. *The Fatherhood of God from Origen to Athanasius*. Rev. ed. Oxford: Clarendon, 2000.

Wilckens, Ulrich. *Der Brief an die Römer*. Evangelisch-Katholischer Kommentar zum Neuen Testament. 3 vols. Zürich: Benziger, 1978.

Wildberger, Hans. *Isaiah 1–12: A Continental Commentary*. Minneapolis: Fortress, 1991.

Williams, Sam K. "'The Righteousness of God' in Romans." *JBL* 99 (1980) 241–90.

Williamson H. G. M. *Ezra, Nehemiah*. WBC 16. Waco: Word, 1985.

Williamson, Paul R. *Abraham, Israel and the Nations: The Patriarchal Promise and Its Covenantal Development in Genesis*. JSOTSup 315. Sheffield: Sheffield Academic, 2000.

———. *Sealed with an Oath: Covenant in God's Unfolding Purpose*. NSBT 23. Downers Grove, IL: InterVarsity, 2007.

Witherington, Ben, III. *The Christology of Jesus*. Minneapolis: Fortress, 1990.

———. *Paul's Narrative Thought World: The Tapestry of Tragedy and Triumph*. Louisville: Westminster John Knox, 1994.

Witherington, Ben, III, with Darlene Hyatt. *Paul's Letter to the Romans: A Socio-Rhetorical Commentary*. Grand Rapids: Eerdmans, 2004.

Wright, Christopher J. H. *God's People in God's Land: Family, Land, and Property in the Old Testament*. Grand Rapids: Eerdmans, 1990.

———. *Knowing God the Father through the Old Testament*. Oxford: Monarch, 2007.

———. *The Mission of God: Unlocking the Bible's Grand Narrative*. Nottingham: InterVarsity, 2006.

Wright, N. T. "4QMMT and Paul: Justification, 'Works,' and Eschatology." In *History and Exegesis: New Testament Essays in Honor of Dr E. Earle Ellis for His 80th Birthday*, edited by Aang-Won (Aaron) Son, 104–32. London: T. & T. Clark, 2006.

———. *The Challenges of Jesus*. Downers Grove, IL: InterVarsity, 1999.

———. *The Climax of the Covenant: Christ and the Law in Pauline Theology*. Minneapolis: Fortress, 1991.

———. *Jesus and the Victory of God*. Minneapolis: Fortress, 1996.

———. *Justification: God's Plan and Paul's Vision*. London: SPCK, 2009.

———. "The Letter to the Romans: Introduction, Commentary, and Reflections." In *NIB* 10: 395–770. Nashville: Abingdon, 2002.

———. "New Exodus, New Inheritance: The Narrative Substructure of Romans 3–8." In *Romans and the People of God*, edited by Sven K. Soderlund and N. T. Wright, 26–35. Grand Rapids: Eerdmans, 1999.

———. *The New Testament and the People of God*. London: SPCK, 1992.

———. "Paul and Qumran." *BR* 14 (1998) 18–54.

———. "Romans and the Theology of Paul." In *Pauline Theology, Volume III: Romans*, edited by David M. Hay and E. Elizabeth Johnson, 30–67. Minneapolis: Fortress, 1995.

———. *What Saint Paul Really Said*. Oxford: Lion, 1997.

Yates, John W. *The Spirit and Creation in Paul*. WUNT 2/251. Tübingen: Mohr/Siebeck, 2008.

Yee, Gale A. "The Book of Hosea: Introduction, Commentary, and Reflections." In *NIB* 7:195–297. Nashville: Abingdon, 1996

Zeller, Dieter, "God as Father in the Proclamation and in the Prayer of Jesus." In *Standing Before God: Studies on Prayer in Scriptures and in Tradition with Essays in Honor of John M. Oesterreicher*, edited by Asher Finkel and Lawrence Frizzell, 117–29. New York: KTAV, 1981.

Ziesler J. A. *The Meaning of Righteousness in Paul: A Linguistic and Theological Inquiry*. SNTSMS 20. Cambridge: Cambridge University Press, 1972.

Author Index

Alexander, Philip S., 16
Andersen, Francis A., 93

Barth, Karl, 158n30
Bousset, Wilhelm, 19, 20
Brower, Kent E., 162
Brownlee, William H., 102
Brueggemann, Walter, 23n25
Bultmann, Rudolf, 19
Burchard, C., 42

Campbell, Douglas A., 66–68, 91, 99, 100n65, 101, 109n91, 116, 135n56, 146, 147, 162
Childs, Brevard S., 19
Chilton, B. D., 134n52, 135n55
Clements, Ronald E., 30
Cousar, Charles B., 15
Crafton, Jeffrey A., 2

Dahl, Nils A., 135n56, 146
Daly, Robert J., 135n56, 141
Davies, P. R., 134n52, 135n55
Deissmann, Adolf G., 11, 12
Dobbeler, Alex von, 138
Donaldson, Terence L., 69
Dunn, James D. G., 4, 51n20, 88, 96, 106, 116, 117, 123, 130, 145, 149
Durham, John I., 21

Eichrodt, Walter, 19
Ellis, Earle E., 15n64
Esler, Philip F., 10, 56

Fitzmyer, Joseph A., 51n20, 96, 120, 124, 149, 150

Garlington, Don B., 83n2, 111
Gathercole, Simon J., 132
Goldingay, John, 27
Gorman, Michael J., 65, 110
Greathouse, William M, 56
Grieb, Katherine A., 4

Hamerton-Kelly, Robert, 136
Hartley, John E., 120
Hays, Richard B., 4, 12–14, 15n64, 65, 98, 99, 104, 106, 110, 116, 119n10, 142, 143, 148
Hengel, Martin, 48
Hodge, Caroline J., 8–10
Hooker, Morna D., 145, 162
Houtman, Cornelis., 23n25
Hurtado, Larry W., 46, 47, 49, 52n20, 142

Jeremias, Joachim, 19, 58, 59
Jewett, Robert, 2n4, 56, 84, 120, 132, 149
Jipp, Joshua W., 119n10
Johnson, Elizabeth A., 8, 10
Jonge, Marinus de, 41n72

Käsemann, Ernst, 64
Keck, Leander E., 76, 155
Kugel, James, 36
Kugler, Robert A., 41n72

Levenson, Jon D., 136
Longenecker, Bruce W., 110, 149

Macintosh, A. A., 33n54
Martyn, Louis J., 99
Matlock, Barry R., 15, 106
Miller, James C., 84, 85
Minear, Paul S., 84
Moberly, R. W. L., 135n52, 135n56, 136, 137, 138, 143
Moo, Douglas J., 65, 83n2, 99, 106, 119n10
Murray, John, 160

Nunnally, Wave E., 20

Rad, Gerhard von, 120, 120n15, 136
Reasoner, Mark, 13
Roberts, J. J., 92

Schlatter, Adolf, 12
Schreiner, Thomas R., 116, 125
Schuller, Eileen M., 40
Schweitzer, Albert, 149
Stanley, Christopher, 15n64, 95n49
Stendahl, Krister, 15n64

Tasker, David R., 1, 19, 23
Thompson, Marianne Meye, 5–7, 55n30

Vermes, Geza, 140n81, 146

Wagner, Ross J., 74, 76n91, 78
Wallace, Daniel B., 83n2
Watson, Francis, 90, 119n9, 123, 153n11, 160
Wilckens, Ulrich, 84
Williams, Sam K., 65
Witherington, Ben, III, 4, 65
Wenham, David, 57, 136
Wright, Christopher J. H., 21, 27, 28, 82
Wright, N. T., 4, 16, 48, 51n20, 52, 78, 86, 89, 116, 130n41, 149, 154, 155, 157, 158, 162

Yates, John W., 63
Yee, Gale A., 34n54

Ziesler, J. A., 51n20

Ancient Document Index

OLD TESTAMENT

Genesis

1–3	51n20
2:7	23
3:5	51n20, 150
3:16–24	150
3:22	51n20
6:1–4	151
11:26—12:3	120
12:1–2	27
12:1–3	25, 131, 138
13:15–16	120
15–17	120ff
15:1–17	122
15:4	136
15:5	120, 124
15:6	85n12, 119, 120–30, 122n22, 132
15:15	138
16:15	136
17:2–8	121
17:3–8	138
17:4	122, 123, 139
17:5	122, 123, 124, 128
17:8	24
21:1–21	136
22	120n11, 122, 135, 135n56, 136–39, 142, 144, 145
22:9	134n52
22:12, 16	135–38, 143
25:2	136
41:45	42

Exodus

2:10	62
2:23	22, 61
4	21
4:22–23	21, 23n25, 33, 45, 48
4:22	3n11, 20, 21, 23, 26, 37, 40, 43, 55, 62
6:5–6	21
6:6	45
9:16	25, 43, 70
13:21–22	61
15:12–13	21
18:21	72
19–24	21, 43
19:4	21
19:4–6	24
19:5	21
19:6	55
20:2	21, 121
20:6	25
25:16–22	108n88
32–34	25
32:11–12	121
33:1	21
34:6–7	25, 79
40:34–38	61

Leviticus

4–5	108
4:2, 13, 22, 27	108n89
5:15, 18	108n89

Ancient Document Index

Leviticus *(cont.)*

7:18	120n15
16:29–34	108
17:1–12	112n99
17:18	120n15
19:34	25
23:32	108n89
25:23	24
25:38	22, 61
25:42–43, 55	22
42–43	61
55	61

Numbers

9:15–23	61
11:11–12	26, 30n44
15:30–31	108n89
18:20–24	24
20:8–10	14
23:19	92
24:17	41
30:27	108n89
35:31–32	108n89

Deuteronomy

1:31	21, 25, 26, 30n44
1:33	61
1:38	24
4:1–14	85
4:6–8	25, 27
4:21	24
4:29–31	35
4:38	24
5:10	25
6:2	72
6:4	86
7:6	55
7:7	66
7:8	45
7:9	24
8:2	137
9	113, 131
9:5	24
10:6–9	66, 85
10:6–16	85
10:9	24
10:16–20	130
10:16	24, 35, 109n89
10:18–19	22, 66
10:19	25
10:20	22
11:8	66, 85
11:26–28	85
12:10	24
12:12	24
13:8–10	66
14:1, 2	20, 22, 24, 31, 35
16:20	24
24:19–22	25
25:19—26:1	24
29:3	101
30:1–10	35, 53
30:6	60, 66, 109n89, 130
30:10	24
31:19	67
32	22, 66, 67, 70, 113, 131
32:4	66
32:4–5	30, 43
32:5	20, 30
32:5–6	23, 25, 55
32:6	22, 22n15, 27, 29, 30, 35, 40
32:6–7	43, 125n30
32:9	22, 24, 31, 40
32:10, 12	22
32:21	32, 70, 101
32:35–42	25
32:36	31
32:43	78, 119
33:9	66

Joshua

7	108n89

1 Samuel

8:2	20
8:5	26
12:14–15	27
13:13–14	26
13:14	126

2 Samuel

7:11–16	50
7:14	20, 27, 37, 40, 50, 62

7:14–15	26, 27
7:15–16	28
7:17	39n65
8:16	20
12:13	108n89
19–20:2	52
22:50	77

1 Kings

8:10–11	61
8:46	71
12:16	52
19:10–18	32

1 Chronicles

1:1	151
17:13	20, 26, 28, 50
17:10–14	26
22:8–10	26
22:10	20, 26
28:5	27
28:6	20, 26
28:7, 21	27
29:10	20

2 Chronicles

3:1	137
10:16	52

Nehemiah

9:7–8	121

Esther

2:7	62

Psalms

1:2	127
1:37	31n48
2	26, 27, 29, 43, 44, 50, 52
2:6–7	26
2:7	27, 50
2:8–9	28, 52, 52n24
5:9	72
10:7	72
11:10	72

14:1–3	104
14:1–7	71
14:2	72
17:31	66
18:43	77
18:49–50	77
30:5	26
32:1–2	113, 126–29
32:11	127
36:1	72
51	108n89
51:9–11	53
53:1–3	71, 104
53:6	71
68:4–6	22
68:5	20, 22
68:7–8	22
77	61
89	29, 44, 50
89:3–4	27
89:3	28
89:19–20	27
89:26	20
89:26–27	26, 50
89:28–29, 34	28
89:36–37, 39	28
103:6, 8	25
103:6–14	44, 45, 55
103:9–13	25
103:13	20
103:17	25
103:18	26
104	61
107:2	22
116:9, 11	71
117:1–2	78–79
118:148	66
143:2	73
145:10–12	39n68
147:19–20	66

Proverbs

3:11–12	26, 27
3:12	20
10	31n48

Ecclesiastes

7:20–21	71, 104

Isaiah

1:1	50
1:2	22
1:9	75
1:10	50, 72n83
1:18	36
9:2–7	50
10:20–22	31, 32, 44, 55
10:22, 23	75
11:1	41, 50
11:10	50, 79
19:24–25	25, 32
24:1–22	92
25:6–12	92
26:1–6, 11, 21	92
29:10	101
35	33
40:3–5	33
40:1–11	31, 61
41:2	101
41:14	31, 92
41:18–20	33
42:6	25, 32, 36, 43, 70, 101
42:16	33
43:1	29, 31
43:14	31
43:25	31, 61, 109n89
44:6, 24	31
45:11	20
45:23	51n20
48:13	125n29
48:20–21	31
49:7	31
49:14–16	7
49:15	26, 30n44
51:4–5	25, 32, 70
51:10	29
51:11	45
52:5	104
52:10	25, 32, 70
52:13—53:12	39
53:4, 5	109n89
53:6	111
53:7–9	147
53:10–12	109n89
53:10–11	111
53:10	109n89, 147
53:10–11	111
53:11	101
53:12	111, 147
55:3–5	28, 44, 50
56:1–8	32, 70
59:7–8	72, 104
59:20	31
62:12	22
63–64	61
63:7, 8, 9	29
63:11	29, 53
63:13–14	29
63:16	20, 21, 23, 29, 31, 43, 44, 45
64:1	32, 44, 45, 55
64:7–8	23, 31, 43
64:8	20, 30, 31, 43, 125n30
64:9	31
65:1	33
65:1–2	101
65:1–8	32
66:10–13	30n44
66:13	38
66:18–24	32

Jeremiah

2:7	24
2:27–29	30
3:3	30
3:4–5, 7–8	20
3:19	33, 36
3:19–20	30
4:4	66, 130
7:1–15	24
9:25–26	130
23:5	41, 44
23:5–6	28, 50
31:1–6	29
31:7	32
31:8–9	32, 44, 45, 55
31:9	20, 23, 33, 60
31:31–34	109n89, 130
33:15	41
50:20	109n89

Ezekiel

3:16–21	36
18:31	36
28:11–19	151
32–36	45
34:1–10	27
34:23–24	50
36:22–23	45, 104
36:22	109n89
39:22	36
44:9	130

Hosea

1:7	34
1:10	33, 34, 35, 74, 75
2:1	33n54
2:8	34, 75
2:18–19	34, 75
2:23	31, 33, 44, 55, 74
3:1	34n54
9:3	24
9:10	33
11:1–3	29
11:1	20, 21, 29
11:3–4	33
11:4	29n44
11:1–8	33

Amos

3:11	24
7:11	24

Micah

6:7	109n89
7:18	31, 44, 55

Habakkuk

1:4	31n48
1:13	91
2:1–3	101
2:3	92, 93
2:3–4	100n64
2:4	16, 90–103, 118n6, 133n50
2:5–20	93
3:2–19	93

Zechariah

3:1–10	109n89
3:8	41

Malachi

1:6	20, 30
1:11	32, 70
2:10	20, 23, 30, 125n30
2:19	43
3:17–18	31

APOCRYPHA

Judith

8:26	139

1 Maccabees

2:45–46	118
2:51–52	122, 139
2:64	122

2 Maccabees

7	109n91
7:28	125n29
7:23, 28–29	124
14:37–46	109n91

Sirach

4:9	37
4:10	37, 38
4:10–16	38
23:1, 4	34, 38, 39, 44, 55
25:24	151
33:10	151
40:1	151, 153
44:20	122, 139
51:1	38n62
51:10	34, 38n62, 55
51:11–12	38

Tobit

1:3	35
8:6	151
13:3–4	34
13:6	34, 55

Wisdom

1:16–24	38
2:12	38
2:12–20	100n64
2:13	38
2:16	34, 38, 55
2:17	38
2:18, 21–24	39
2:23–24	151
9:17	53
10:1–2	151
11:25	125n29
14:3	42, 44, 55

PSEUDEPIGRIPHA

Apocalypse of Adam

21:1	151

Apocryphon of Ezekiel

Fr.2	36, 55

Apocalypse of Moses

14; 32:1, 2	151

2 Baruch

17:3	151, 153
21:4	124, 125n29
23:4	151, 153
48:8	124
48:42	151, 153
54:15, 19	151, 153
57:2	122

1 Enoch

6:1–6	152
7:1	152
10:8–9	152
38:2	100n64
44:10	55
53:6	100n64

2 Enoch

30:17	151

4 Ezra

3:7	151, 153
4:30	151
3:21–27	151, 153
6:58	55
7:48	151
7:118	151, 153

Joseph and Aseneth

11:7–14	42
12:8, 12–14	42
12:14–15	62
12:15	42
15:7–11	42
20:7	124
23:10	55

Jubilees

1:19	36
1:21	53
1:22–26	35, 60, 130
1:24–26	131
1:24	36
2:20	55
3:17–31	151
4:15, 22	151
5:1–15	151
7:21–25	151
14:1–16	122
15:7	122
17:15—18:13	139
17:17–18	122, 139
18:15–19	139
19:15–31	37
19:19–29	37
19:25	152, 155
19:29	34, 37
21:1–3, 5	122
23:10	139
23:23	37
31:15	37

3 Maccabees

6:3	34
6:3–4	37

6:8–9	37, 44, 55	*Sibylline Oracles*	
7:6	36	1: 50–54	151

4 Maccabees

Testament 12 Patriarchs

6:27–29	109n91
14:20	140
16:20	110n91
17:20–22	109, 109n91
18:3	140
18:12	110n91, 139

Testament of Judah

24:3–6	41, 43, 70

Testament of Levi

14:3–4	43, 70
17:2, 8	41
18:1–11	41, 53
18:2	53
18:3	43, 70
18:6, 9	41, 53
18:9–11	55
18:11, 14	41, 53

Psalms of Solomon

2:31, 34	39
8:7	39
13:8–10	39
14:15	39
15:12	39
17:15, 19	71n80
17:17–31	39
17:21–32	50
17:26–32	41, 41n73
17:44	41n73
18:4	39

Testament of Naphtali

8:3–4	43, 70

Testament of Simeon

3:4	72

Pseudo-Philo *Bib. Ant.*

18:3, 5	140
32:2–4	139n74, 140
40:2	140
44:2	151

Testament of Job

33:3	39, 44, 55
33:9	39
40:2–3	39
47:11	39
50:3	39

ANCIENT JEWISH LITERATURE

Josephus *Ant.*

1:20	42
1:225–36	140
1:230	42
2:152	42
13:318–19	118

Philo *Decal.*

51, 61	42

QUMRAN SCROLLS

CD III	55, 152, 155, 158	4Q372	40, 44, 55, 58
4Q225	139	4Q460	40, 59
4Q246	50	4Q504	40, 53, 59
4Q369	36, 44, 59	4QFlor	41, 44, 50

Ancient Document Index

1QH	40, 59, 71n80, 158
1QpHab	94, 98, 102, 118n6, 130
4QMMT	122, 126–28, 126n34
1QS	53, 152, 158
1QSb	53

NEW TESTAMENT

Matthew
12:40 — 150

Mark
14:36 — 58

Luke
23:47 — 100n64

John
1:29 — 147n100

Acts
3:14	100n64
7:38	66
7:52	100n64
13:32–33	52n24
15	113
22:14	100n64

Romans
1:1–15	3
1:1–17	117
1:1	2, 68
1:1–3	76, 77, 79, 88, 101, 105
1:2	57, 88, 160
1:2–3	64
1:2–4	99
1:3	10, 17, 49
1:4	47, 49, 51, 52, 60, 160
1:1–5	47, 54, 63, 68, 70, 84–89, 101, 110, 125, 129, 147, 148
1:5	12, 48, 52, 53, 54, 57, 68, 70, 83n2, 84, 86, 87, 89, 96, 98, 133, 142, 148
1:6	56, 97
1:1–7	49, 51n20, 73, 106, 149
1:7	46, 47, 55, 56, 86
1:8	86, 97
1:9	2, 17, 49
1:15	2
1:16	57, 70, 83, 117, 132, 132n48
1:16–17	46, 70, 90, 96, 97, 105, 106, 149
1:17	4n11, 16, 64, 73, 84, 87, 89, 90, 95n48, 96, 99–101, 133n50, 144, 158, 162
1:8–15	2
1:18—3:20	10, 11, 83, 110, 112, 117, 154
1:18—13:9	155
1:18—12:29	70
1:18–32	62, 71, 86, 104
1:18	65
1:20–23	154, 154n14
1:23	155, 156, 158
2:1	57
2:5	70
2:6	98, 133
2:6–11	98
2:9	86
2:9–10	98, 133
2:11	57, 70
2:17—13:20	104
2:17–29	67, 86, 113
2:17–28	62
2:17–24	3
2:21–24	104
2:25–29	130
2:28–29	130, 133
2:29	65, 86, 102
3:1–20	86
3:1–9	10
3:1–8	67, 68
3:1	65, 67, 67n73
3:2	65, 66, 67
3:2–3	52
3:3–22	117
3:3	12, 65, 67, 97, 157, 161
3:4	65, 66, 67, 70, 97, 113, 117
3:5, 7	65, 68

3:6, 8	68	4:14	131
3:9	67, 67n73, 71, 86, 104, 130	4:15	105, 155, 160
3:9–20	155	4:16	12, 124, 131, 134, 142
3:10–20	67, 71–73, 86, 104	4:17	102, 119, 124, 131, 142, 144
3:21–31	119	4:18–22	125
3:21	4n11, 46, 51, 57, 64, 65, 70, 73, 76, 76n91, 83, 88, 89, 98, 102, 108n88, 112, 160	4:18–19	124
		4:18	120, 124
3:21–25	64, 77, 96, 101, 105, 125, 126, 128, 129, 130	4:20	133, 144, 145, 156, 158, 159
3:21–26	4, 12, 17, 73, 75, 83, 84, 87, 100, 101, 102, 103, 104–14, 111, 117, 142, 145, 146, 147, 149, 158, 159	4:21	131, 133, 144
		4:22–23	102
		4:23	119, 143
3:21—24:25	99	4:23–25	83, 134, 162
3:22	3, 11, 12, 46, 51, 52, 70, 73, 76, 87, 88, 97, 105, 106, 107, 108n88, 114, 117, 119, 128, 141–44, 146	4:24	47, 98n58, 111, 113, 125, 144
		4:24–25	101, 124, 125, 148, 159
		4:25	111, 128, 144, 146
3:23	83, 97, 107, 155, 158	5–8	62
3:24	3n11, 46, 64, 113	5:1–21	4, 125
3:25	100, 105, 109, 112, 128, 135n56, 147	5:1–12	159
		5:1–11	149, 156, 157
3:26	11, 105, 106, 107, 146	5:1	159
3:27—24:25	117	5:2–21	112
3:27–31	3, 117–19, 119n10, 128	5:2–3	114
3:27	3, 118, 119, 132	5:2	47, 156, 158
3:28	155	5:5–8	56
3:29–30	86	5:5	61
3:29	73, 118	5:8	107, 113
3:30	118, 130	5:9	4n11, 75, 159
3:31	76n91, 98, 119	5:10	47, 49, 75, 146, 159, 162
4:1–25	117ff, 143, 159	5:11	4n11, 10, 87, 132, 133, 157
4:1	119n10	5:12–14	150, 153
4:2–5	132	5:12–21	11, 13, 18, 46, 50, 52, 83, 87, 101, 103, 107, 110, 129, 141, 142, 143, 144, 145, 148, 149, 150, 154, 159
4:2	124		
4:3	123		
4:4–5	49, 132		
4:4–6	130		
4:5	86	5:13–14	155, 161
4:6–8	126	5:14	156
4:6	113	5:15–21	156
4:9–15	130	5:15–19	84, 101, 148, 156
4:9	86, 128	5:15	111, 156, 157
4:10	73, 133	5:17–21	157
4:11–13	86, 159	5:17–18	96, 162
4:11	65, 70, 73, 74, 123, 129	5:17	157
4:12	12, 73, 74, 123, 129	5:18–19	87, 100, 155, 156, 159
4:13	63, 113, 134, 159	5:18	101, 159
4:13–14	63, 160		

Ancient Document Index

Romans (cont.)

5:19	3, 11, 12, 17, 54, 83n2, 87, 97, 103, 110, 111, 112, 144, 154, 158
5:20	155, 157, 160, 161
5:21	103, 110, 157, 158
6:1–23	145
6:1–11	75, 103, 159
6:4–23	51
6:4	3, 46, 47, 48, 48n9, 96, 112, 144, 146, 156, 158, 158, 162
6:5	48, 103, 147, 162
6:6	87, 158
6:7	48
6:8	96, 125
6:11	162
6:12–13	98, 161
6:14–15	155
6:15	48, 96
6:16	161
6:18	4n11, 51, 64, 96
6:19	161
6:22	48
7:6	86
7:7–25	155
7:12, 14	97, 155
8:1–27	4, 129
8:1–17	54n28
8:3–4	102, 103, 156, 161
8:3	3, 47, 49, 50, 54, 64, 76, 89, 98, 105, 111, 112, 128, 146, 147, 155, 156, 160
8:4–14	162
8:4	161
8:5–11	54
8:9–15	107
8:9–11	102
8:9	60
8:11	47
8:12–17	64
8:14	60, 61, 148
8:14–15	61
8:14–17	4n11, 6, 10, 47, 54, 57, 58, 80, 83, 86, 88, 103, 110, 112, 125, 131, 145, 158, 160
8:15	46, 48, 54, 55, 58, 61, 77
8:15–27	60
8:16	60
8:17	102, 107, 156, 158
8:18–27	63, 64, 125
8:18–21	80, 96, 103, 159
8:19–25	75
8:21	46
8:22–25	80
8:23	3n11
8:27	56
8:28–29	63
8:29	47, 49, 54, 60, 63, 75, 80, 87, 112, 145, 156, 158
8:29–30	88, 107
8:31–39	56, 135n53, 142
8:38–39	153n10
8:38	153n10
8:32	47, 49, 54, 120n11, 134–35, 141–48
8:34	47
8:35	56
9	63
9–11	8, 57, 68, 78, 160
9:1–6	75
9:1–5	49, 68
9:3–8	131
9:4–5	10, 66, 68
9:5	10, 62, 63, 67, 68, 160
9:6–22	124
9:6–13	74, 134
9:6–9	131
9:6–7	63
9:7–8	75, 131
9:7	123, 130
9:8	74
9:13	56
9:23–29	74–75
9:24–29	58, 63
9:25–26	56, 69
9:29	80
9:30—10:4	111
9:30–32	113
9:31–33	99
9:31	113, 161
10:2	112
10:3–4	77
10:4	4, 70, 76, 98, 102, 105, 112, 119, 129, 161
10:5ff	128
10:6–16	133
10:6–11	162

10:9–10	125, 144
10:9	47, 83
10:11–13	143
10:12	160
10:14–18	58
10:16	86, 101, 111, 148
10:19	66, 85
10:19–21	101
11:1–10	56
11:1	10, 68
11:1–2	69
11:8	101
11:11–32	146
11:11	68, 73, 143
11:12	57, 73, 143
11:13	57, 73
11:14	74
11:17–21	3
11:21	143
11:25	10, 57
11:25–26	68
11:26	56
11:28	56, 68
11:26–32	75
11:28–32	58
11:30	143
11:32	74
12:1	85, 145, 162
12:1–2	58, 112
12:3	3
12:9	98
12:19	66, 85
14:1—15:7	3
14:11	80
15:4	102
15:6	46, 47, 48
15:8–13	77–80, 88, 160
15:8–12	63, 69
15:8–9	6
15:8	57, 68, 77, 133, 160
15:10	66, 69, 85, 119
15:12	50
15:14–33	2
15:14	3
15:15–18	68
15:18	65
15:19	83n2
15:21	101, 111, 148
15:27	57, 68
16:2, 15	56
16:17–20	3
16:19	86
16:25–26	13, 88–89
16:26	12, 57, 70, 83n2, 86–89, 98, 133

1 Corinthians

4:9	153n10
6:3	153n10
10–13	2
10:4	14
10:11	102
11:10	153n10
15:3	107
15:3–6	162
15:20–22	156, 162
15:42–49	156

2 Corinthians

5:17	162
11:3	153n11
12:17	153n10

Galatians

1:8	153n10
1:11–16	113
2:7–9	9n40
2:11–21	113
2:15	9n40
2:16	12, 106
2:19	106
2:20	49
2:21	106
3:11	95n48
3:13–14	148
3:16	124
3:22	12
4:6	58
4:14	153n10
4:21–31	9n40
5:13–25	98
6:16	56

Ephesians

3:3–6	88

Philippians

1:29	12
2:5–11	13, 52, 106
2:10–11	80
2:8	12
3:9	106

1 Timothy

2:14–15	153n11

Hebrews

5:12	66
7:3	150
9–10	108n88
10:38	95n48, 100n64
11:17–19	137, 144

1 Peter

1:19–20	147n100
3:18	100n64
4:11	66

1 John

2:1	100n64

www.ingramcontent.com/pod-product-compliance
Lightning Source LLC
Chambersburg PA
CBHW070325230426
43663CB00011B/2228